MANUAL OF GRAPHIC TECHNIQUES 2

FOR ARCHITECTS, GRAPHIC DESIGNERS, & ARTISTS

TOM PORTER AND SUE GOODMAN

Astragal Books · London

Acknowledgments

The authors would like to thank the following architecture students at Oxford Polytechnic, who contributed project works:

Paul Baker, Henry Busiakievicz, Philip Campbell, Colin George, Peter Ireland, Gary Jemmett, Kikkan Landstad, Richard Partington, Mike Richards, Sue Stewart, John Stewart, Andrew Ozanne, Peter Traves, and the late Martin Beranek.

They would also like to thank Paul Chemetov (Atelier d'Architecture et d'Urbanisme) and John Craig (Aldington, Craig, & Collinge).

Special thanks are due to Iradj Parveneh for all photography, and to Richard K. Chalmers, George Dombek, Maelee Thomson Foster, Martin Gordon, Ron Hess, Pat Jackson, Steve Maybury, Gordon Nelson, and William Taylor for their encouragement, help, and technical advice.

Astragal Design Series

First published in Great Britain 1982 by Astragal Books, an imprint of The Architectural Press Limited, London.

First published in the United States of America 1982 by Charles Scribner's Sons, New York.

ISBN 0 906525 24 1

Printed in the United States of America

TABLE OF CONTENTS

Introduction

Manual of Graphic Techniques 2 has developed specifically as a companion volume to its forerunner, Manual of Graphic Techniques 1. Based on teaching experiences in graphics workshops presented in both the U.S.A. and U.K., it is aimed at the beginning design student who is often baffled, needlessly, by the mystery that tends to surround the image-making process.

Because timid and bland images are inefficient in graphic communication, this manual is dedicated to aiding a visually exciting and convincing artwork. It begins by explaining the basic ingredients of images, together with techniques to assemble them and an understanding of visual response patterns in viewers.

Also critical to the creation of potent artwork is the selection of a graphic vehicle and a medium appropriate both to its intended message and to its ability to be produced (and reproduced) quickly. Therefore, ensuing sections concentrate on the range of representational modes--with emphasis on perspective--plus a step-by-step review of the characteristic effects of various rendering techniques.

Finally comes a section comprising easy-to-follow methods which, in concerning itself with experimental graphics and the mixing of drawings and photographic prints, is devoted to the rapid achievement of professional-looking design graphics. This is followed by a concluding review of the options that await the designer presenting his ideas. Amongst others, transformation into a page, an exhibition panel, and screen formats are considered as stimulating alternatives to the physical display of artwork.

1 ANATOMY OF AN IMAGE

Graphic Ingredients: Dot, Line, and Plane

The dot is the most basic graphic element. Having no scale, it signals an energy point within the visual field. A network of dots can be interpreted by the eye as connected by invisible force lines that, when constructed visually, allow assembly into identifiable images. Colonies of dots also create value structures, as in dry-transfer screens, stippling, spray-painting, and half-tone printing.

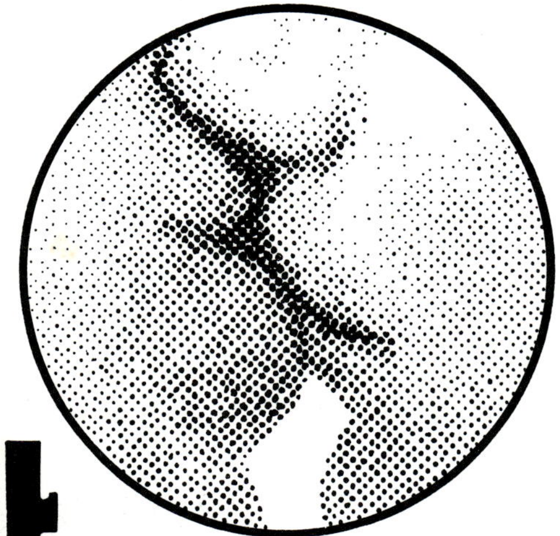

1

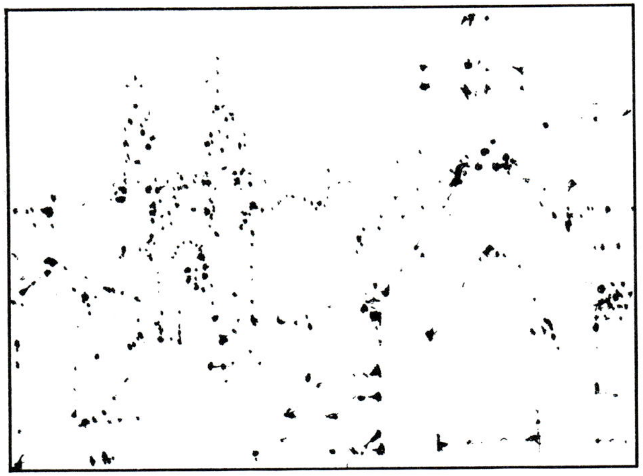

2

Experiment with making images composed of dots. This drawing, for example, uses dots to locate points at the corners of objects in space, and the points at which--if a line drawing--lines would begin, end, and intersect.

When a dot is animated, as on the tip of a pencil or the nib of a pen, it becomes a line. This is the most common graphic element. Lines are used to create all forms of image making because, in concentrating graphite and ink into dense, precise areas, they are relatively easy to control and conducive to modern systems of reproduction.

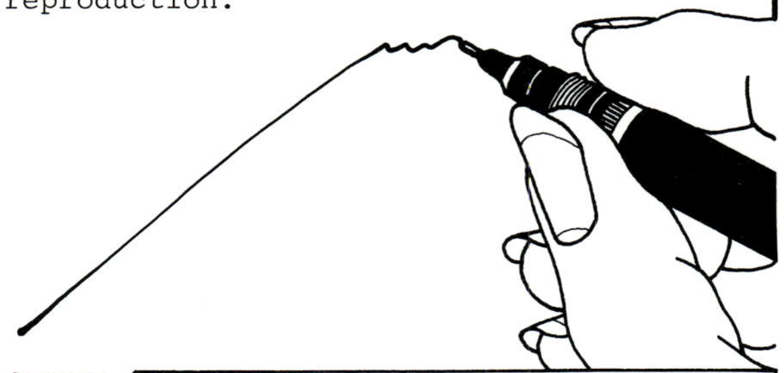

3

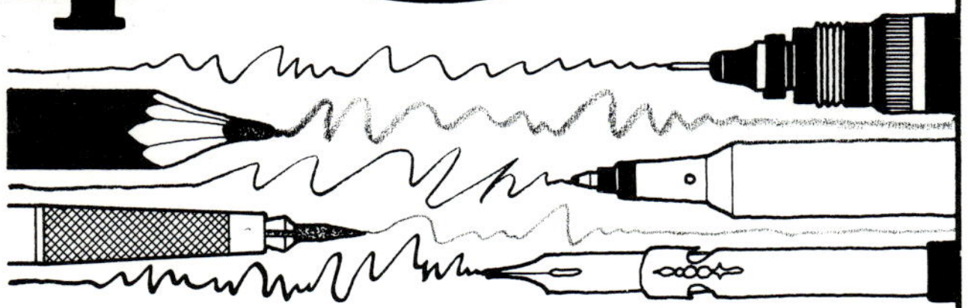

4

Lines generate expression. For instance, they can appear "wooden" and insensitive, or when drawn with feeling appear filled with nervous tension. A drawing is often considered crude when executed mechanically in one heavy delineation. Sensitive qualities, on the other hand, are associated with lines that "breathe," such as lines of various thickness, density, or weight. These attributes are achieved by degrees of pressure when using pencils or pens with nibs that offer variable line qualities--a quality extendable by the different grades of graphite or ink applicators, such as technical pens, that include interchangeable nib sizes.

5

Experiment with various line qualities. For example, lines appear in tension when apparently stretched between two anchor points. As a general rule, exert more pressure where lines begin, end, change direction, and meet or intersect.

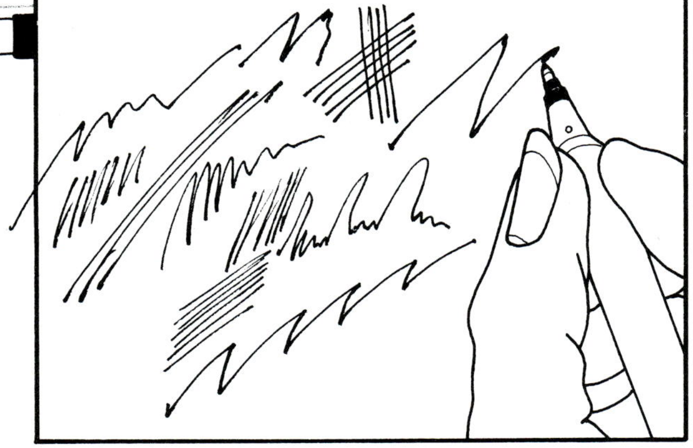

6

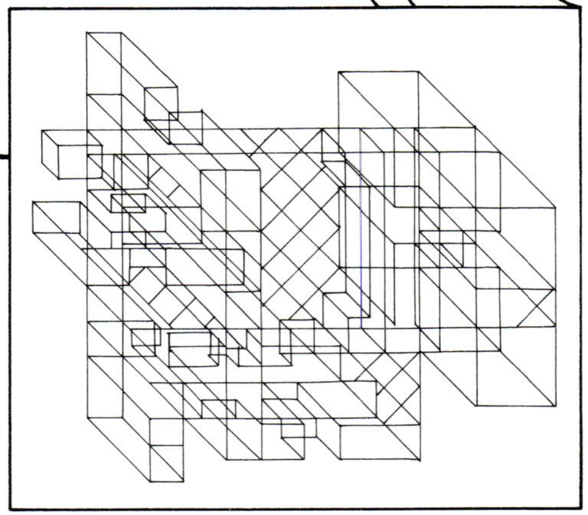

Although lines as such have little to do with the image as visually or mentally perceived, the delineation of objects or concepts is a drawing convention almost universally accepted as a means of communication. As part of this convention, the plane--like the dot and the line--makes visible our concepts of space in two dimensions. Being defined by lines, their illusory presence defines the boundaries of volume.

N.B.: The surface on which an image is created is called the picture plane. As part of the image-making illusion, the ingredients of graphics can be made to appear to exist on, in front of, or behind this plane.

Graphic Ingredients: Shape, Form, and Value

1

When the two ends of a line are connected in a drawing, the contained area is seen as a shape--a defined figure that appears detached from its surrounding area. This is a figure-ground phenomenon in which the container line is relegated into sub-servience.

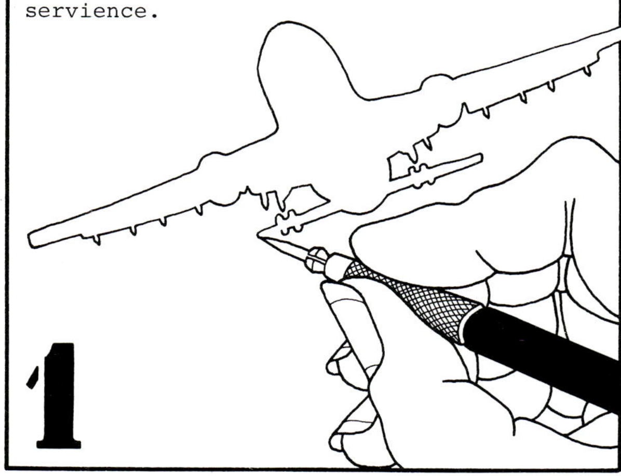

2

Shapes are delineated by edges; edges are contours in perception. Depending on the nature of their edge, i.e., the nature of the route taken by the eye, shapes can exert powerful visual impact. They can appear static, perform directionally, or generate movement.

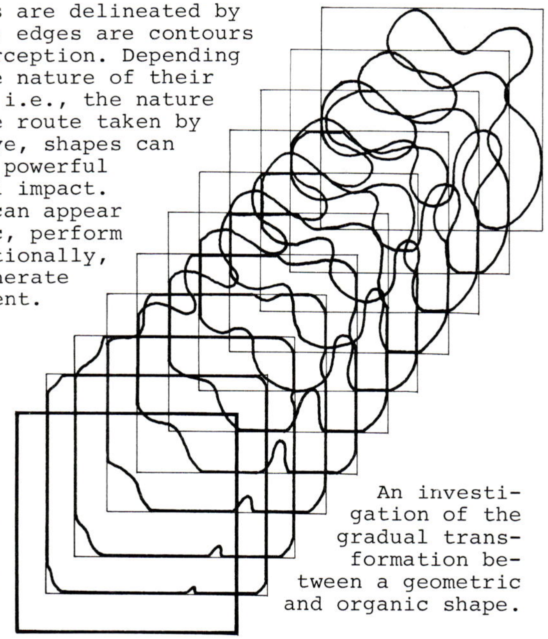

An investigation of the gradual transformation between a geometric and organic shape.

3

Positive form is substance--seen as existing in and thereby defining space. Space is realized as negative form that surrounds and thus defines substance.

Illusions of positive form can be defined using any one of the graphic elements used either individually or in combination. For example, lines can describe the edges of form, texture, pattern, and (with or without color) can describe its surface and scale.

4

Value can describe the solidity of form. Its inclusion in a graphic introduces an additional wealth of information such as the quality, direction, and level of light, a description of the surface quality of form and the inclination of plane, and indicates the extent of surrounding space.

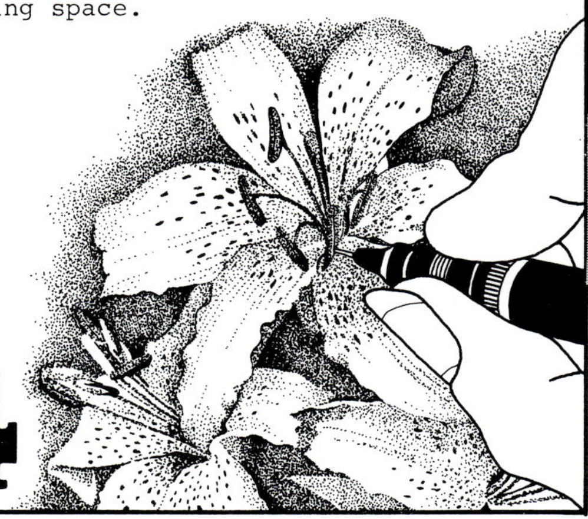

5

The basic graphic function of value is structural, i.e., a regulation through degrees of contrast of the rhythm and balance of darker and lighter areas in a composition.

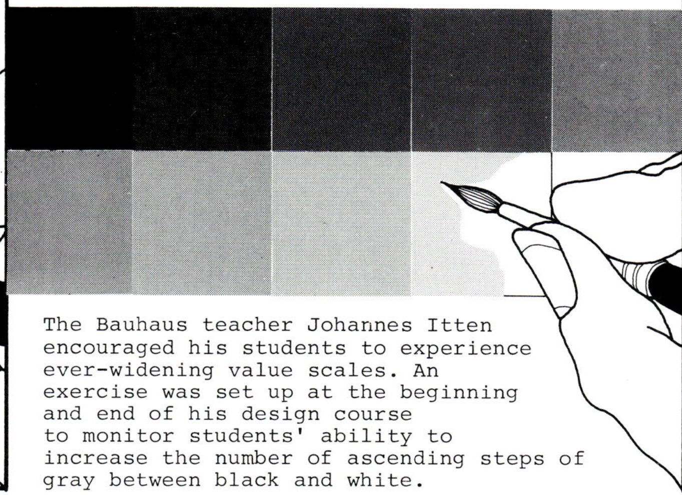

The Bauhaus teacher Johannes Itten encouraged his students to experience ever-widening value scales. An exercise was set up at the beginning and end of his design course to monitor students' ability to increase the number of ascending steps of gray between black and white.

Graphic Ingredients: Pattern, Texture, and Color

Pattern is the regular repetition of an arrangement of marks that may comprise lines, shapes, and units of color.

1

2

Often, patterns of paving, brickwork, blockwork, and other mortar joints is the only means of indicating a sense of scale in architectural drawings devoid of human figures.

There are two kinds of texture: optical and tactile. Essentially, tactile texture is what is experienced via the sense of touch. It can be classified along scales of rough-smooth, matte-glossy, warm-cold, etc.

Strictly speaking, tactile texture in graphics is the surface texture left behind after the application of mediums. However, a popular definition is of a simulation, i.e., the literal depiction of a surface.

3

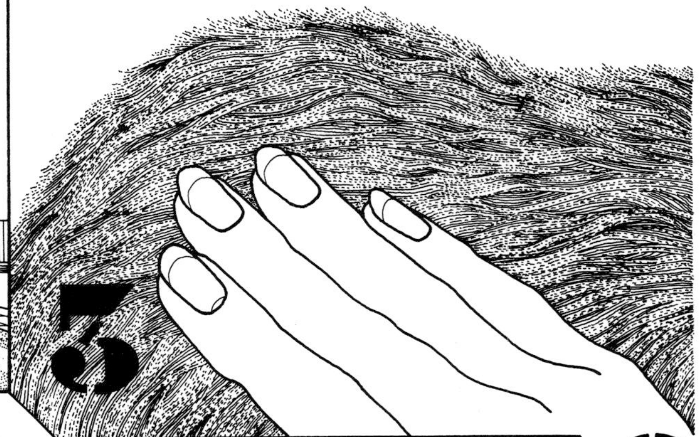

4

Optical texture is the designed or accidental creation of visual surface effects. In hatching or stippling, for example, lines or dots describe tonal value, but their textural grain will also describe optical texture--an effect that may or may not be incidental to the image being communicated.

5

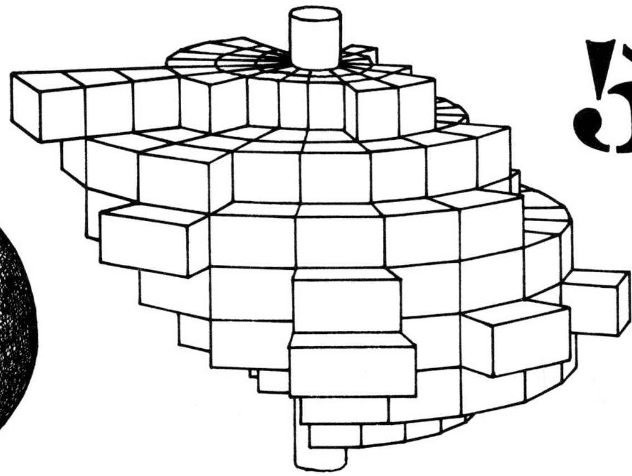

Color is considered to have three dimensions: hue, chroma, and value. Hue is that quality which is commonly accepted as color in defining its redness, greenness, etc.; chroma refers to the strength of a color; value describes the lightness or darkness of a color.

The three coordinates form the basis of the color solid, a conceptual structure that conveniently houses the world of color.

6

Value is the most important dimension of color for the designer. Its considered handling in graphics is central to the structuring of paintings and colored artwork. Degrees of contrast in the components of an image are related directly to the steps between one color value and another.

N.B.: The color experience is simultaneously modified by a supplementary experience of all the other graphic ingredients. In other words, color is texture, pattern, form, etc., for we perceive each as a facet of all the others.

Graphic Ingredients: Figure-Ground

1

Our perception of this classic reversible figure can be alternately shifted at will to see either two faces or a central vase. Whichever is seen, however, its sister image (or "negative") is as vital to the perception as the positive, each having an interdependent life of its own.

2

Similarly, whenever a mark is introduced to a surface, a positive-negative or figure-ground, relationship is established.

3

Op Art graphics are exercises in highly tuned positive-negative relationships because, in creating graphics with near-equal figure-ground pulse rates, the eyes are bombarded with constantly fluctuating information caused by a rapid and involuntary reversal of positive and negative roles.

4

On the other hand, extreme concentrations in the role of one will intensify the apparent condition of the other. In this image, for instance, a heavy concentration of black heightens the "whiteness" of white.

5

Interval--the space between positive elements--is another version of negative or ground. For example, meaningful arrangements of lettering rely upon controlled intervals. Disturb this arrangement and meaning is lost or reduced.

IN TERV AL,I.E.,T HE
SPA CEBETW EE NP
OSIT IVEE LEM ENT
S,ISA NOT HERV ER
SI ONOF¨NE GAT IV

N.B.: In design it is the quality of refinement of both interval (negative) and letterform (positive) that denotes the difference between good and bad lettering.

6

It is good design experience to make objective drawings that throw searching lines around negative shapes, the forms that lie between solids in a field of view. This not only exercises awareness of the dynamic role of negative pattern but opens the door to further graphic techniques (see page 90).

Graphic Ambiguity

1

The creation of graphics is a process of making optical illusions, an arrangement of pigment on a flat surface having the potential of conveying both powerful emotion and a high degree of realism. However, within the graphic vocabulary, certain structures are ambiguous and in themselves create further illusions. These have been exploited by many artists, such as M. C. Escher, Salvador Dali, and Josef Albers.

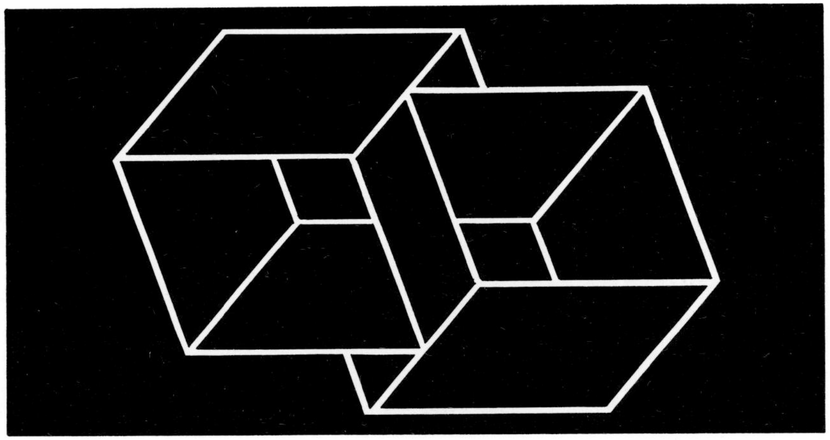

2

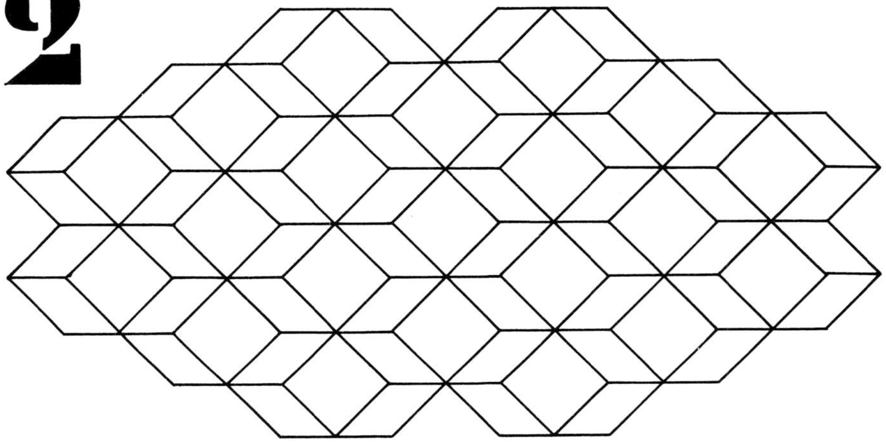

Optical illusions also turn up as party games. For example, how many boxes do you see in this drawing? (The answer is contained in Frame 5).

3

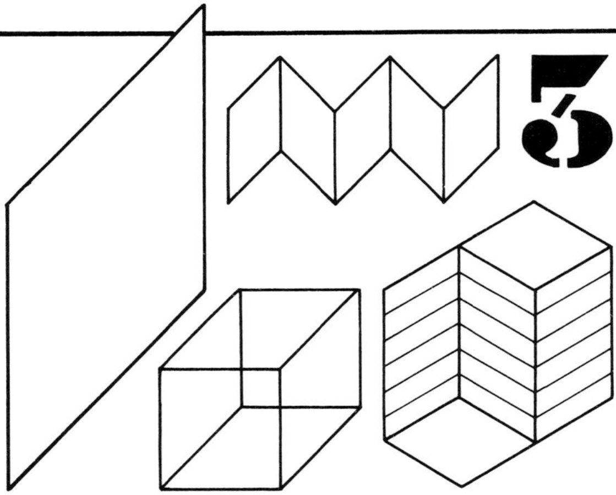

The generators of these reversible-figure illusions are the rhombus and parallelogram, shapes that the eye refuses to see as being flat. Their ambiguity allows two different and reversible versions of their graphic description of a plane in two-dimensional space.

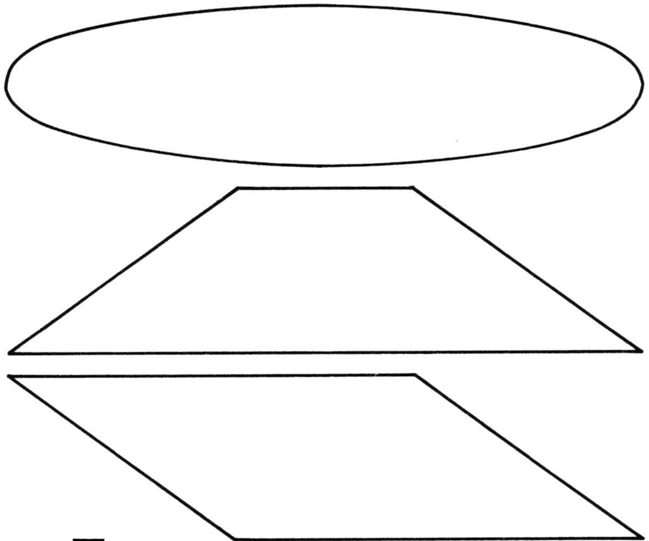

4

There are a series of other shapes that our eye and brain refuse to perceive as flat.

5

The reason for this ambiguity is that we live in a rectangular world of space defined by buildings and boxlike forms characterized by straight lines and right-angled corners. Overexposure to this kind of environment has meant that, in a subtle way, our vision, being continually bombarded with rectilinear information, has developed a highly conditioned and specialized perception. Furthermore, this conditioning to illusions is not found in cultures such as that of the Zulus, who live in nonrectangular settings.

Designers should be aware of this potential visual distortion in their graphics, and be alert to the power of the secondary depth cues, which can, to a degree, correct it.

Solution 63

The Secondary Cues to Pictorial Depth

1 Our visual experience of three dimensions relies upon a hierarchy of primary and secondary optical functions. However, the static nature of pictorial displays permits only a translation of the secondary cues as graphic depth signals.

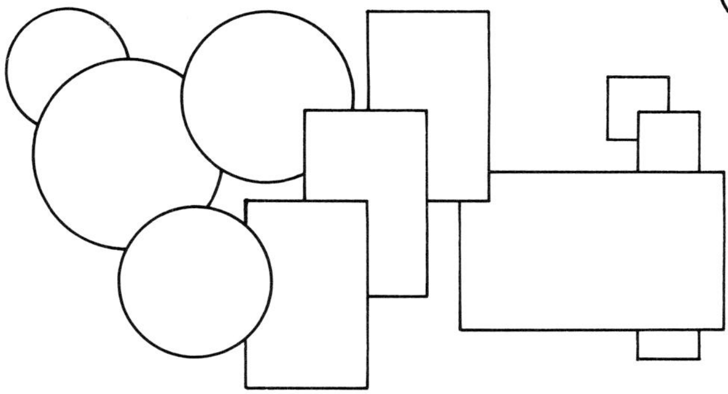

Overlap is the most powerful graphic depth cue--the appearance of one object partially blocking off another, establishing a two-dimensional spatial sequence.

4 Light and shade. Shadows in graphics are potent depth cues because they indicate intensity and direction of light, relative positions of overhanging features, profiles, and--depending on the degree of sensitivity of applied tone--the surface texture of form.

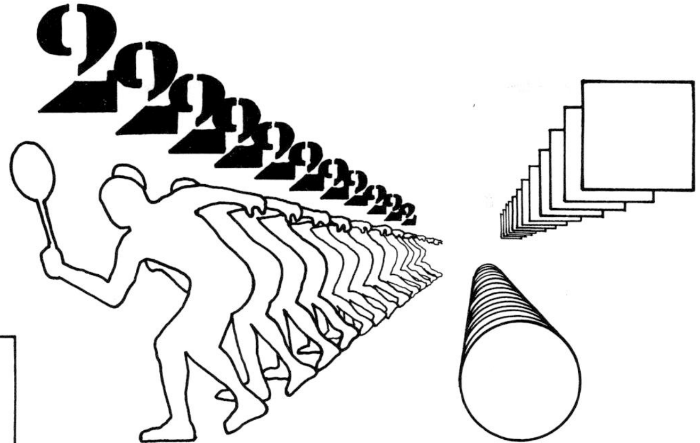

Apparent size. In Western perspective, two similar-sized objects shown at different distances from the viewer will appear to be different in size, the nearer appearing larger than its more distant counterpart. This drawing system uses convergence as the means of coordinating apparent size within the illusion of graphic space.

5 Texture gradients are the diminishing surface patterns that are important to our visual judgments of both scale and distance.

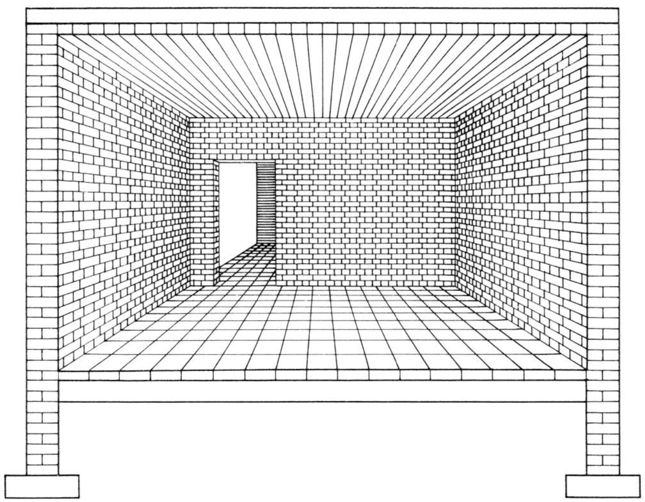

3 A further aspect of apparent size is the relative location of objects in the visual field. This association of juxtaposed forms with distance is related to our perceptual stance in which more distant objects usually appear as more elevated relative to the viewer's position.

6 Atmospheric haze (aerial perspective) is determined graphically by employing scales of color or value which at their extremes describe darker or richly colored (saturated), sharply defined foreground information against lighter or grayer (nonsaturated), diffuse backgrounds.

Depth Representation and Constancy Scaling

1 A further consideration in graphic representation is the phenomenon of constancy scaling--the difference between the image that enters the eye and the same image reconstructed by the brain. It can be illustrated by the appearance of spectators' heads in a crowded football stadium or cricket ground; all the heads will look much the same size and yet the retinal images of the nearest heads are far larger than those at the back. This phenomenon refers to a "zoom lens" capacity of the brain, which compensates for the shrinkage of objects with distance.

4 In viewing a photograph, we find that constancy scaling does not readily occur, because the mechanical eye of the camera reproduces a visual image that has not been modified by the brain.

2 This is a drawing made from a photograph. Photographic images do not account for constancy scaling, and foreshortening distortion results.

5 The common distortion of increased depth in constructed perspective drawings--especially those of "tunneled" spaces--happens because, as in the camera, the mechanical rules of perspective respond to visual rather than cerebral images. Many artists overcome this problem by bending perspective laws to record what they perceive.

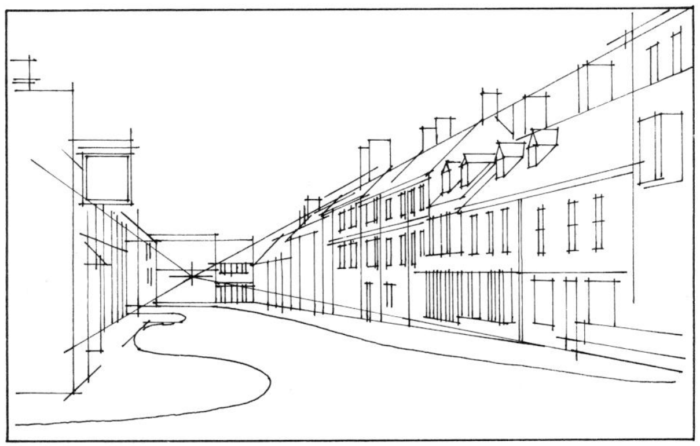

3 Constancy scaling operates in horizontal perception, but it reverses when we look along the vertical plane. For example, if we look down from tall buildings, the ground plane appears more distant than it actually is. Only those such as steeplejacks and spidermen have adjusted their perception in order to experience the true distance.

6 However, objective freehand drawings are not subject to mechanical rules but, instead, spontaneously respond to the reconstructed image of the brain. In this sketch the effect of constancy scaling operates. Note the advanced position of the back wall in relation to the eye (and brain) of the viewer.

Graphic Illusions of Movement

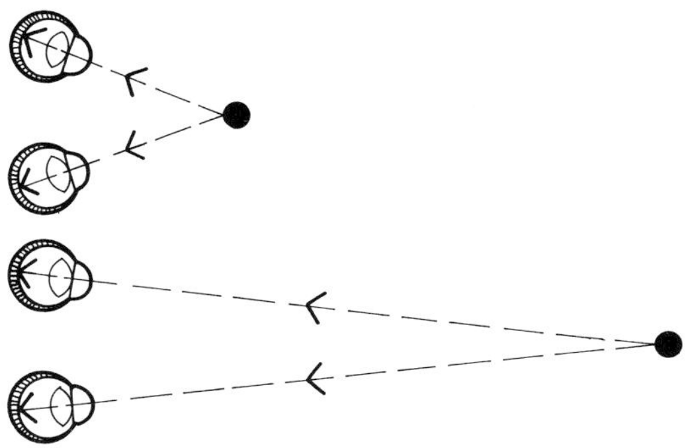

1

The primary visual signals to depth perception are binocular vision and motion parallax. Binocular vision is the pivoting action of our two eyes when adjusting to nearer and farther objects, plus their ability to converge and focus upon one point at a time, with each eye receiving a slightly different version of the object in view.

2

Movements of the head and eyes give motion parallax, movement at right angles to a line of vision altering the relative position of two unequally distant objects.

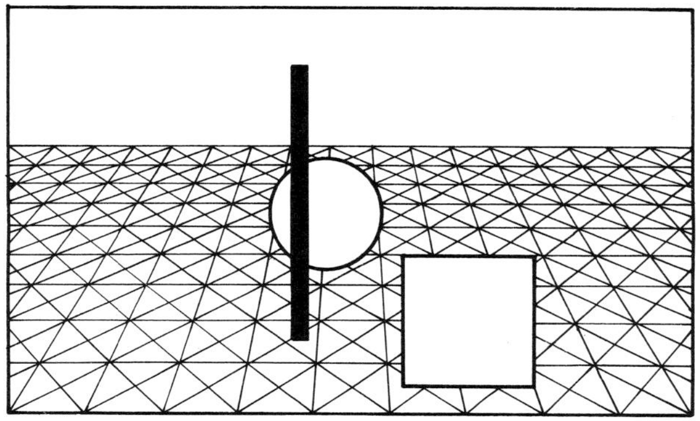

This experience cannot function in graphics for, despite the depth illusions in this perspective, object-to-field relationships do not change in response to different viewing positions.

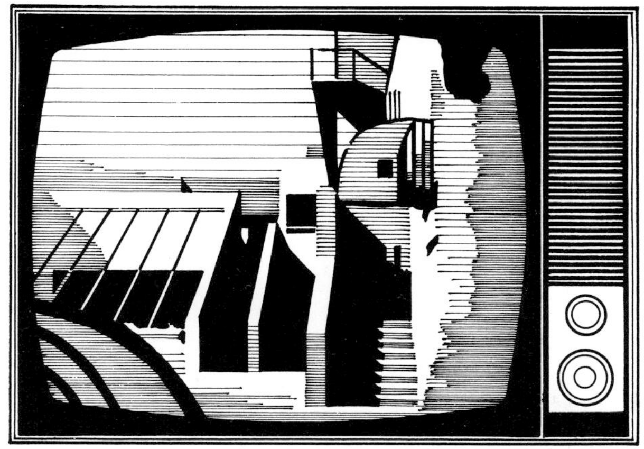

3

If motion parallax is required, the designer has to turn to those mediums that offer movement in picture making, such as film or video, or to three-dimensional graphics, such as holograms (three-dimensional photographs), which allow movement around their illusion of solidity.

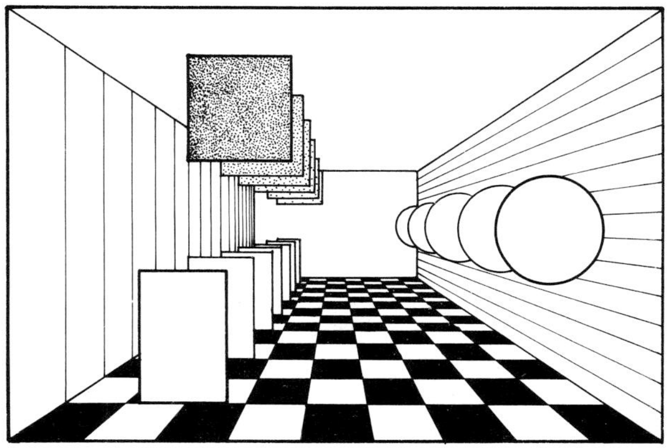

4

All flat and static forms of graphics equate to a one-eyed person's view of the world around him, but from fixed points. As with this frozen, "monocular" perception, graphics must instead rely exclusively upon the secondary cues in order to convey pictorial impressions of depth (see page 11).

5

Throughout the ages, artists have attempted to simulate movement graphically. These range from using echo lines for the contour of objects moving relative to the observer, to the reduction of forms to a blur, to the Cubist-like dismembering of forms for a graphic reassembly in dynamic fashion.

6

However, designers and artists also seek to portray an abstract movement by means of dynamic forms and compositions and in the vibratory pulses between positive and negative elements.

Two-Dimensional Force-Fields

1

When confronted with blank rectilinear formats, our perception generates invisible lines of energy, with the edge of the format functioning as their visual container.

The Union Jack flag exemplifies a basic design response to these energy lines.

2

The natural impulse to divide formats in response to basic force-fields is also illustrated in the more formal graphics of schoolchildren. For instance, when they are asked to design Christmas cards, it is common to find this predictable relationship between message area and format edge.

3

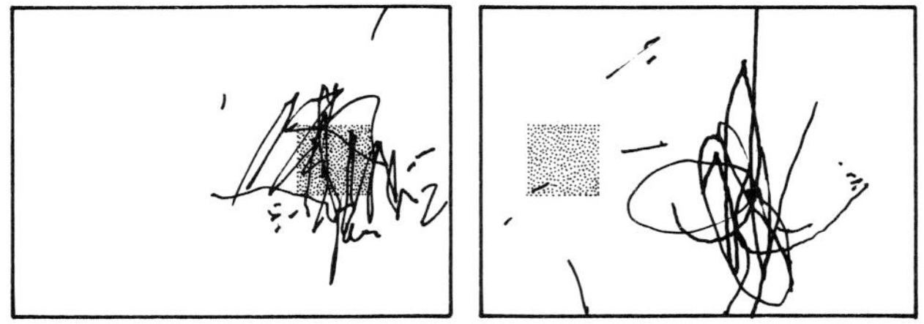

Tests with chimpanzees have also demonstrated this search for balance in graphic displays. When confronted with a sheet containing a square located in an off-center position, the chimp either marked inside it or introduced a scribble in order to effect graphic balance.

4

When confronted with another sheet, having two squares equally distanced on either side of the center, the chimp marked both squares but also made a third mark in the central blank space, as if to introduce a visual fulcrum to the arrangement.

5

When the designer introduces marks to the sheet, these force-fields react in response to their relationship with the format. A second mark again modifies these energy lines which, as the marks continue, shift and alter until the final graphic design determines their ultimate structure.

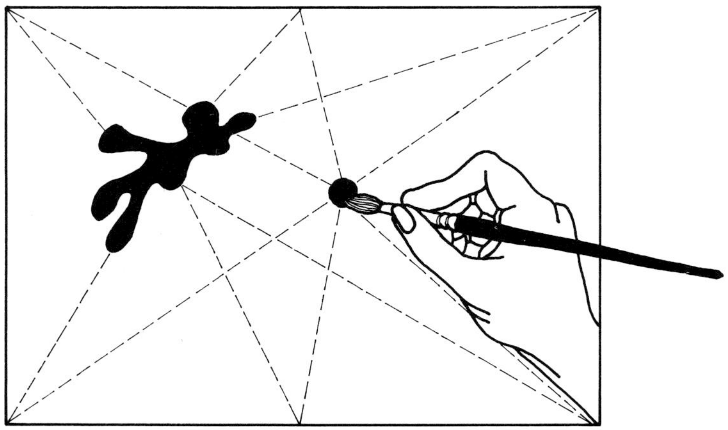

6

Force-fields, and the graphics that generate them, are sensed against the frame of reference (the edge of the picture). If a physical or graphic frame does not exist, the eye then seeks another visual container. For example, the frame of reference for this drawing is its linear boundary, but the frame of reference for this page is the edge of the book.

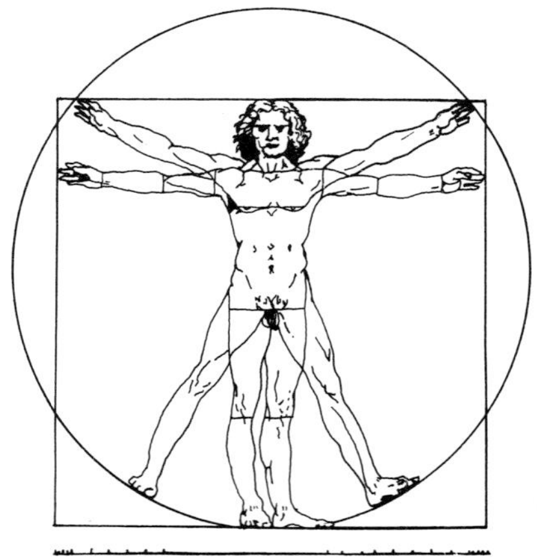

Image as Distance Regulator

Pictorial images automatically regulate the physical distance between viewer and viewed. This image--constructed from dots like a pointilliste painting or a newspaper photograph--has little figurative meaning when viewed from this distance. However, if the page is moved away from the eyes, the dots are assembled into a tonal pattern that can be readily interpreted as an identifiable picture.

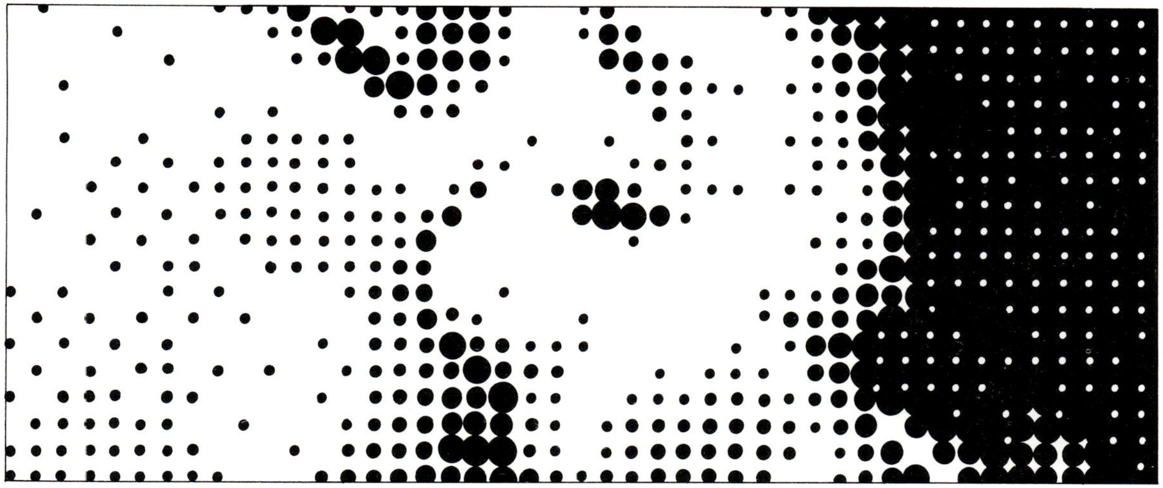

1

2

Many types of design drawings comprise pictures and words, in order to communicate a complexity of information. Often these are orchestrated to be perceived from different viewing distances. This drawing functions for two viewing relationships: first, overall visibility of layout, titles, and a basic impression of the plan; second, more detailed information contained within the plan, necessitating a closer inspection by the viewer.

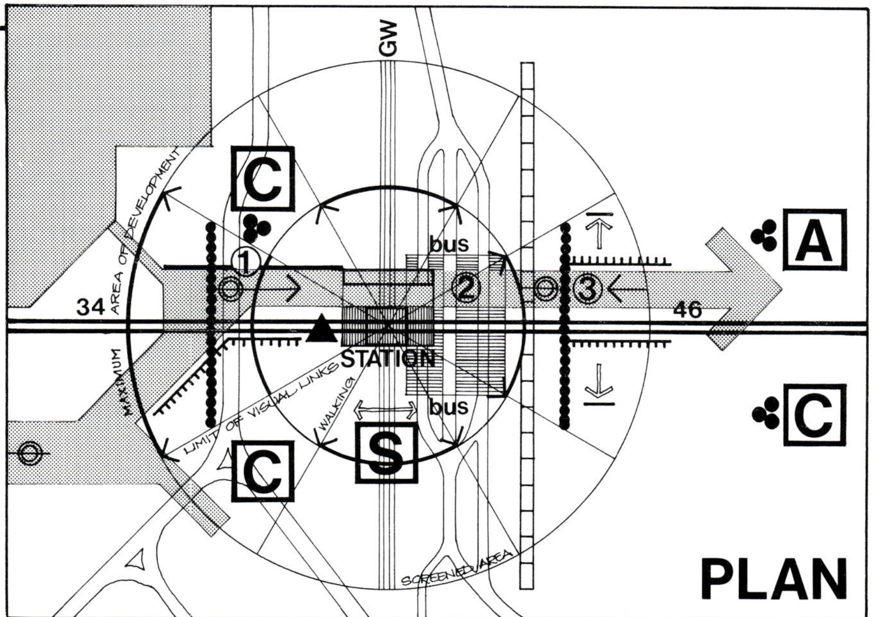

3

An awareness of viewing distances imposed by graphics is important in design, for it is central to an ability to communicate.

When designing sheet layouts and multiple displays, check their degree of readability by assuming the predicted viewing position of the intended audience. This process is echoed in the way artists stand back from their canvases to judge visual effects from vantage points beyond the point of execution.

Scale in Graphics

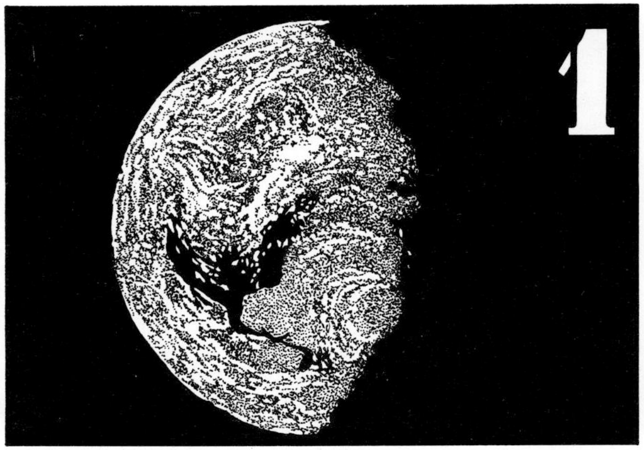

The size and scale of an image automatically introduces both a physical and a mental viewing distance when either making or viewing pictorial information. For instance, this representation, many million times smaller than its actual size, rockets the spectator's mental viewing stance several thousand miles into outer space.

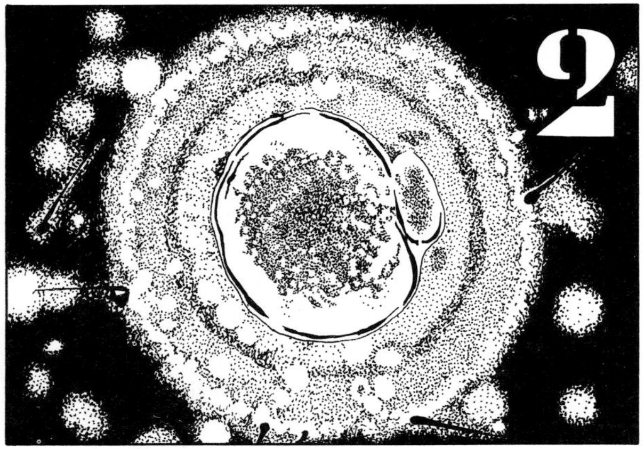

On the other hand, this drawing of a human egg cell takes us into the world of inner space, making possible conceptually what is impossible physically. Although the graphic size of this image is identical to that in the preceding frame, its scale is several thousand times larger than that of the cell in reality.

Selecting scale in graphics and orthographics is the way to regulate the distance between the designer's (and viewer's) mental stance and the size or degree of complexity of a concept. For example, plans, sections, and elevations are usually drawn at 1/4" = 1'-0" or 1/8" = 1'-0" (metric equivalents 1:50 or 1:100), but a scale of 1/2" = 1'-0" (1:20) allows details to be focused.

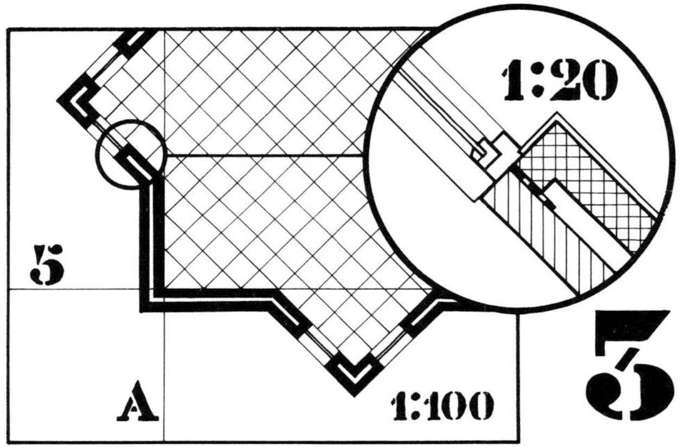

Increasingly larger buildings and building complexes can be shrunk along decreasing scales of 1/16" = 1'-0" (1:200) or 1:500. Thus, in selecting a scale the designer not only regulates the distance of an idea from his eye but also regulates its graphic size so that it fits within the confines of his drawing board.

As it is usual for environmental designers, for practical reasons, to visualize at reduced scales, it is important to immerse a developing idea in different scales. In this fashion a prowess at visualization is enhanced and a new idea is allowed to "breathe."

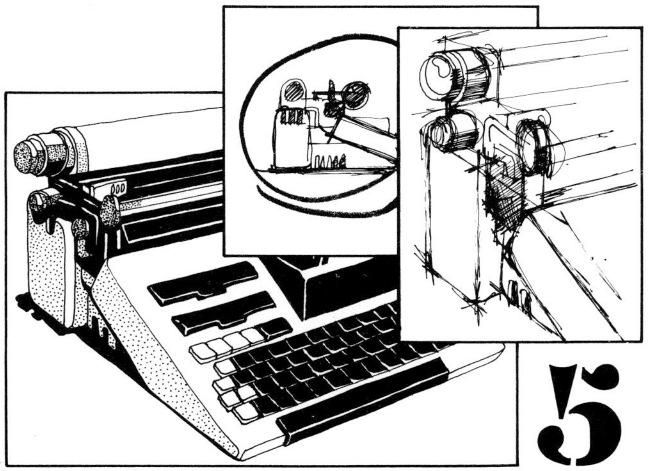

Whenever possible in the design process, it is a good idea to realize plans in a scale at which human figures can be identifiably represented as something other than dots. This metamorphosis begins to occur in 1/8" = 1'-0" (1:100) scale. The adoption of this and larger scales in both design and presentation functions as a check by allowing the depiction of materials and furniture and, of course, the people they relate to.

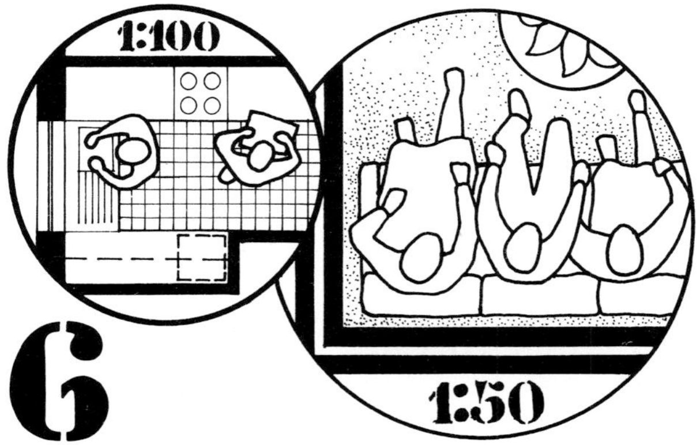

The Influence of Graphic Size

1 Selecting the size of an image requires giving equal weight to the nature of the picture in the mind's eye (i.e., its degree of content and complexity), its function in context with other images, audience size, and the related question of the appropriate medium.

Another factor in the selection of size is the question of aptness. For instance, artists find that two-dimensional ideas can dictate their own size, with a representation appearing visually appropriate at one size but losing this appropriateness when transformed to another. In other words, a well-designed postage stamp intended for individual consumption may not always magnify successfully into a billboard with proportions intended for mass consumption.

2 By affording increased readability over greater distance, graphics transmitted on larger formats take visual precedence over their smaller counterparts. Also, by filling the visual field with graphic information, extra-large images can induce a profoundly dramatic effect on the viewer.

3 However, when presenting graphic displays to groups of observers, such as critique panels, avoid overmixing extremes in format size, because miniature formats invite close scrutiny, whereas larger ones interpose greater viewing distances. Such mixtures can result in the breakup of the observer-group and thus a breakdown of communication.

4 The creation of very small images exercises the fingers and hand, whereas the production of larger ones can involve movement by the whole body. Larger formats require the adoption of mediums, applicators, and techniques having a scale and intensity compatible with their size. For example, to execute a large, complex design drawing in hard-grade graphite is to render its image practically invisible from viewing points beyond arm's length.

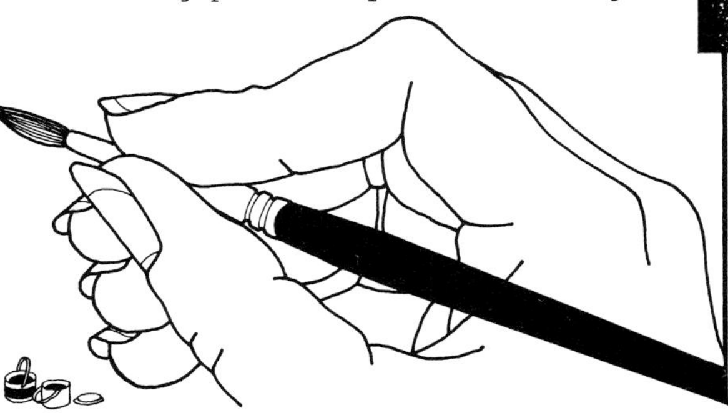

5 It is imperative that the beginning designer experience the creation of artwork to different format sizes. Those who work exclusively on smaller formats find extreme difficulty in switching to larger versions, whereas those with a command of the bigger sizes can easily scale down their work to more modest proportions.

How the Eye Scans Images

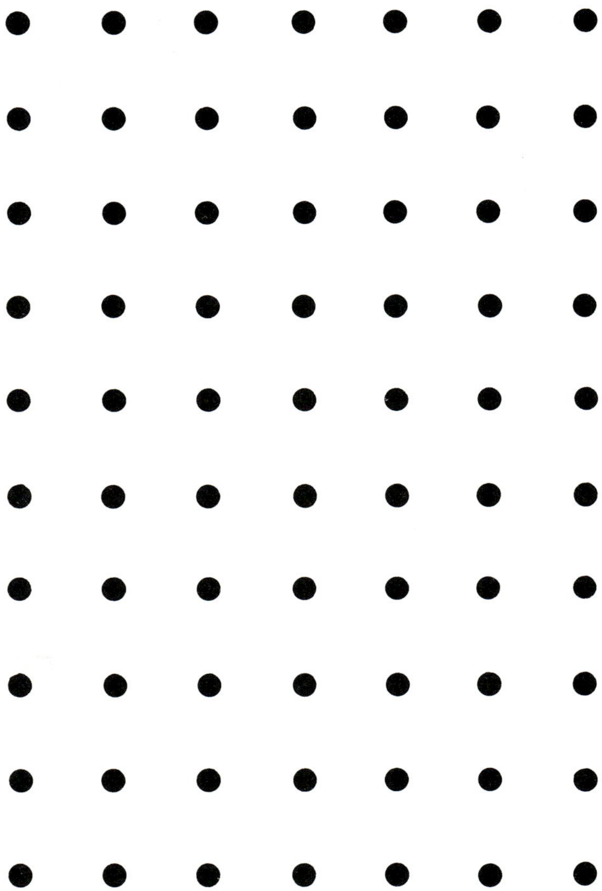

1

The act of seeing is a dynamic and creative process involving participation between viewer and viewed. For example, in denying the viewer a focus for his attention, the regularity of the dot configuration in this classic perception experiment causes the eye to search continuously for a stabilized image. In doing so, the eye scans the ordered arrangement, constructing and reconstructing a changing sequence of rows and squares. However, if just one dot had been drawn larger than the rest--thereby reducing its surrounding space--it would have immediately become the center of attention.

Pictorial images are also reconstructed visually in a similar fashion and--depending upon the interests or motives of the observer--certain points of focus in a composition will act as a visual anchor from which to perceive the remaining information.

2

3

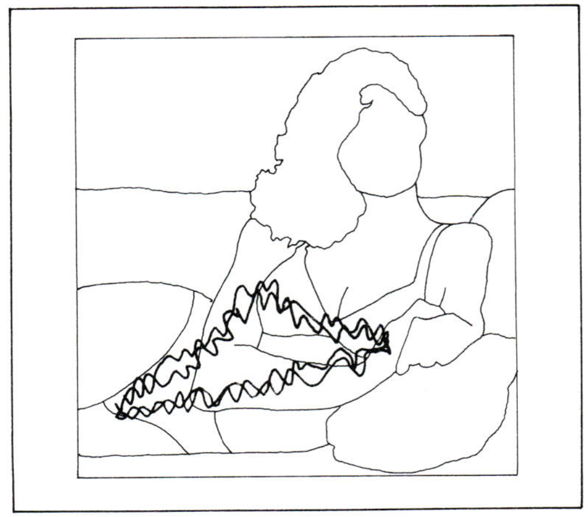

An instrument called an Eye Movement Recorder, much used in assessing the communicative effectiveness of commercial ads, can track the movements of the eye as it views images. The scanner produced this pattern of eyeball movement when recording a male observing the image on the left.

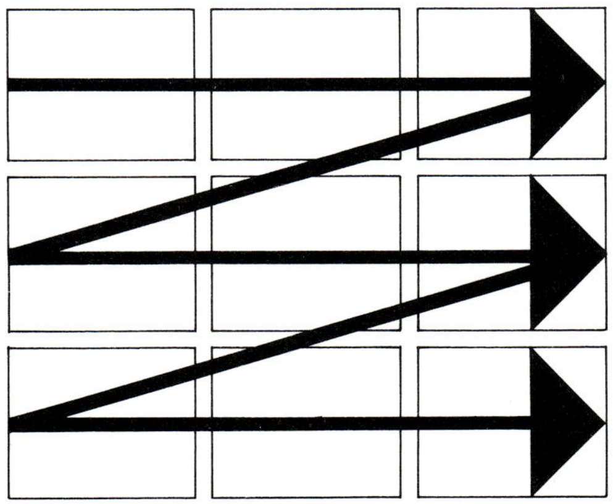

4

People in the Western world tend to "read" bland arrays of pictorial information in much the same way text is read, working downward and scanning from left to right. However, because images take precedence over written material and large images tend to attract the eye before smaller ones, the beginning designer can proceed to program visual priority into graphic communication.

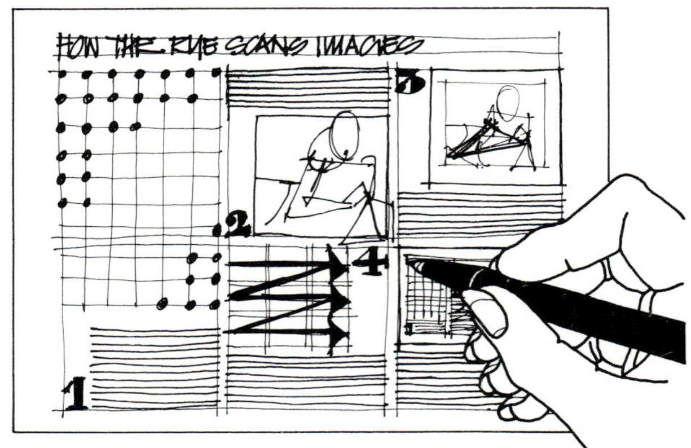

The preplanning of visual pathways through individual images, the various elements in a display sheet, and a hierarchy of information in multiple sheets of presentation graphics is an essential part of composition and layout design. The pathways can be determined initially by means of thumbnail sketches made to explore the sequencing of words and images to best advantage.

5

The Pictorial Zones

1

When perceiving or memorizing images, or reconstructing pictorial versions, it is important to understand their basic zones.

When observing a funneled or blinkered view, we experience a natural frame of reference. The eyes are steered directly to the heart of an image for closer scrutiny by the positive framing of its limits.

2

Panoramic vistas, on the other hand, require the superimposition of a frame of reference. In vision, this is represented by the edge of the visual field; in graphics, this is a compositional decision in the placement of a selected boundary or pictorial frame.

3

Pictorial zones are best understood if visualized as a stage set. For instance, the background of a picture acts as a backcloth against which the "performance," or graphic message, is examined. In providing a stop to the image, background information is less distinct than other zones comprising more specific degrees of detail.

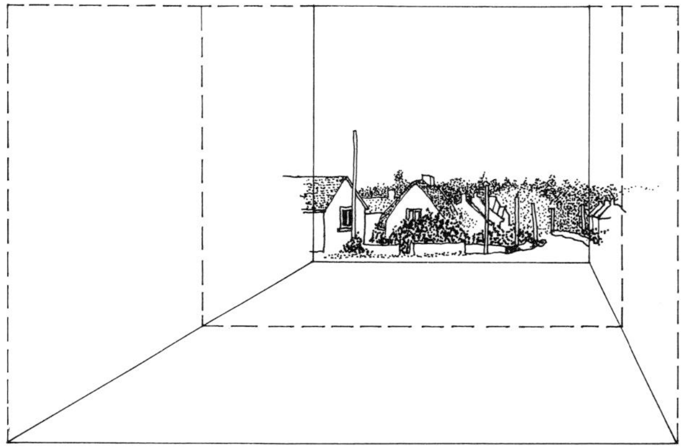

4

"Center stage," or middle distance, functions as the core zone. In graphics, this is where the main reason for communicating takes place, an event that is represented by the designed form, as in, for example, elevations. In this key sector, objects usually appear as complete and in some degree of detail.

5

Objects or events that occur at the very front of the "stage," i.e., in the foreground, appear as incomplete. They are larger, generally darker, and in sharp detail. Great care must therefore be taken with their positioning. Avoid blocking the middle distance, or unintentionally disrupting the frame by projecting elements.

6

The handling of the area around the frame--especially to the left--is crucial in composition, as this is where the eye enters the picture. With experience, various devices can be employed to guide the eye inward to the message zone by using either direct or diverse routes.

Focus and Focal Points

Although the amount of information absorbed by the eyes at any one moment is enormous, our field of vision varies in its degree of focus. For instance, peripheral vision (the information around the outer edge of our visual field) is blurred, but the small area at the center is in sharp focus. This focal zone occurs where the viewing angle of our two eyes converges in the close scrutiny of objects within the field of view.

Here are the two basic forms of graphics that articulate focus and focal points in different ways.

1

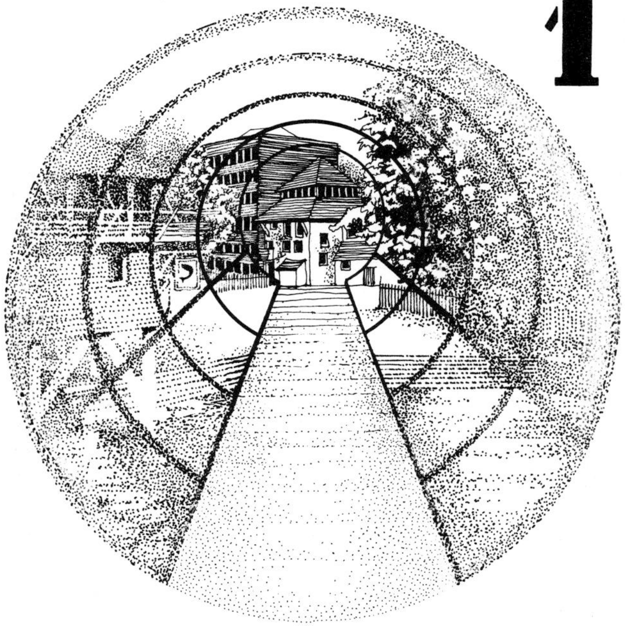

The single-glance graphic usually contains one focal point. It presents information apparently seen--but intended for visual consumption--in a single, stationary perception. These range from ads (sometimes absorbed from the "corner" of the eye) to French Impressionist paintings, the latter portraying diffuse "impressions" of the behavior of light on objects with one center of focus. This drawing illustrates a general defocusing of information for an at-a-glance communication.

In "switched-foci" graphics, the total area of a pictorial display is evenly in sharp focus. Rich arrays of detail invite a close visual encounter and provide the wandering eye with high degrees of information. Perhaps the best example of this type is Pre-Raphaelite art, which filled large canvases with meticulously painted detail. This drawing also operates on a high focal level, inviting the viewer to make a visual journey around its format.

2

How to Create Focal Points

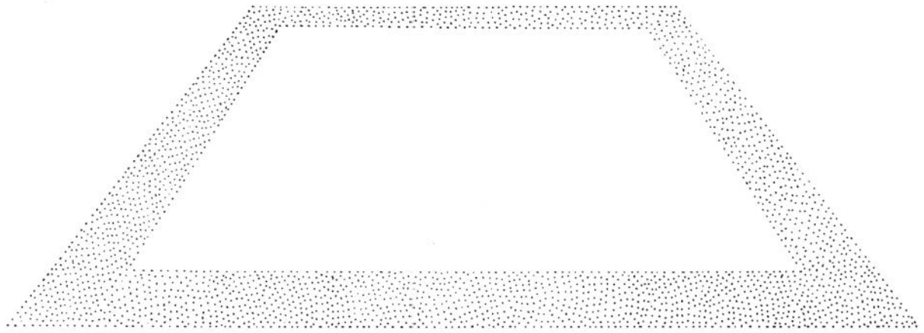

Perception experiments demonstrate that the human eye quickly tires of bland images. For example, during a test in which a subject was asked to look at this display for an extended period, it was found that the retinal image of this work simply faded away, even though it remained fixed in the gaze.

1 The basic function of the eye is to detect movement and change in the stimulus. When the stimulus is graphic, the eye is immediately attracted to areas of contrast. These function as centers of attention, or focal points, and can be introduced into artwork and graphic displays in a variety of ways.

2 Varying degrees of detail in a drawing will entertain the eye more than a completely bland display. Highly detailed areas of information command the attention of the viewer because they signal important zones.

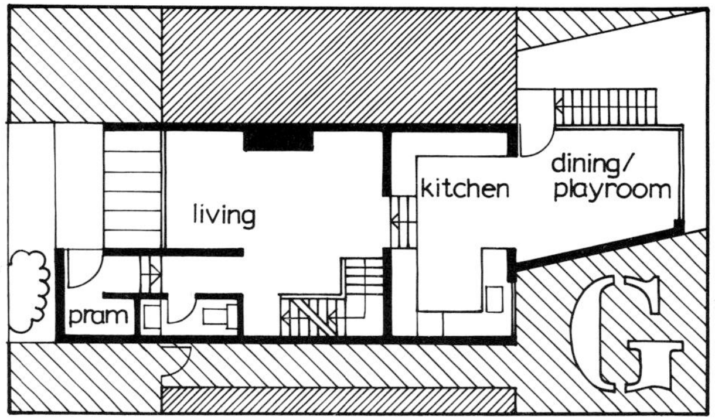

3 Color change--for instance, the use of a single hue in an achromatic graphic, or an intense stab of red in a predominantly green-based scheme--is another means of directing the eye to the key points. This effect can also be achieved using tonal contrasts--with a light value contained in a field of dark or, conversely, a dark center of attention in an area of light tonal value.

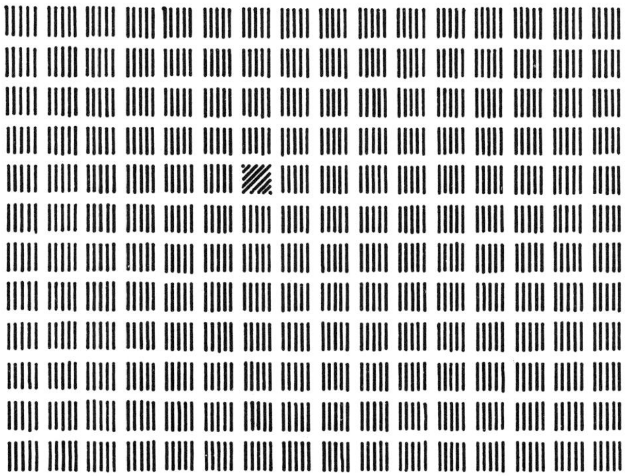

4 Changes in the use of a technique or between mediums within a single format or a wall display comprising multiple presentation units will also function as a focal point.

5 Contrast is also created by introducing visual changes in the components that make up an image or a multiple display. For example, one contrasting element in a field of regular ones will immediately draw attention to the information within the dissonant element.

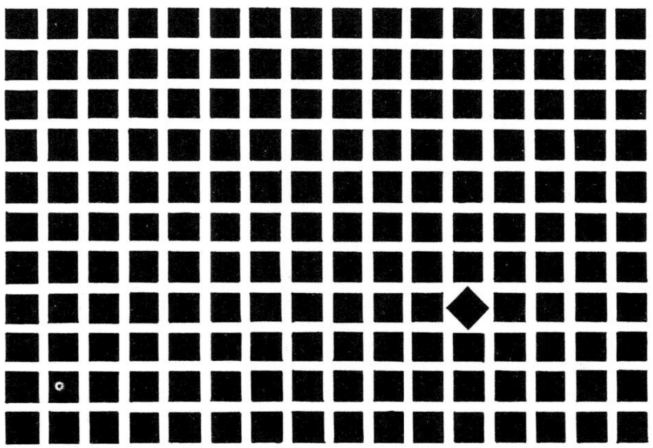

6 A key aspect of creating centers of attention is to control the interval between graphic elements, the spatial relationships between positive and negative information. If a single unit is isolated from those in close proximity, it will attract attention. Conversely, if this relationship is reversed, units in close proximity will take visual precedence.

Animating the Message Area

When designing a graphic it is important to make sure that its focal points coincide with its intended message. Generally, message areas should occur around the central region of a format, but shifts in emphasis during the rendering phase can pull the eye to a variety of different centers of interest.

For instance, the subsequent treatment of a basic line drawing can isolate the message area in totally different zones when the treatment is animated in response to what the image is meant to communicate.

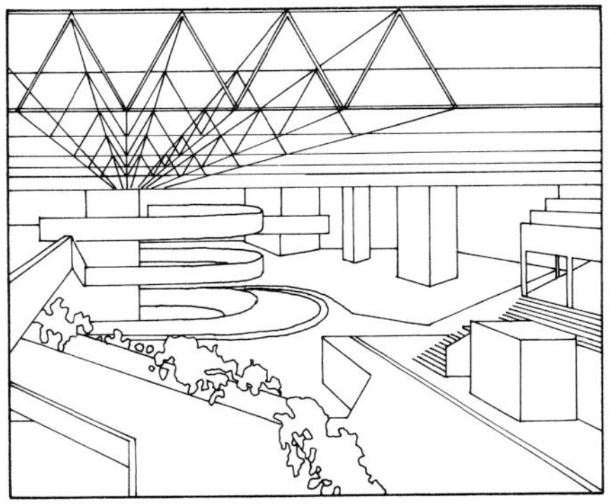

1

2 In this interpretation, a detailed explanation of the roof structure confines the message area to the ceiling plane.

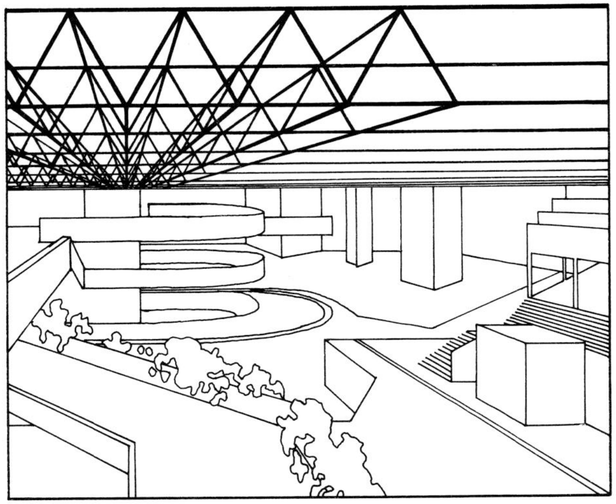

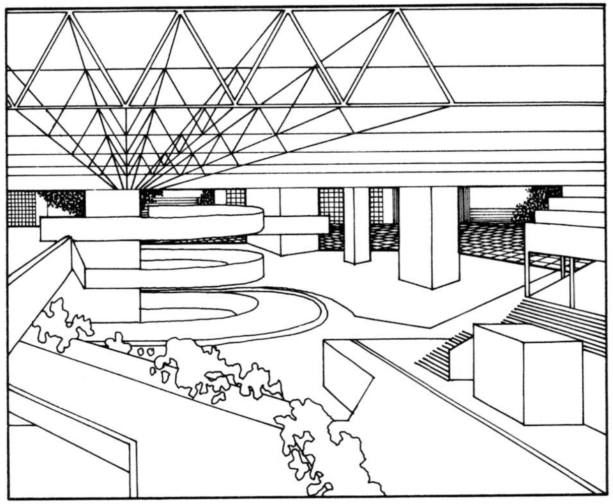

3 The emphasis shifts when the point of the drawing responds to interior-to-exterior visual links.

4 The analysis of lighting effects draws the eye to illuminated zones within the format.

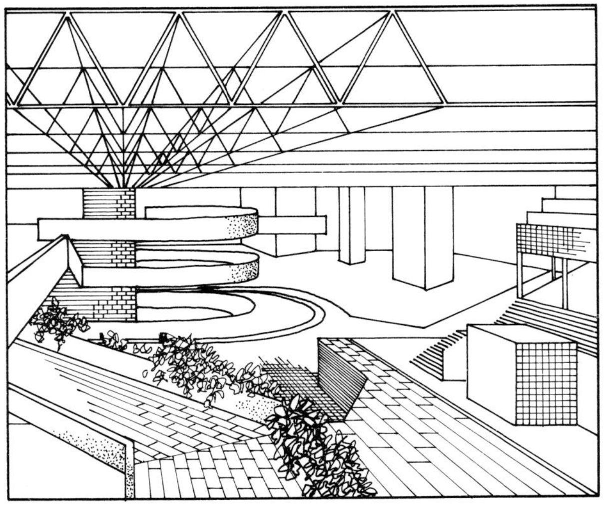

5 Another investigation--this time studying the nature of materials and their finishes--spreads the location of message areas.

6 Yet another dimension is brought to graphics when words and symbols are introduced to direct the eye to multiple points of annotated information.

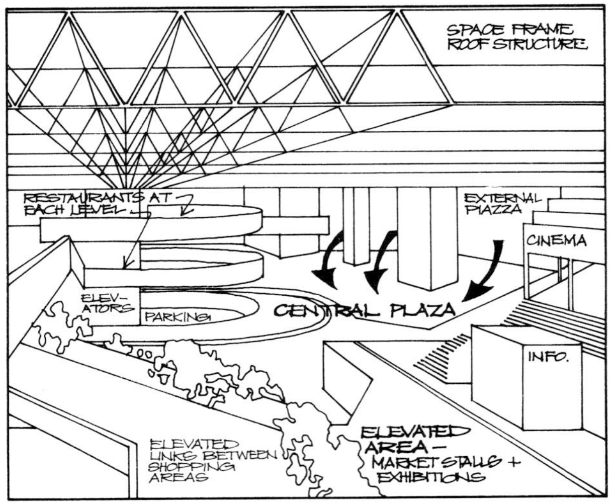

The Art of Basic Composition

1

Regular artwork formats divide into three basic types: square, portrait, and landscape.

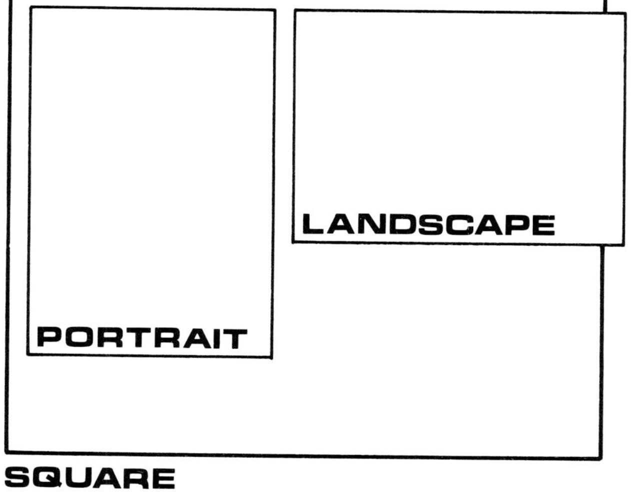

2

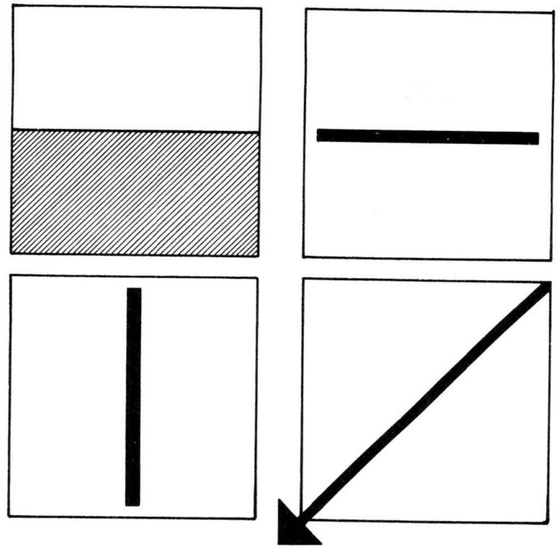

Whichever format is selected, it is important that basic compositions avoid horizons, or other horizontal features, together with vertical or diagonal divisions that cut the format into equal halves.

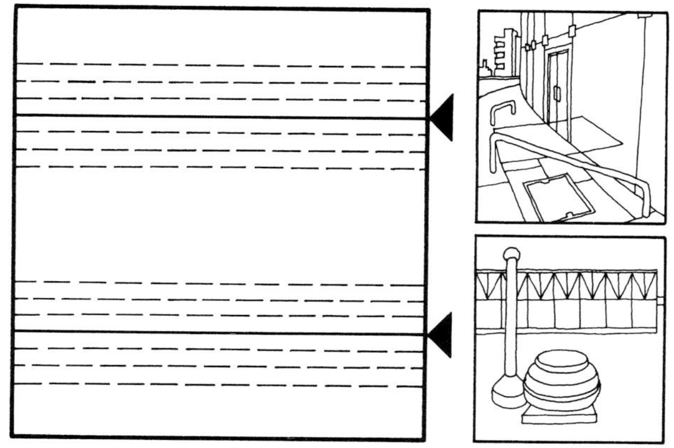

3

Formats should not be divided equally because symmetrical compositions make for deadly dull artwork, information divided centrally being boring to the eye. Therefore, locate major horizontal elements nearer the top or bottom of formats, and seek off-center locations for vertical and diagonal elements.

4

Also, avoid the regular displacement or isolation of both repetitive and irregular forms. This is a common trap that leads to bland pictorial displays.

5

Instead, aim to juxtapose objects along scales of depth, allowing them to vary in size and to overlap in clusters. In this fashion, graphics move toward our perception of objects in space, profiles of overlapping groups of objects providing the potential for more exciting contours.

6

Finally, avoid dead-central vanishing points in perspectives, as they tend to lead the eye directly to the heart of symmetrical compositions. Instead, allow degrees of unpredictability or the information's content to guide their location.

Various Graphic Formats

1

By being associated with windows through which images are viewed, conventional graphic formats are usually square or rectangular. Picture frames enhance this illusion and are often simulated in unmounted drawings by a clearly defined edge, which is sometimes reinforced with a dark line that isolates the drawings' pictorial illusion from surrounding space.

However, if we examine the outer shape of our peripheral field of vision, we find it more related to the circle than the square. Elliptical formats--much used by Victorian photographers--can be exciting, as are circular and even free-form formats, which have been used successfully by many artists, such as Pablo Picasso.

Experience with the more unconventional shapes offers an exciting challenge to the designer in search of visually dynamic images.

One method of achieving dynamic formats is to allow important elements within a composition to break through the confines of a frame.

2

3

A popular format is the soft-cornered square or rectangle, because of its obvious associations with film and the shape of television screens. Its use conveys a sense of immediacy, especially when conveying serial images.

4

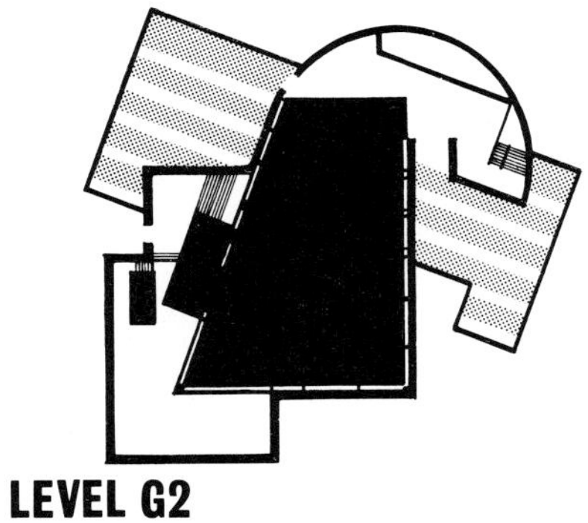

Visual drama can also be achieved by allowing an image to float on the sheet and find its own format shape. However, because the eye seeks stability, such images should be designed in a conscious relationship with the shape of their support sheet and, whenever possible, "anchored" by using, for example, title blocks.

To complement the blur at the periphery of our visual field, some designers allow artwork to fade at the edge. However, such images should be worked on smooth surfaces. For instance, if a perspective is drawn on heavily textured paper without a crisp edge or clear frame, the surface grain will invade and optically confuse the image, thus negating any illusion of depth.

5

The Nature of the Frame of Reference

When composing a graphic, it is wise to remain open to the potential uniqueness of its format. For example, during the image-making process a preparatory thumbnail sketch might explore the possibility of how an evolving orthographic or perspective might achieve a more creatively shaped expression. The following are basic examples of graphics that, under different influences, have "found" their own shaped existence, both on and off the sheet.

While echoing the main theme of the image, this container immediately focuses the viewer on the center of attention.

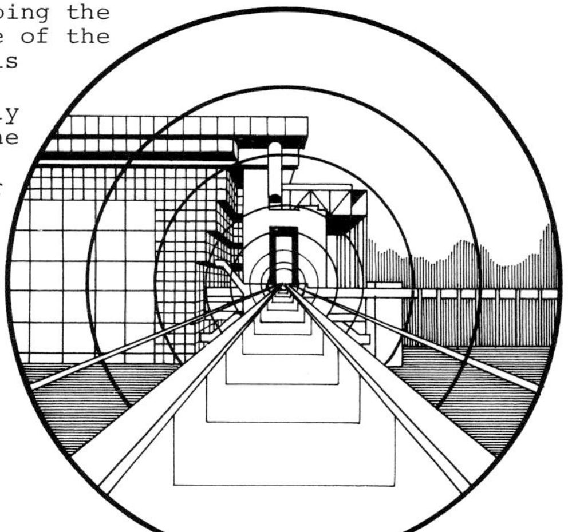

1

2

A line drawing with its extremities cropped by an "invisible" boundary creates illusions of being simultaneously "fixed" and "free."

This aerial view is shaped by the natural limits of its subject matter. In this case, its "floating" impression can be arrested by adding labels or a title block.

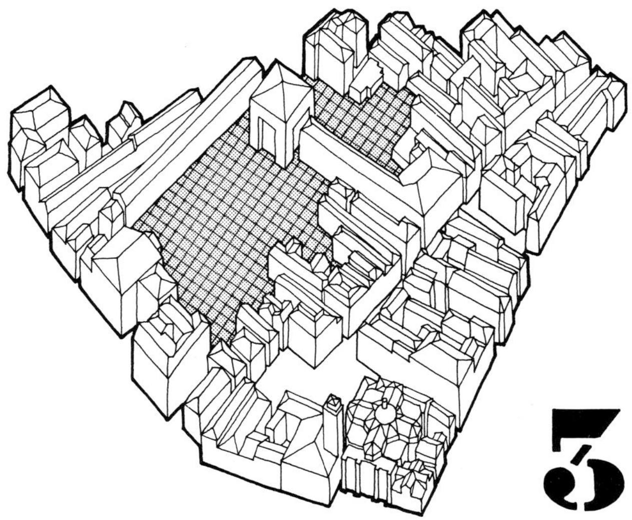

3

4

In being associated with the spontaneity of quick sketch techniques, the controlled, "unplanned" appearance of formats can function as refreshing focal points, particularly within large orthographic displays.

For example, the dynamic edge of this drawing derives from a recognition of its perspective structure.

5

This irregular but consciously designed frame results from an erosion caused by a selection of its contained elements attempting to "escape".

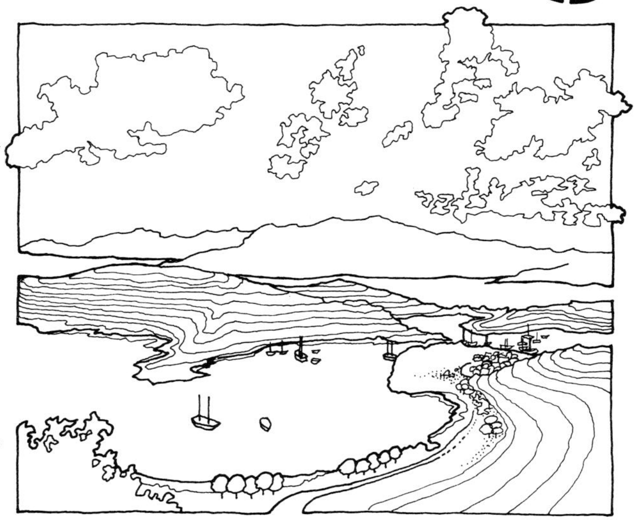

6

Interestingly shaped orthographics and axonometrics can be cut away from their sheet and card mounted for a presentation which, against modular displays, act as a center of attention.

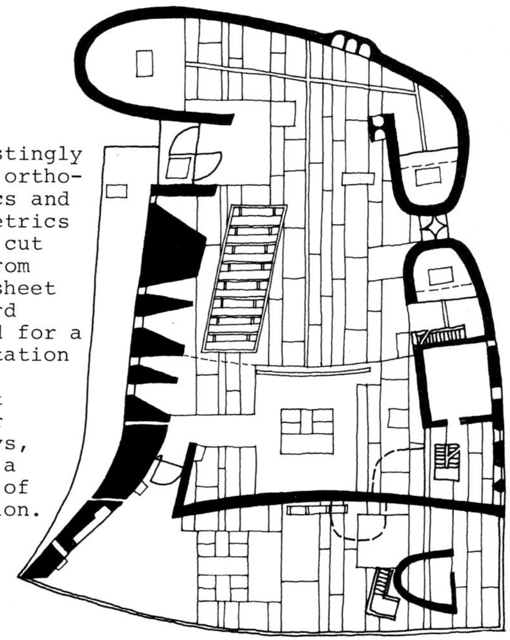

Deciding the Framework of an Idea

1

Prior to organizing the various graphic ingredients into the anatomy of an image, there are certain decisions--often ignored, or taken for granted--that should be made. For example, what is the message that is being communicated? Is it an abstract concept best served by words and diagrams or, if a figurative picture, which drawing system will best act as a vehicle for its communication? Would a freehand sketch function better than a measured drawing or orthographic projection? Would an axonometric design perform better than a perspective? Will a single image suffice, or does its complexity demand a multiple set of drawings?

2

In any event, before embarking on finished artwork, it is worthwhile predesigning the graphic in sketch form. Ideas can be quickly evolved on tracing paper overlays--each layer refining the impression of the last--before rescaling and transfering it to the drawing board.

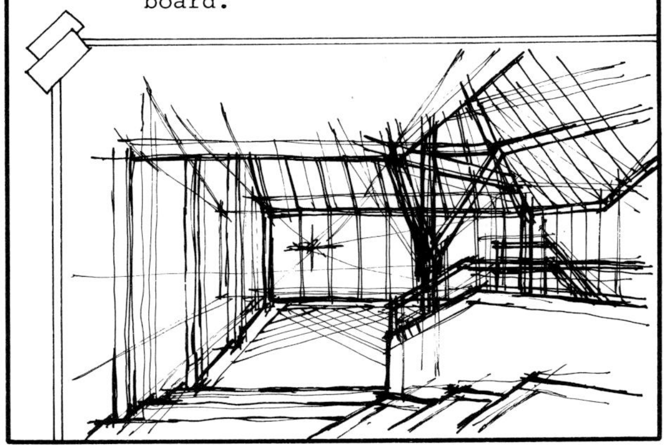

3

During this preview, make sure that the most important information areas in the composition coincide with the focal points or optical centers of attention.

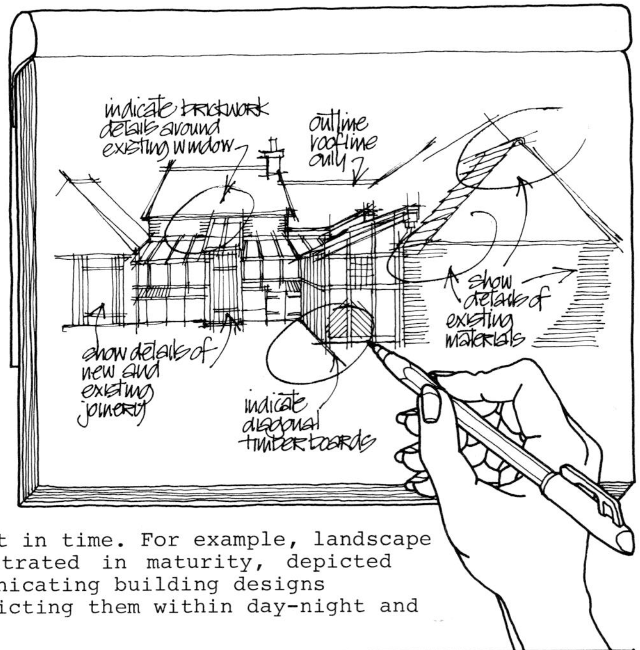

4

A further factor in the organization of an image--embodied in the choice of graphic vehicle--is the need to determine the best possible viewpoint of its subject matter. The selected point of view obviously will be assumed and shared by future observers.

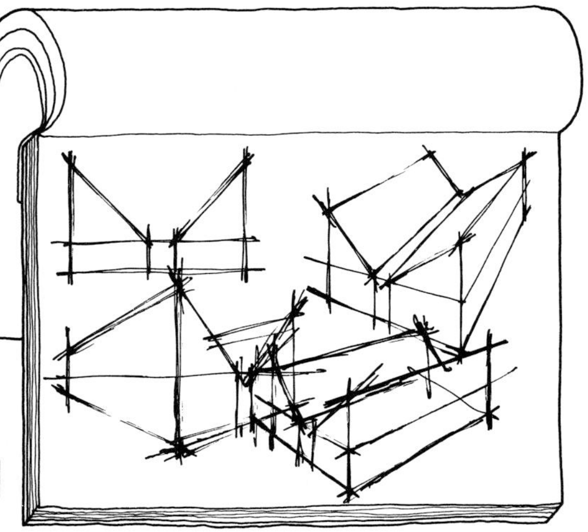

5

Always fix pictorial images at a point in time. For example, landscape design and planting should be illustrated in maturity, depicted in a future setting. Also, when communicating building designs consider any advantages gained by depicting them within day-night and seasonal contexts.

2 MECHANICS OF REPRESENTATION

The Plan and the Section

Plans and sections represent the most important drawings in orthographic projection. They are both sectional cuts, the former being made in a horizontal plane, the latter in the vertical plane. In presentation, design plans and sections communicate the form and spatial quality of an object or building and are generally drawn to a small scale. Additional sections, called "production" or "working" drawings, are drafted to larger scales in order to describe materials, constructional methods, and assembly of details.

N.B.: The key to successful plan and section drafting is the sympathetic use of line weights--in other words a hierarchy of line thickness that responds both to degrees of importance in drawn elements and to their spatial position in relation to the eye.

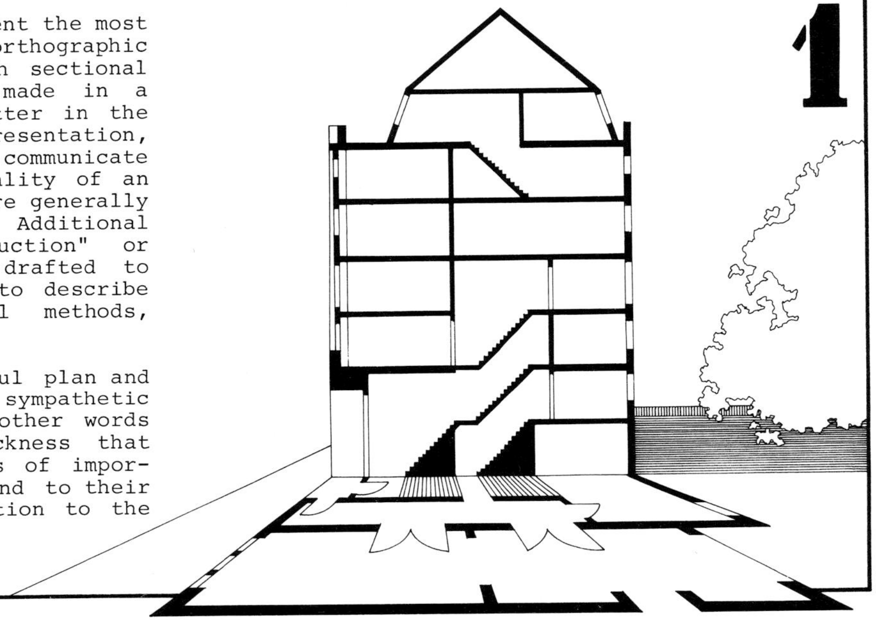

1

The plan is a dimensioned drawing that, being quick to set up, is found to be the most receptive when describing the formation of a design idea; indeed, le Corbusier suggested that it was the generator of ideas. It is also the drafting generator of the vertical section, the elevation, and the axonometric.

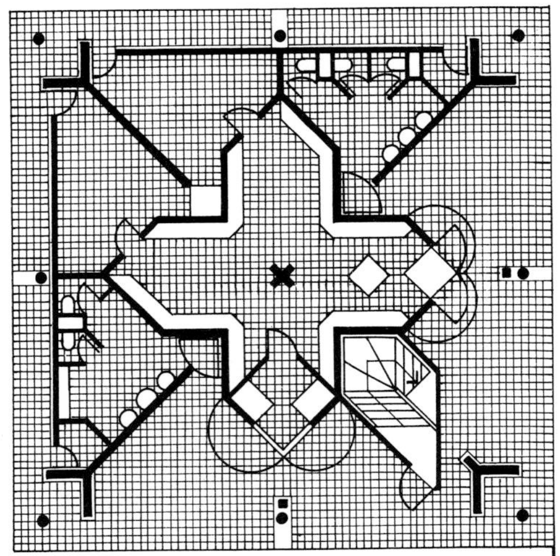

2

In order to show openings such as doors and windows, the plan usually slices through a building design at a point around 5'-0" (1.5m) above ground or floor level.

N.B.: As a general rule, when setting up the plan, drafting is worked after establishing fixed points such as columns and structural walls. Another aid to accuracy is to draw all curved lines before straight ones.

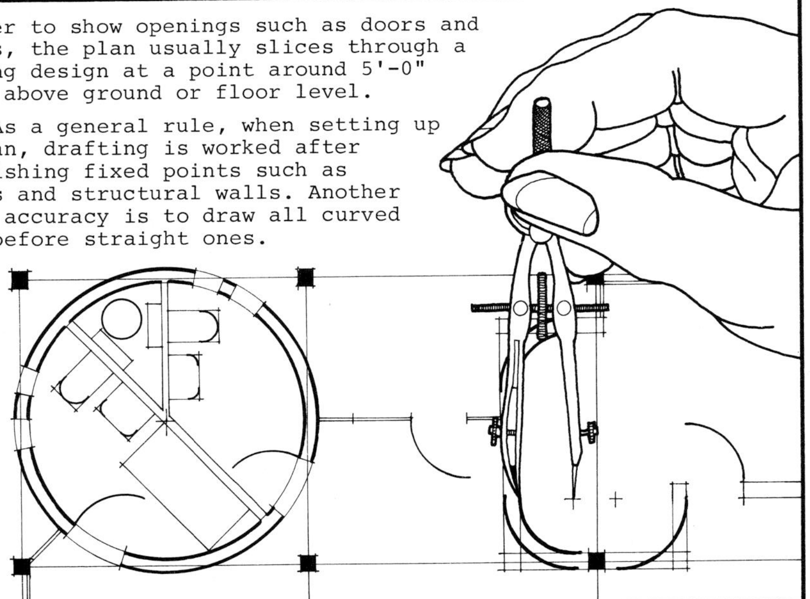

3

4 A·A

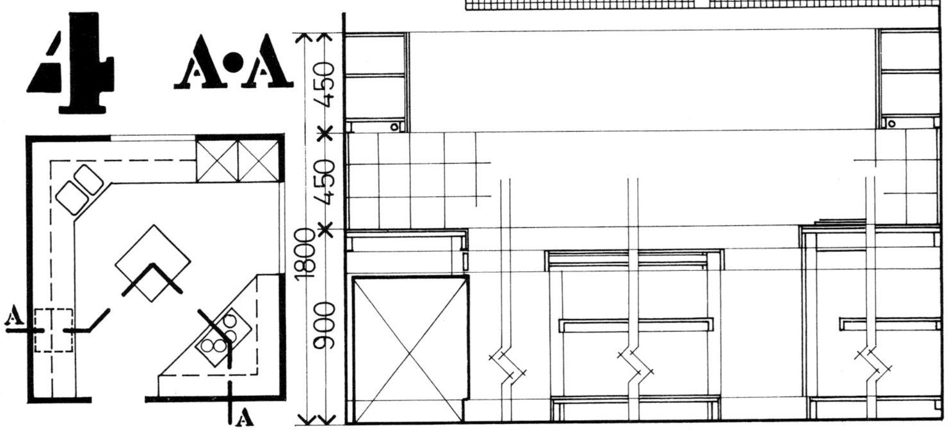

Incision points of vertical sections can differ in response to the kind of information being conveyed. For example, in order to explain important areas occurring at different points in depth, this production section is staggered selectively, its route being referenced on the accompanying plan.

N.B.: Depending on its relationship to the main axis of an object or building, the vertical section is usually termed a transverse, cross, or longitudinal section.

The Elevation

1 In elevations, all planes parallel to the drawing surface and perpendicular to the observer's line of vision retain their true size, scale, shape, and proportion. In design, elevations function to assess or convey the all-around massing and silhouette of a designed form and, together with sections, are used as a check on the planning stage.

Elevations represent a section taken in front of a form. This can be located at various points, such as 1'-0" (300mm), 10'-0" (3m), 15'-0" (4.5m) forward of the façade under study. This initial decision includes or excludes objects in the line of vision.

2 Decide also how much contextual information to include in the image, especially left and right of the façade. This can be determined by making a preliminary thumbnail layout sketch.

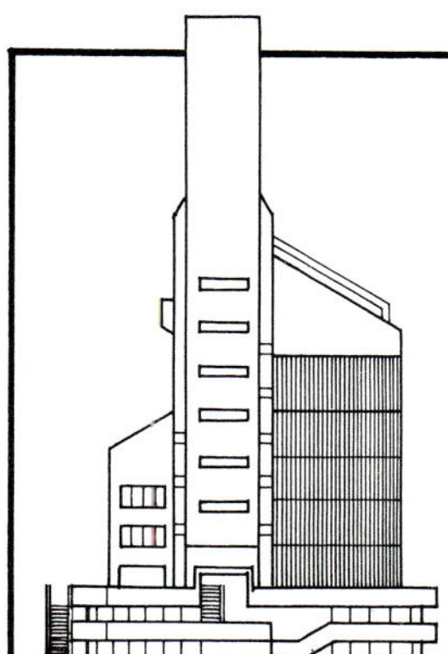

3 The scale selected for elevations should be appropriate to the degree of detail required for communication.

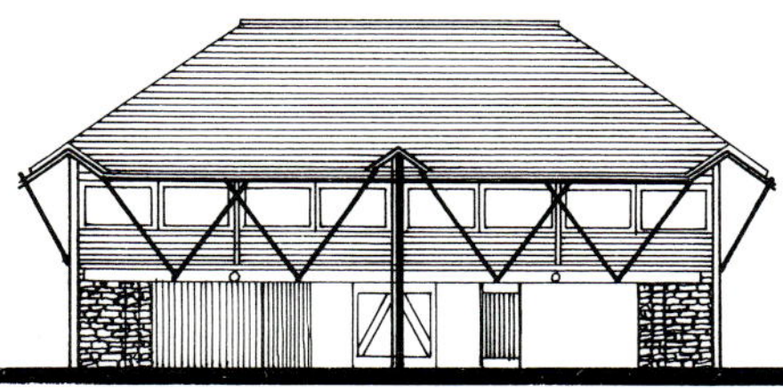

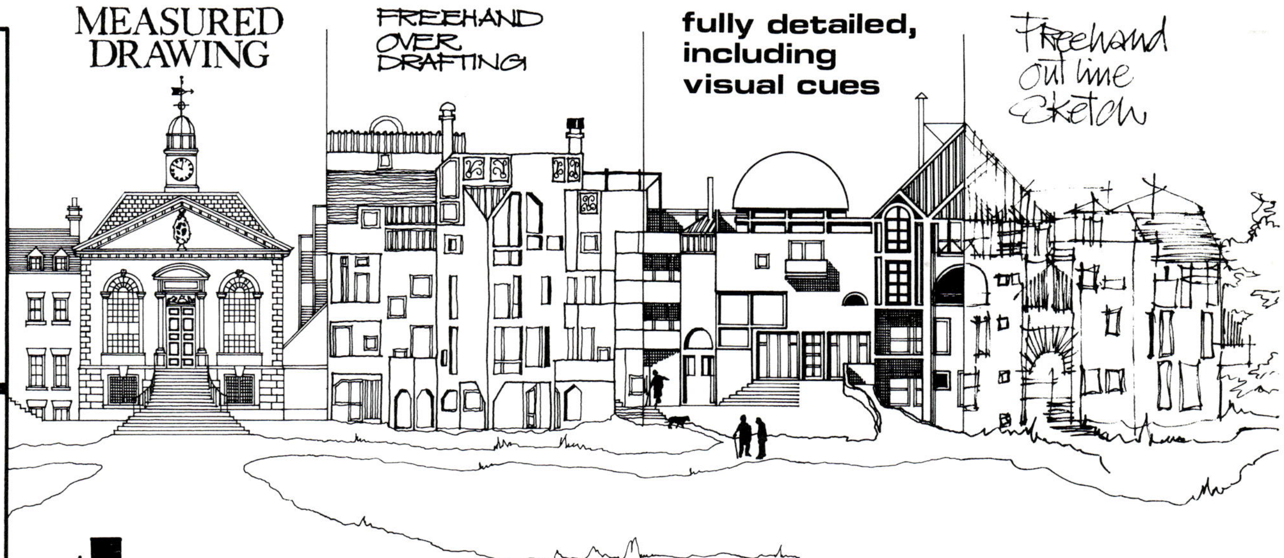

4 The choice of drawing technique should be directly related to the function of the orthographics in presentation, the amount of time available, and the experience and graphic ability of the designer.

The Axonometric and Isometric

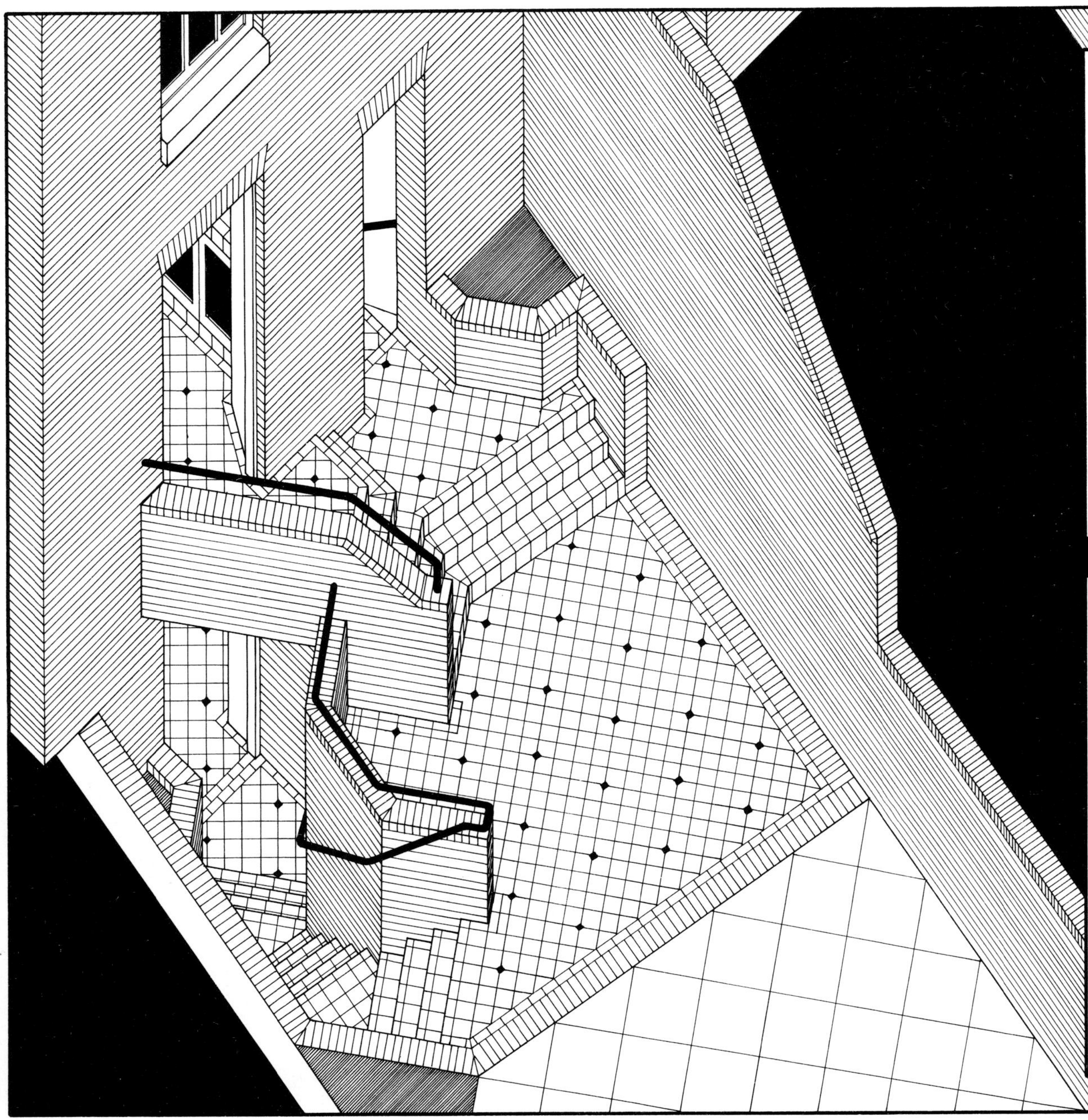

Axonometrics and isometrics are among the most widely used graphics in modern design. Their essentially cubic nature can exert great influence on a design idea. Simple to construct, they have obvious roots in Cubism, having been made popular in architectural graphics by Le Corbusier and Herbert Bayer.

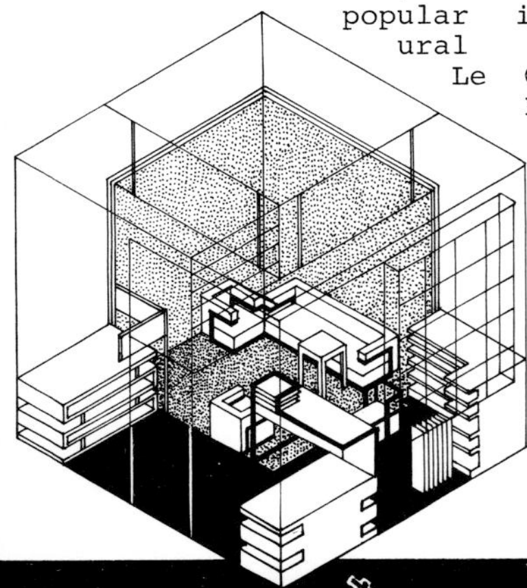

1

2

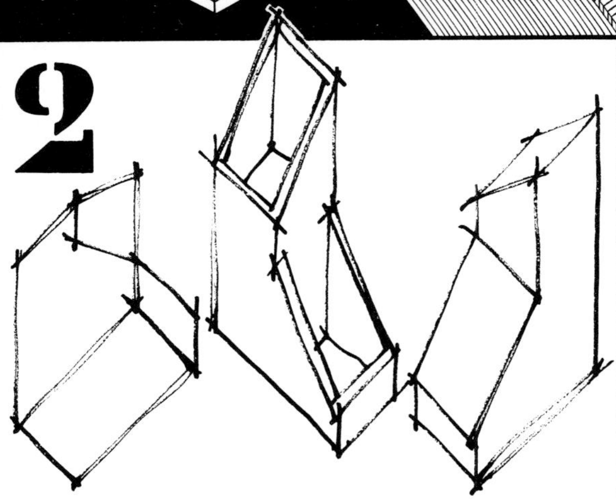

Prior to constructing an axonometric on the drawing board, a thumbnail sketch will find the optimum corner or side as a vantage point for looking into, onto, or up to a design concept.

Axonometrics in Action

1

Designers often refer to axonometrics as three-dimensional drawings because, like perspectives, their projections occupy a graphic illusion of the third dimension. However, being paraline drawings, they are fast and easy to construct, with or without the plan. Also, provided their inherent distortion is acceptable to the concept, they are highly useful design tools to explore and communicate cubic forms.

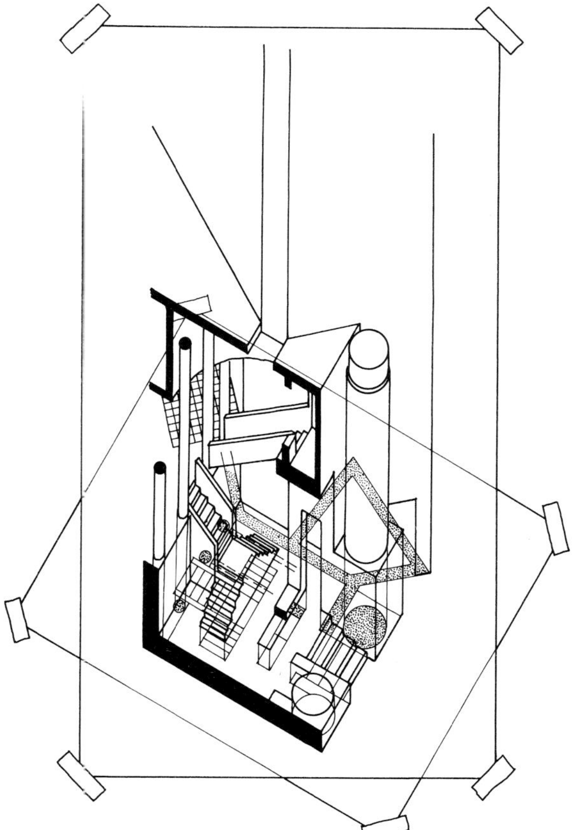

2

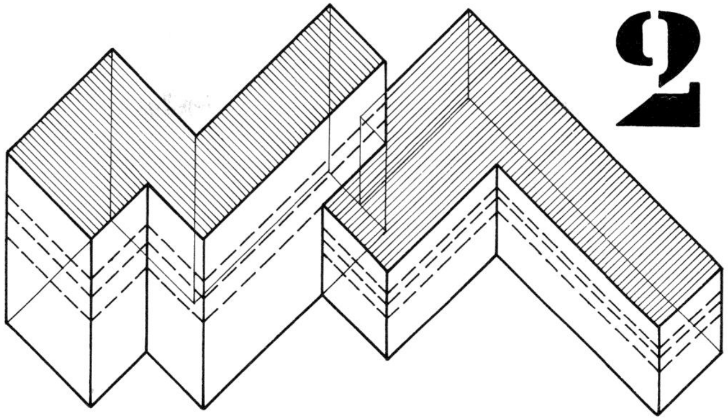

The plan oblique is an axonometric projection particularly useful when visualizing more complicated arrangements of form. In coinciding with the picture plane (the plane of the drawing surface), the true plan shape is projected vertically with all sets of parallel lines retaining true size.

N.B.: If required, a vertical depth distortion can be corrected along a scale of 3/4, 2/3, or 1/2 reduction.

3

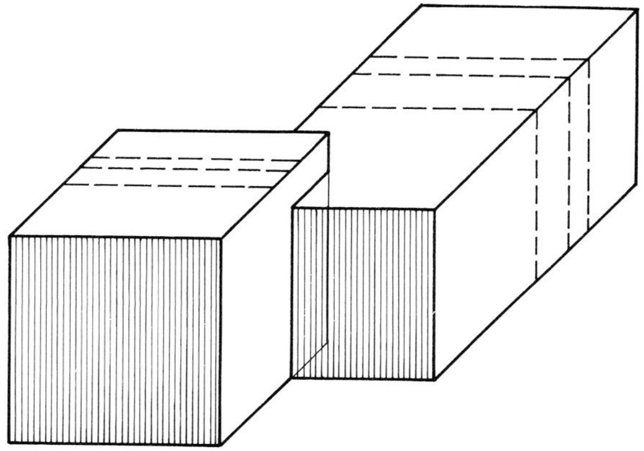

The elevation oblique is a horizontal axonometric projection from a true elevation shape coincident with the picture plane. Again, if required, horizontal depth distortion can be adjusted by reducing the scale.

4

The real ability of the axonometric is to diagram analytically the various facets of a design concept. For example, this sequence of "eroded" views of a building design functions as X-ray views concentrating on:

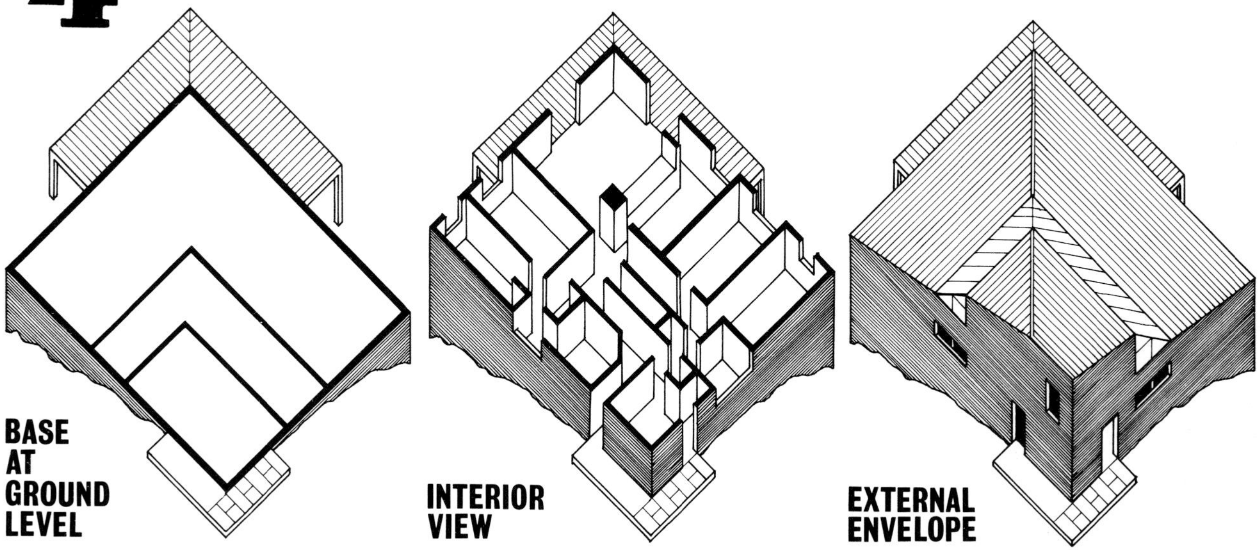

Peep-Show Graphics

The choice of drawing mode means selecting the graphic container that best illustrates a point of view of an object or of a design concept. As the subject matter becomes more intricate, kinds of graphic convention and their mixtures with others can be usefully employed.

1

The most common use of the section-axonometric combination is removal of a "lid" from a hollow form to allow aerial glimpses of internal workings.

However, in multilevel designs the cut can slice at different points and levels, to allow comparison among a variety of internal areas.

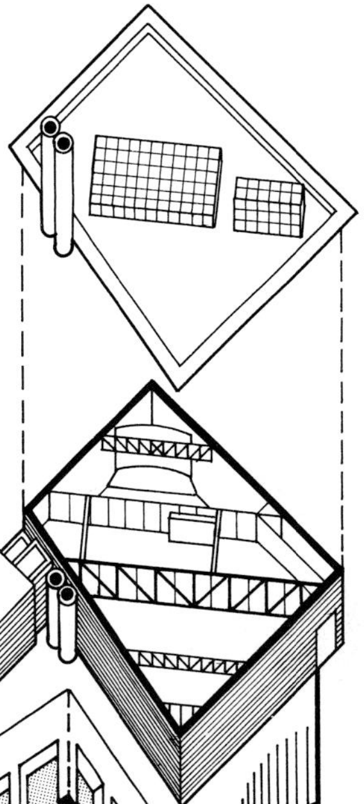

When cutting into axonometrics, it is important to control the degree and extent of incision in response to the amount of information to be communicated.

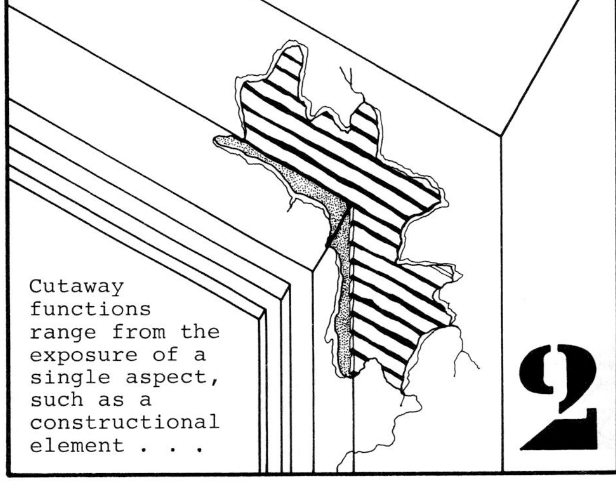

Cutaway functions range from the exposure of a single aspect, such as a constructional element . . .

2

. . . to a more total erosion of the outer mass.

In this case, visual confusion is lessened by annotating interior cells with an accompanying legend. Also, including a smaller, adjacent axonometric of its uncut form will aid a mental check of its complete impression.

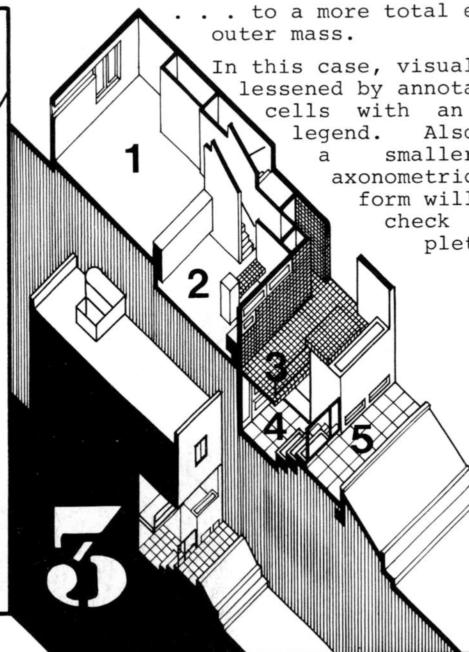

3

4

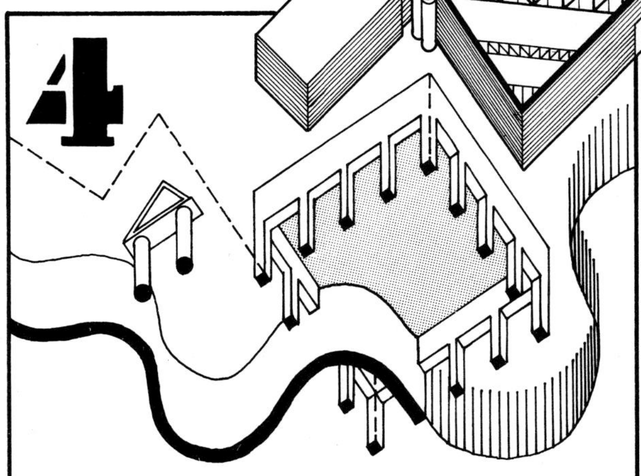

In exploiting the ambiguity of paraline drawings, the worm's-eye-view axonometric detaches the plan for an upward glimpse of interiors. Potentially confusing to the uninitiated, this version is not widely used, except as in Frame 2, to show construction details.

In all cutaway graphics it is important that the sectional cut be carefully designed around the area to be exposed. There are three basic types of cut continuity:

5

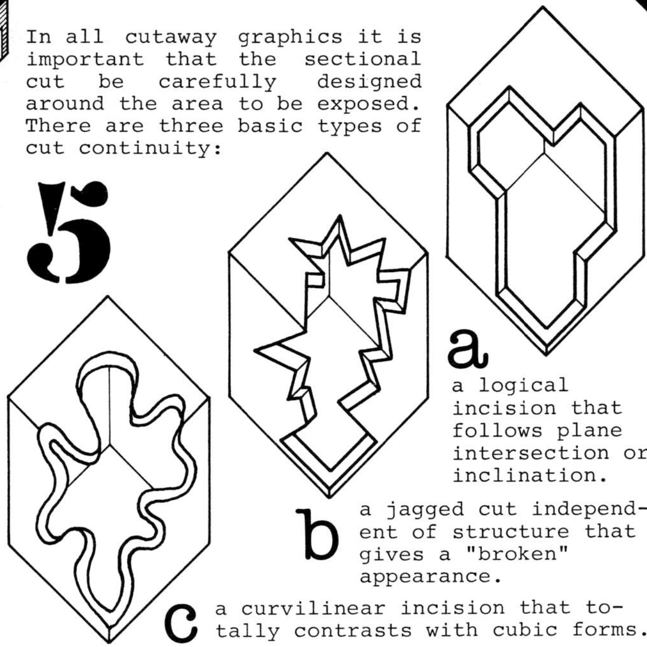

a a logical incision that follows plane intersection or inclination.

b a jagged cut independent of structure that gives a "broken" appearance.

c a curvilinear incision that totally contrasts with cubic forms.

Confusion is also avoided by clear depiction of the cut. Depending on scale, medium, and intensity of image, the cut can be contrasted in white, black, hatching, or be picked out in dry transfer tone or colored.

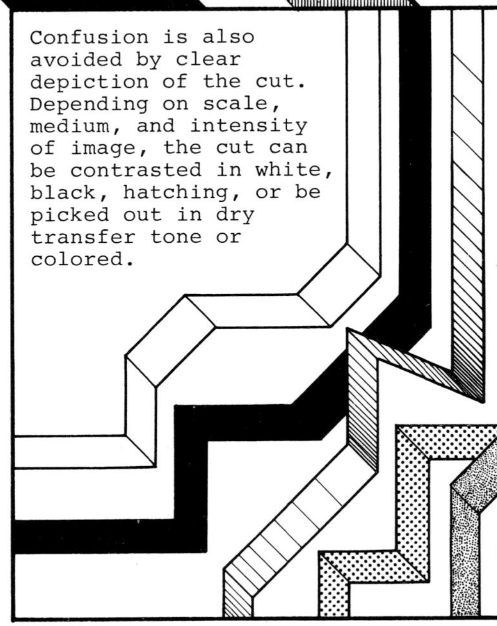

6

Peep-Show Graphics

7

The transparent, or X-ray, axonometric can use two degrees of line weight together with continuous and broken lines for a simultaneous description of interiors and exteriors. It displays most of its "hidden lines," i.e., those usually concealed in regular drawings by overlapping planes.

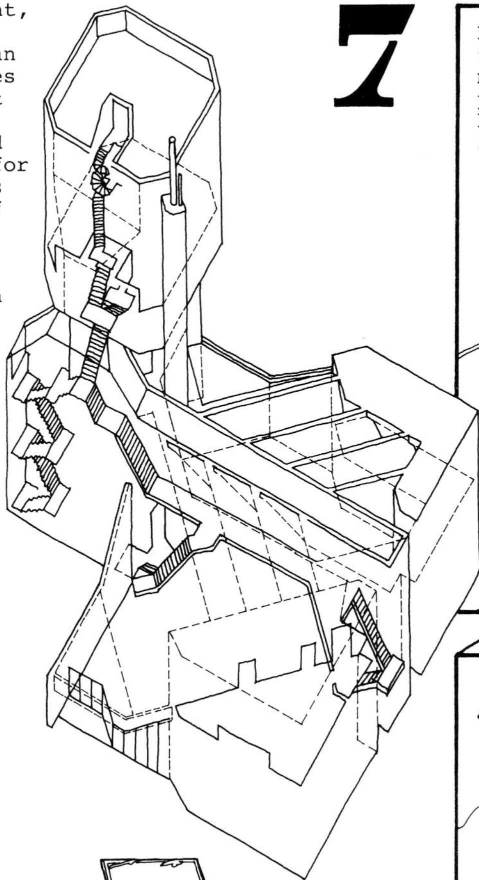

8

Here is another simultaneous view, this time of planning and massing. This combination of plan and axonometric works best with repetitive, linear forms.

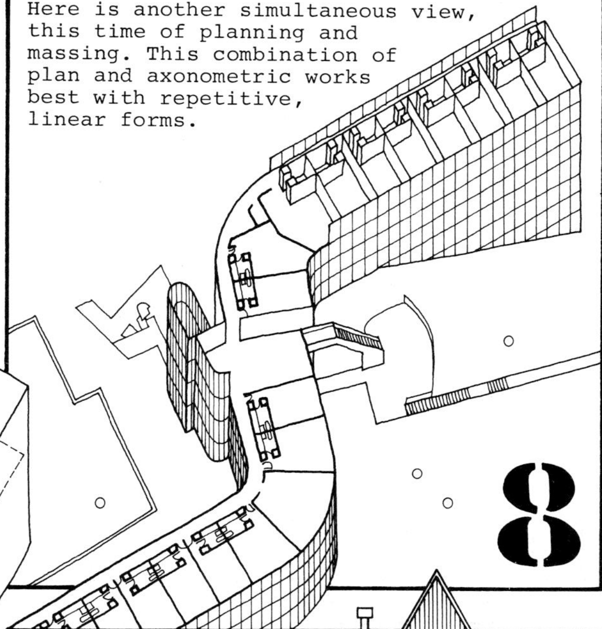

9

A marriage between the design section and the perspective can convey more complex information than can either in isolation. The viewer is presented simultaneously with realistic glimpses of internal and external features.

10

Cutaway perspectives hold tremendous potential in probing the inner secrets of more complicated forms. This drawing illustrates a series of cuts through layers of space, each allowing a peep into the next.

11

The pseudo-perspective places a true-to-scale elevation drawing within a perspective setting. This is a fast method of creating realistic-looking elevations and is extremely useful when communicating with clients (see page 85).

12

The cutaway elevation. Selected areas of the façade are here removed to expose parts of interior or structural elements. In this example, the dotted tree stands in front of the façade and the shaded tree is located behind the building.

Specialized Graphics: Exploded Images

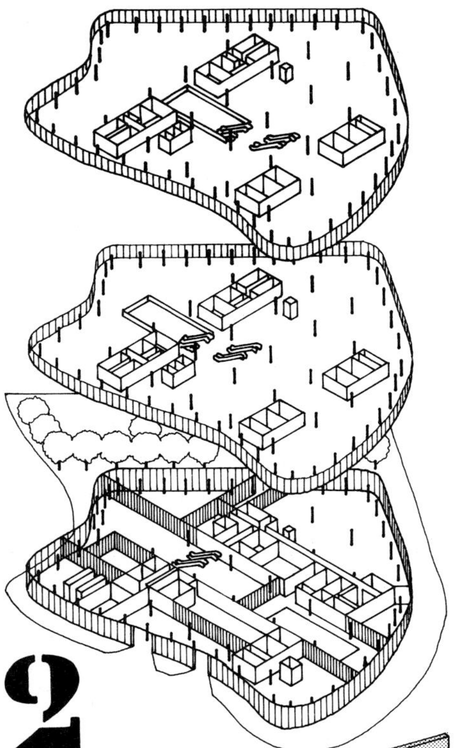

1

The expanded drawing stretches the dimensions of an object or idea for greater clarity of communication. For example, the space between this set of isometric floor plans has been expanded vertically to provide an unimpeded view of each of its levels.

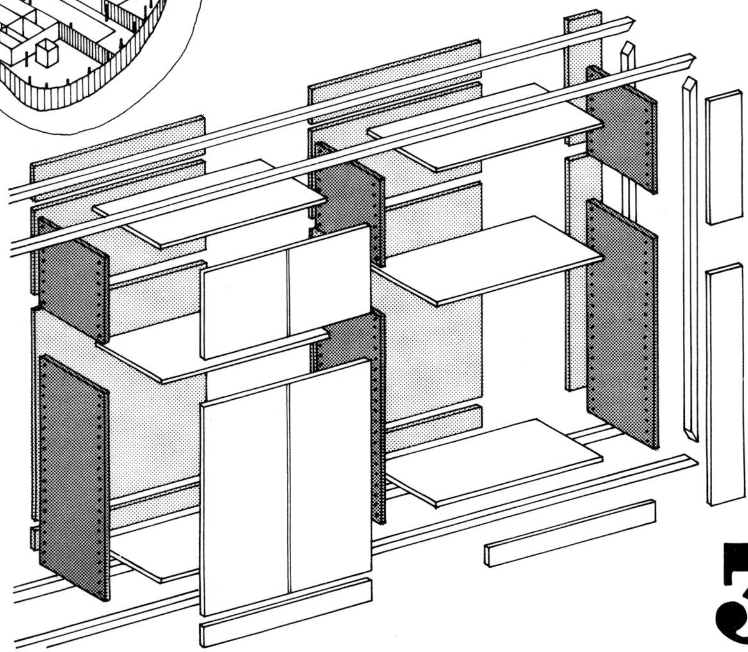

2

Exploded drawings stretch the space between the components of a designed form in all directions, with the "explosion" being frozen graphically at the moment that best explains the relationships among parts. Both expanded and exploded graphics use axonometric and perspective formats.

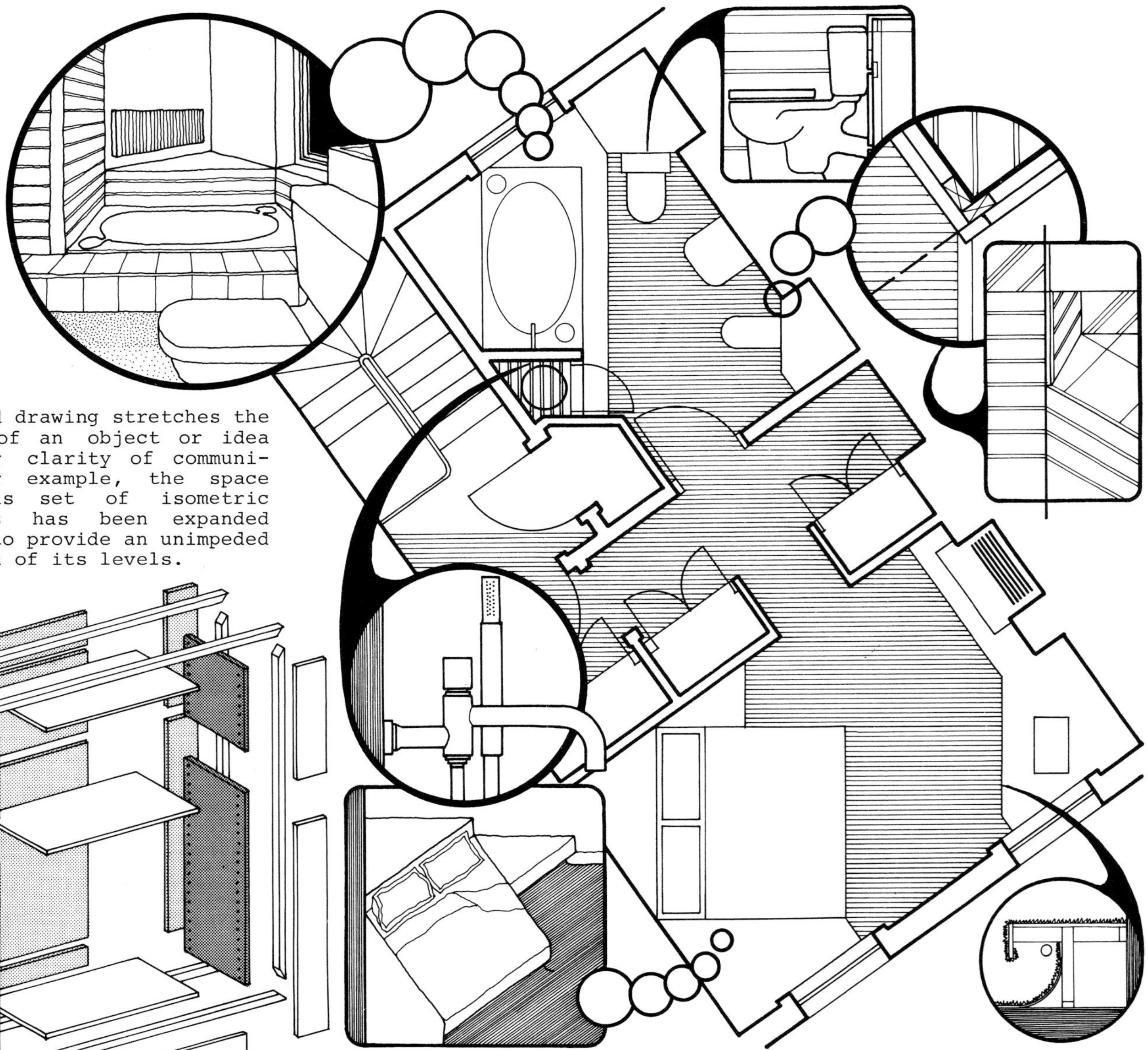

3

More complex layers of information can be explained in a veritable potpourri of graphic conventions. In this format, perspectives, axonometrics, and so on have been employed to explain details which, having been extracted from the drawing, are projected onto the picture plane for closer inspection.

Specialized Graphics: Serial Images

1 In combining multiple views of the same object, the fragmented graphic has obvious roots in Cubism. It is much used in fine art, graphic design and especially advertising, as a means of communicating different aspects of an idea, design, or product. This type of composite image works well in posters, brochure covers, and the like and can work to effect in wall-display communications of all kinds.

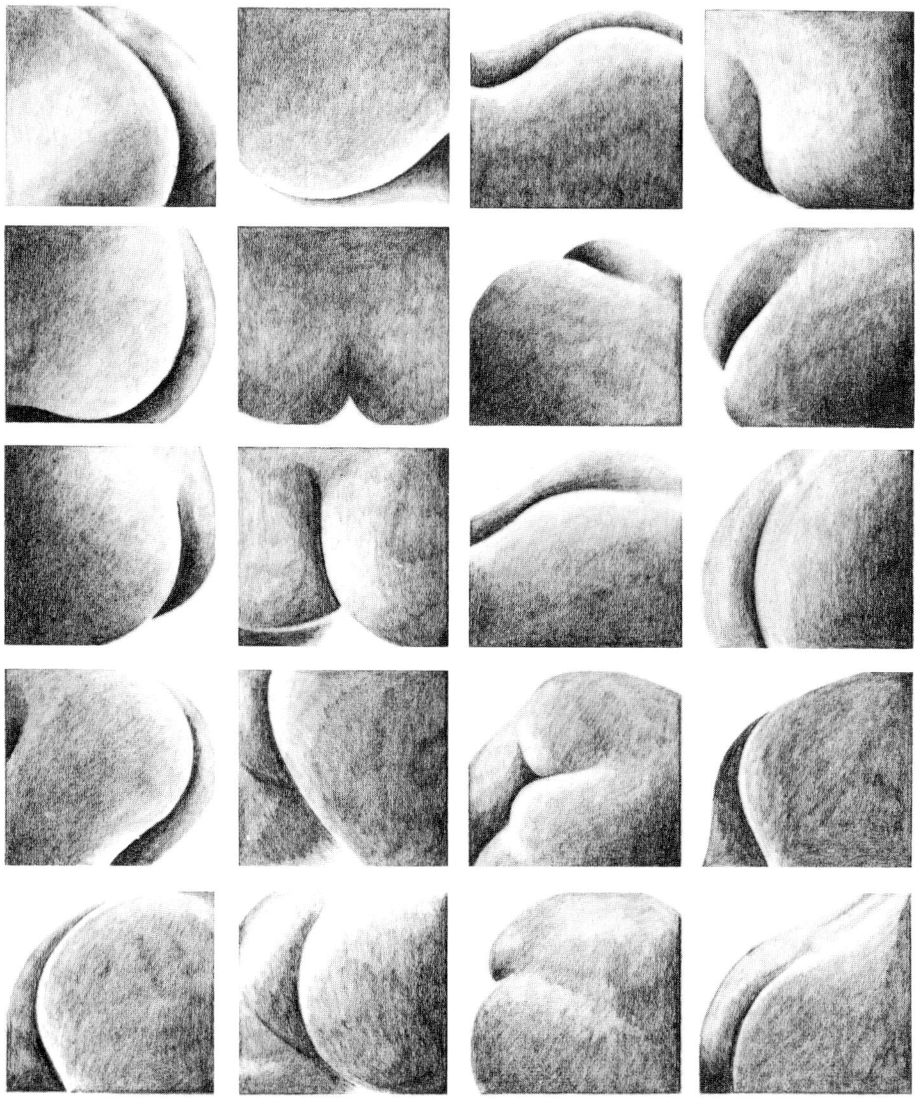

In order to convey images in a digestible form, the developmental graphic represents a controlled accumulation of sequential information. Each successive frame introduces elements not present in the last, such as the evolutionary phases of a design concept, the stages in the assembly of a structure, and the steps in a how-to operational graphic.

2

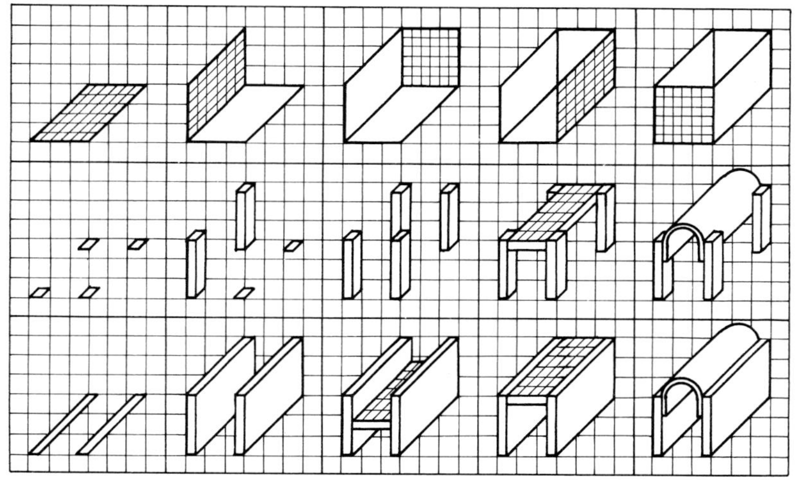

Story-telling graphics are one method of taking viewers on a "walk around the drawing board." Usually shown as perspectives, they function graphically as guided tours around the inside and outside of design ideas. Each frame in the series provides related vantage points from which to view a simulation of movement through space. These also work well when presented as thumbnail sketches.

3

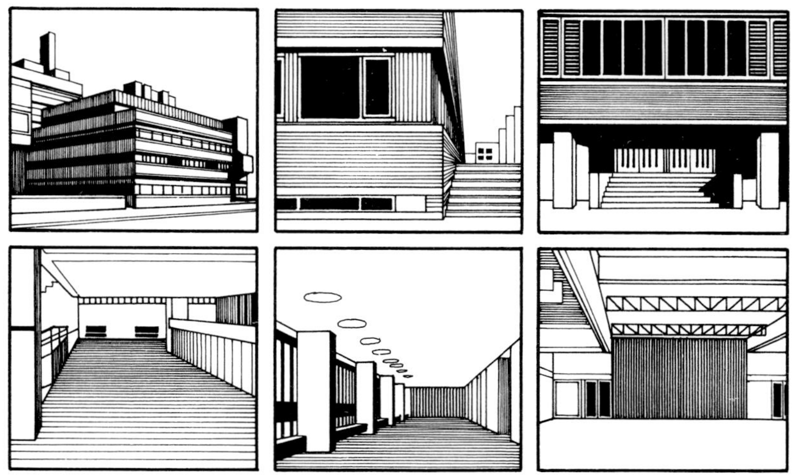

Grids as Design Tools

Used throughout history as a proportional device, grids have lurked behind the structure of paintings and been responsible for the ordering of elements in plans and façades. In the twenties, however, sophisticated versions created in black, white, and primary colors were to become exposed as a neoplastic artform in the work of the Dutch artist Piet Mondrian.

1

2

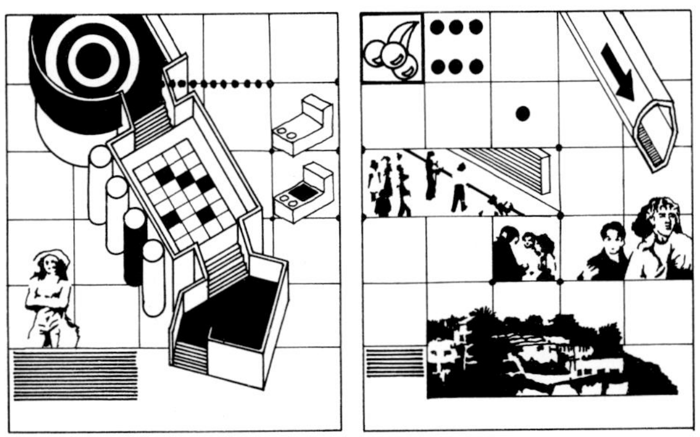

Similarly, this updated presentation format employs a visible grid as a kind of scaffolding from which to hang, compartment, frame, background, but above all harness a diversity of graphic elements.

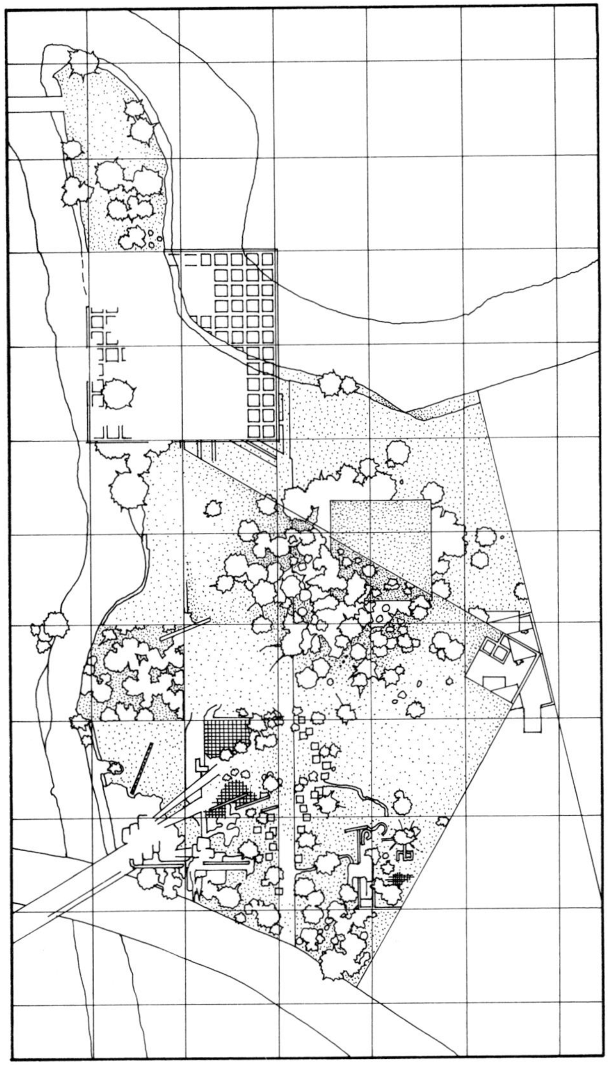

3

Usually, grids and graphs remain visible only during the early design stages. For example, this developmental plan of a leisure park landscape design by a second-year architecture student was organized purely in response to its grid, the latter "disappearing" in the final presentation.

4

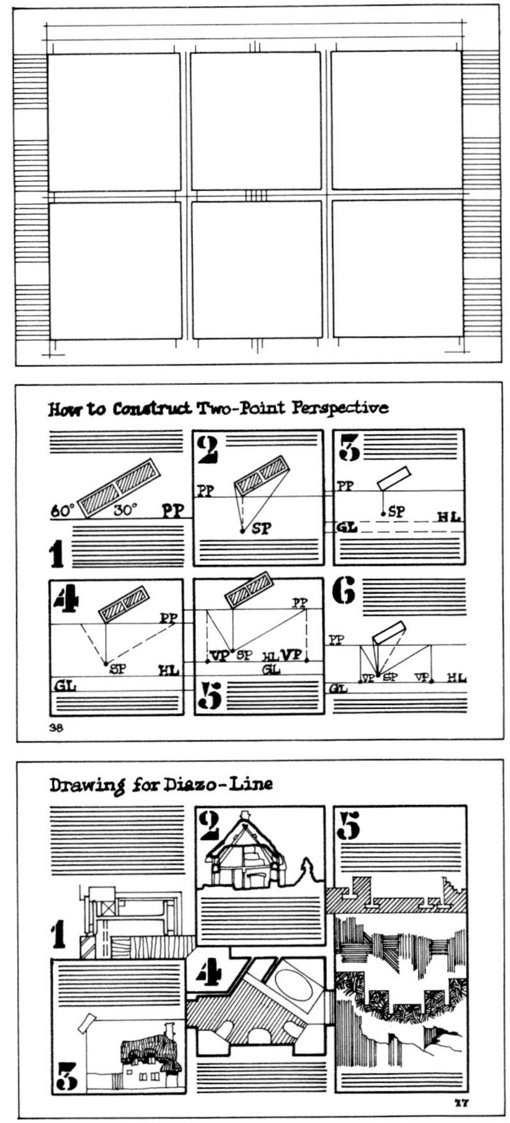

The use of "bespoke" grids is invaluable when composing all forms of layout such as in presentation sheets, wall displays, brochure pages, and exhibition panels. The underlying sense of order generated by such grids allows a great variety of format.

Basic Perspective Coordinates

Perspective is a mechanical device for pictorial illusion-making. One of the fastest ways of understanding its mechanics is to retrace the coordinates over a photograph showing two faces of a cubic object.

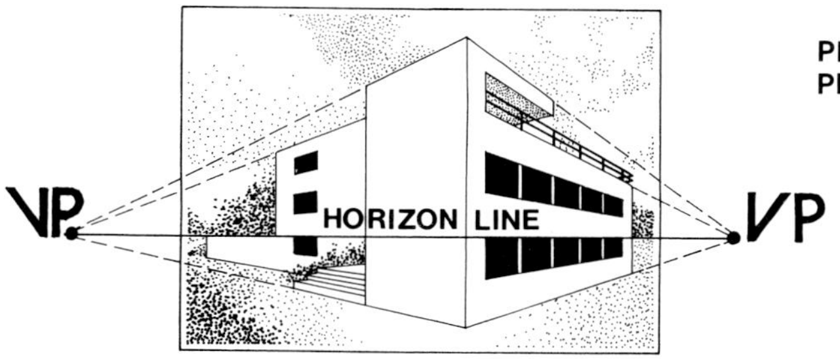

1

Using a ruler and a pen, project all horizontal edges. Where these lines converge to the left and right of the object are the vanishing points. If these are connected, the horizon line (also known as the eye level) is established. This is a horizontal line corresponding to the height of the observer's eye from the ground.

2

The bottom edge of the photograph simulates the ground line. Draw a line completely framing the photograph to define the picture plane--an imaginary plane or window through which the object is viewed.

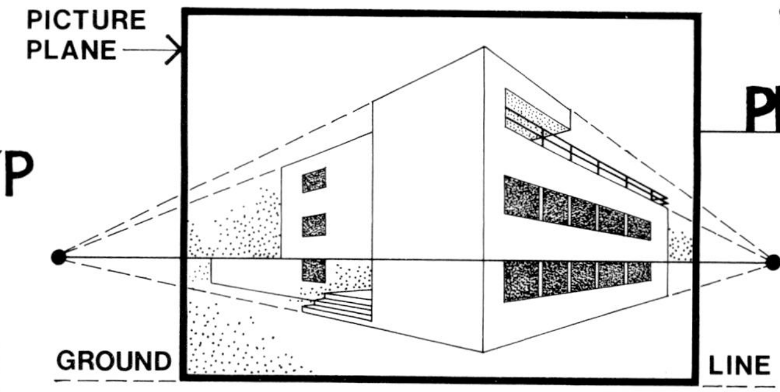

The picture plane is perpendicular to the observer's line of sight and is simulated by the actual drawing surface. The ground line, therefore, is simply a line intersecting this vertical "window" with the horizontal ground plane.

3

This plan diagrams the observer's relationship to the picture plane, a relationship that regulates the size of subsequent perspective drawings.

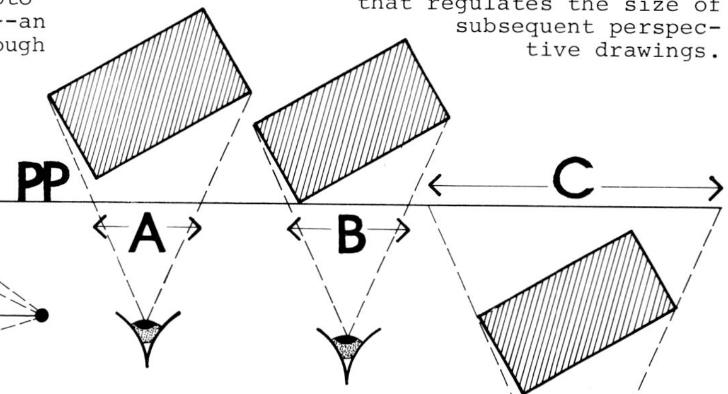

A Objects behind the picture plane will appear smaller.

B Points at which objects touch or pass through the picture plane retain their "true" size.

C Objects in front of the picture plane will appear larger.

4

The horizon line in "normal" perspectives (those viewed from a standing position) is located 5'-3" (1600mm) above the ground line.

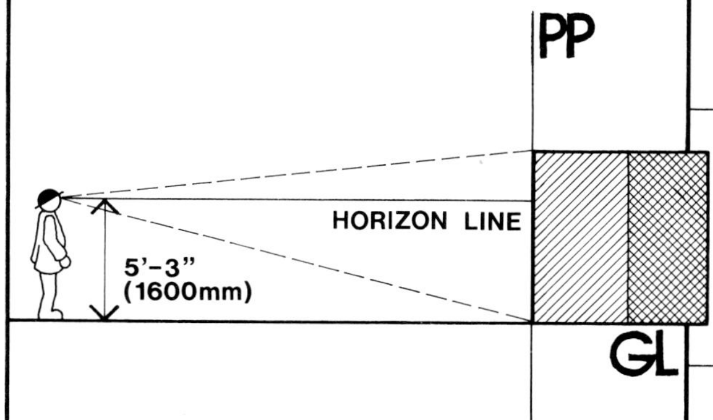

By sliding the horizon line upward or downward, different perspective views can be achieved (see page 40).

5

The station point simulates the observer's location, i.e., the distance between the viewer and that which is viewed. It also controls the relative position and proximity of the vanishing points to the object.

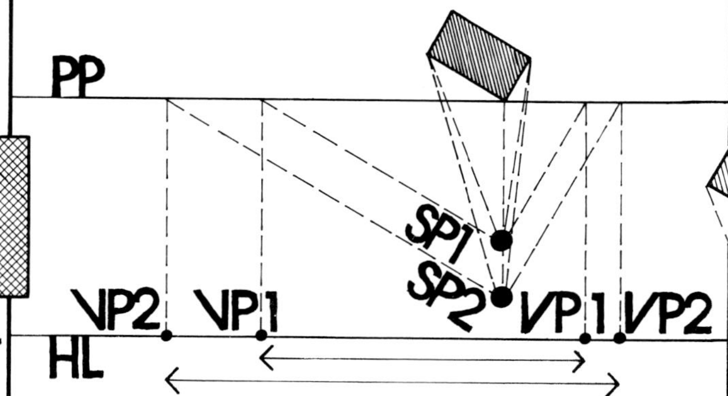

For example, the nearer the station point to the object, the closer the vanishing points to the object; the farther the station point, the wider apart the vanishing points.

6

The orientation of the object in relation to the station point determines the angle of vision. For instance, if the object presents two equal faces to the observer, they will appear equally foreshortened. If the object is rotated to present two unequal faces, the faces will vanish at different rates.

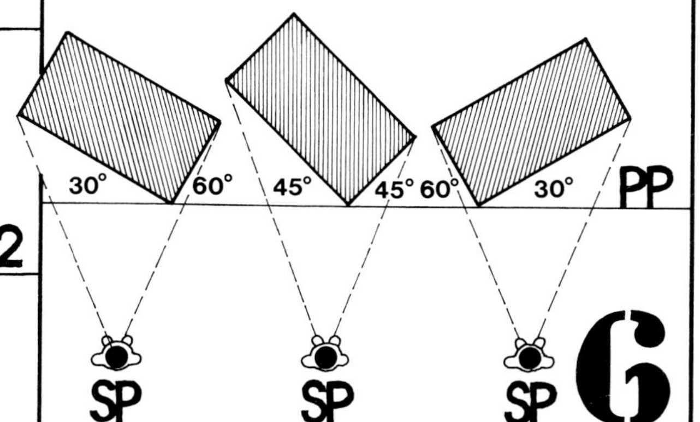

How to Construct Two-Point Perspective

The plan projection method of perspective described here is a means of translating accurately the dimensions of a plan and elevation into a three-dimensional illusion of an object or building.

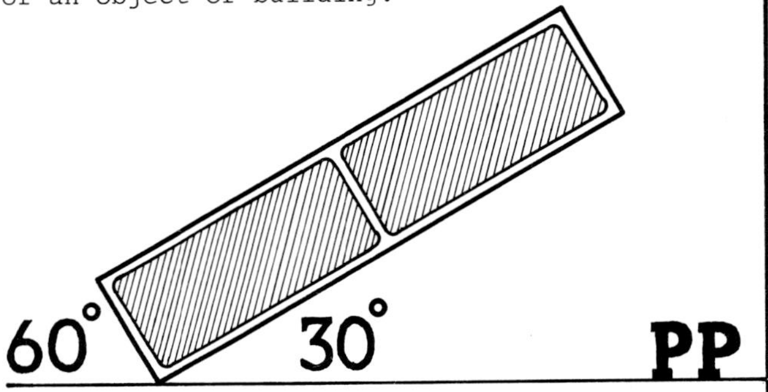

1

Draw the line of the picture plane and, in relation to it, establish the plan.

N.B.: Remember that at this stage you are determining the relative size of the object and, indeed, the size of the ultimate perspective drawing in relation to the plan.

2

Select and locate the station point (viewing position) at right angles to the picture plane.

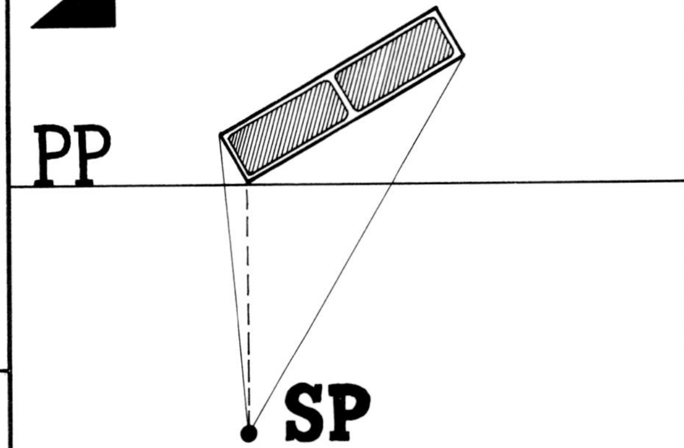

N.B.: Remember that the amount of distance between the station point and the plan regulates the acuteness of the angles of perspective convergence.

3

Next, locate the ground line lower down on the drawing sheet. Above it and parallel to it, establish the horizon line (eye level).

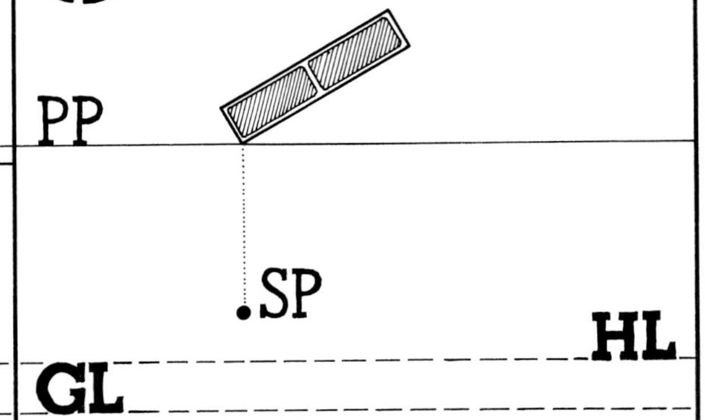

N.B.: In this instance, the horizon line represents a scaled version of the "normal" viewing height, i.e., 5'-3" (1600mm) above the ground line.

4

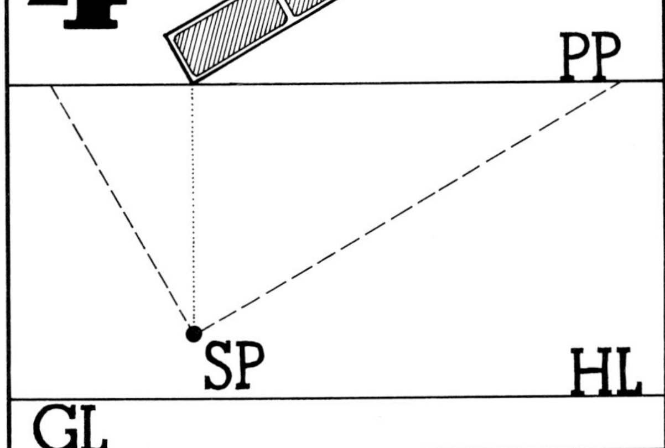

Project lines from the station point, drawn parallel to the two faces of the plan, so that they intersect the picture plane.

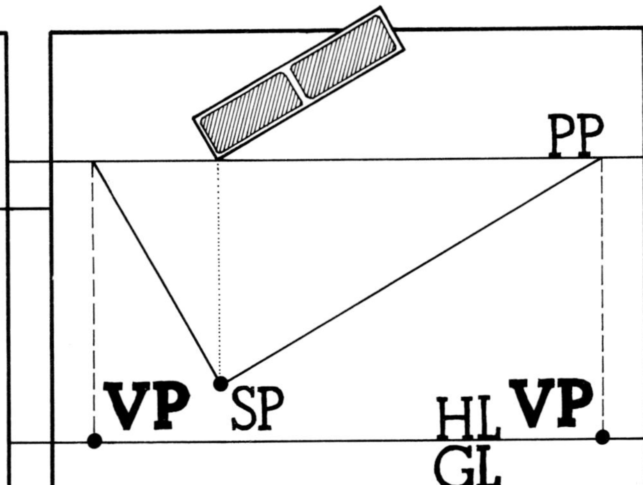

5

Then transfer vertically each intersection down to the horizon line. This establishes the vanishing points for the two-point perspective.

6

Project lines from the station point to all "visible" corners of the plan. The points at which these projections intersect the picture plane establish the further limits of the receding sides of the object.

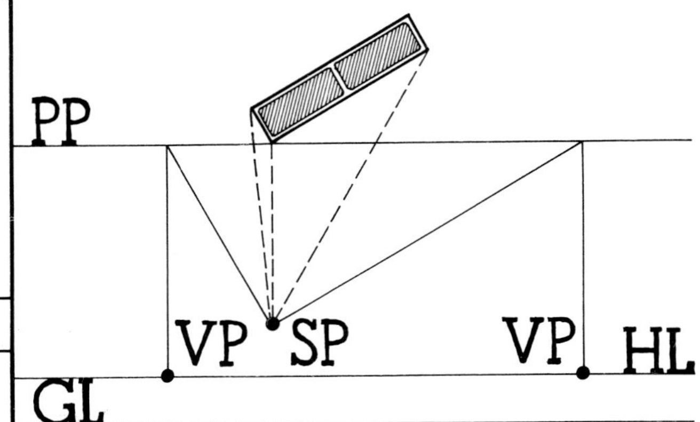

N.B.: In representing the angle of vision, these lines also correspond to our cone of vision, which is between 40 and 60 degrees.

How to Construct Two-Point Perspective

7 Transfer the corner of the plan that is opposite the station point down to the horizon line and ground line.

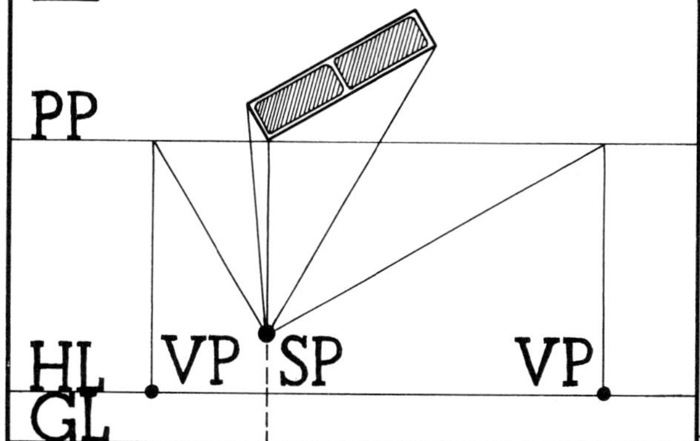

N.B.: Because this line is a bisection of the angle of vision, it is called the center of vision.

8 As, in this case, the plan actually touches the picture plane, the "true height" of its projection from the ground line can be conveniently determined via the elevation.

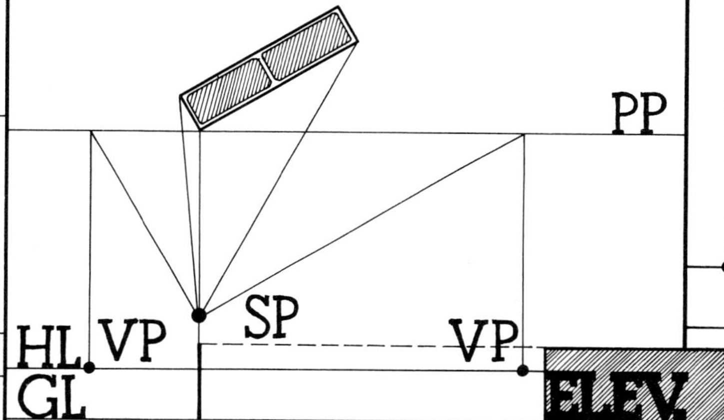

N.B.: For plans occurring in front of or behind the picture plane, see page 40.

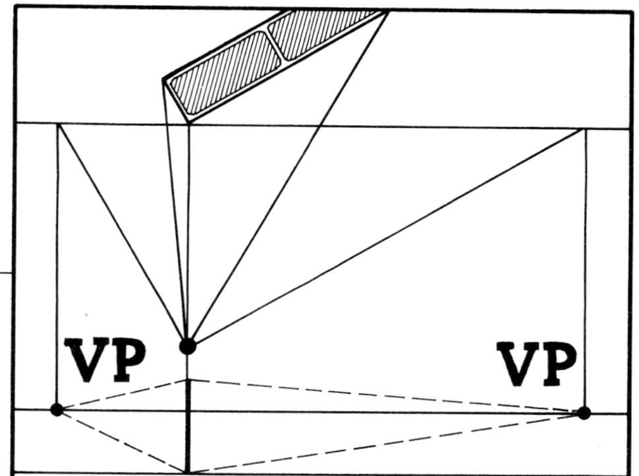

9 Project lines from the top and bottom of this front edge so that they converge at the vanishing points.

10

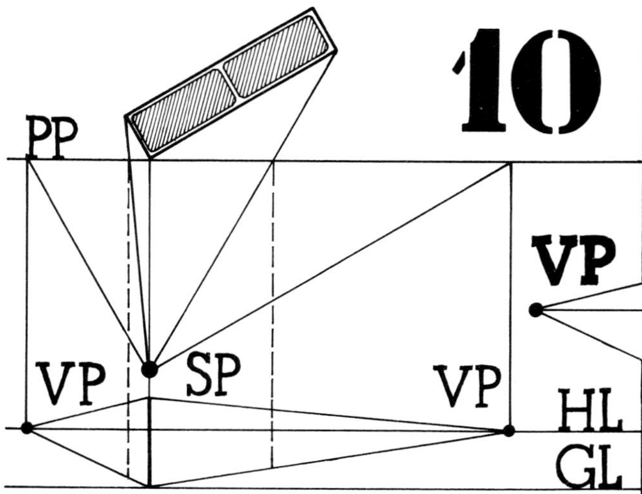

In order to establish the further, vertical edges of each receding plane, transfer the points at which the angle of vision intersects the picture plane down vertically to the horizon line.

11

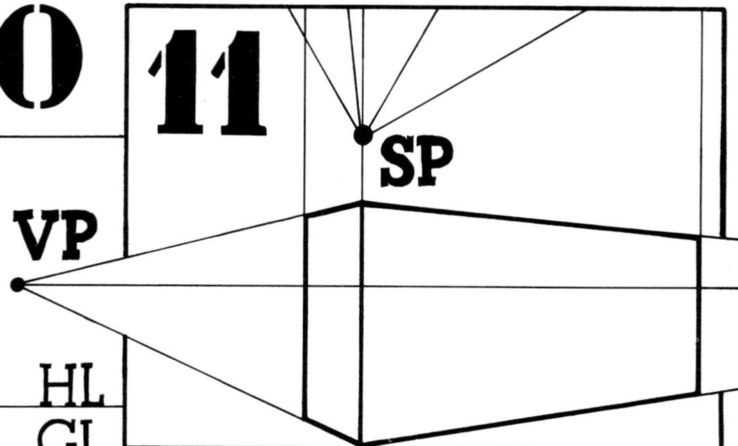

The point at which these intersect the vanishing lines completes all the coordinates for the three-dimensional reconstruction of an object from its plan and elevation.

12 The completed perspective drawing now acts as the container for the rendering of your choice.

How to Animate Perspective Coordinates

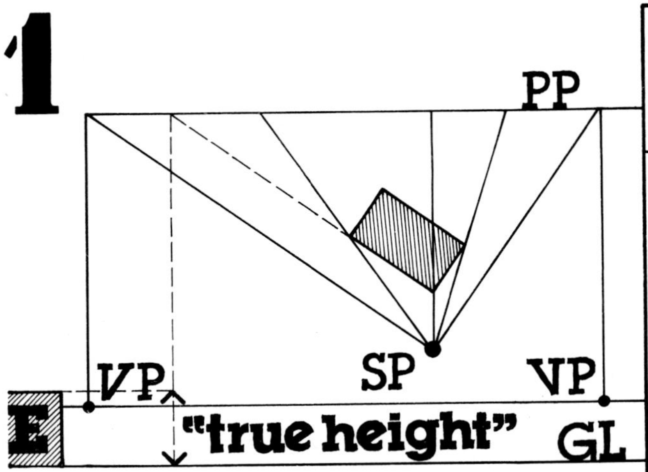

In order to establish a "true height" measuring line when the plan is located in front of the picture plane, project one of its sides up to the picture plane. Then, after transferring down to the ground line, determine the "true height" from the elevation.

2

From the adjacent vanishing point, project the "true height" into its enlarged version, occupying a space in front of the picture plane.

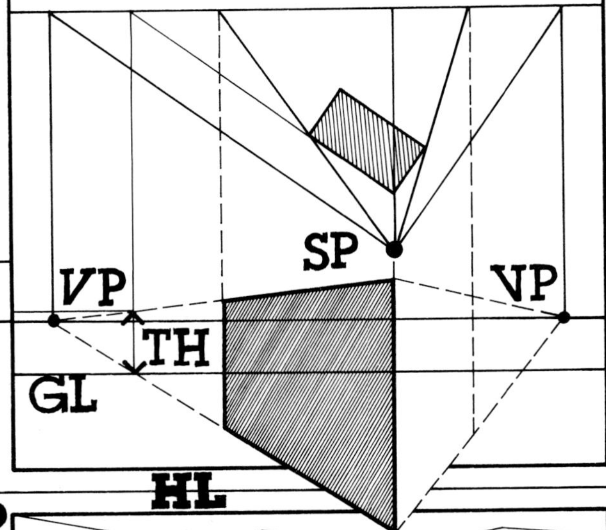

In order to establish a "true height" measuring line when the plan is located behind the picture plane, project one of its sides down to the picture plane. Then, after transferring down to the ground line, determine the "true height" from the elevation.

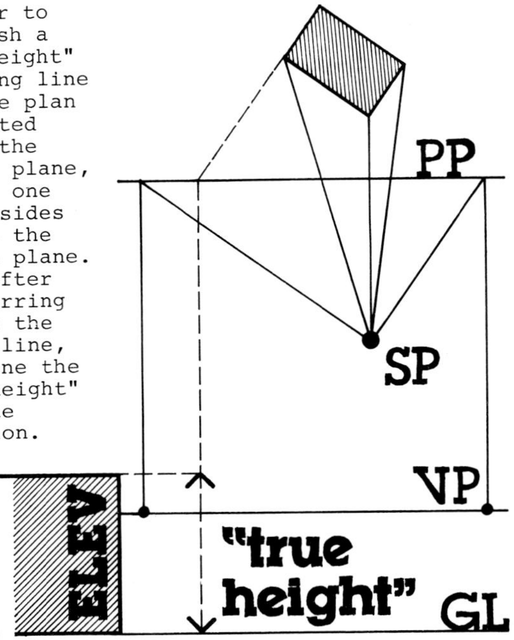

From the opposite vanishing point, project the "true height" into its diminished version, occupying a space behind the picture plane.

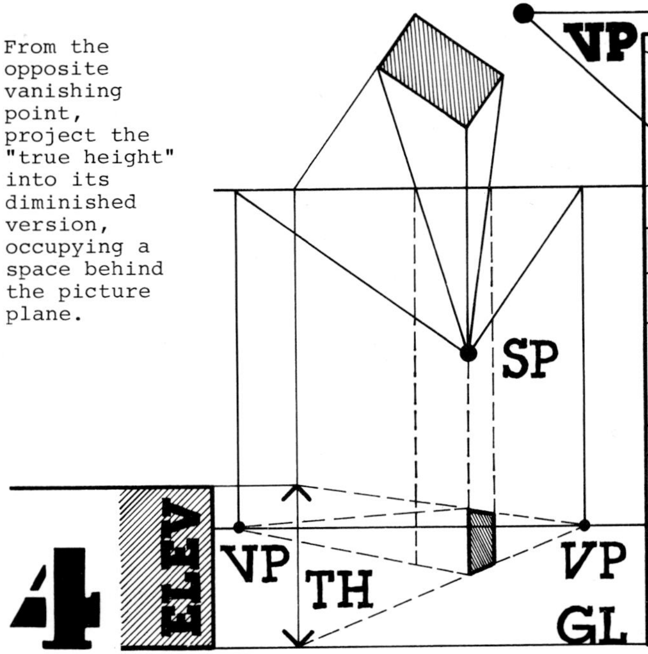

5

By moving the horizon line into an elevated position above the ground line--and using the same projection method--an aerial, or bird's-eye view, can be constructed.

A worm's-eye view is achieved when the horizon line and the ground line coincide as one line.

N.B.: For views that look underneath objects, the horizon line should be positioned below the ground line.

How to Animate Perspective Coordinates

7

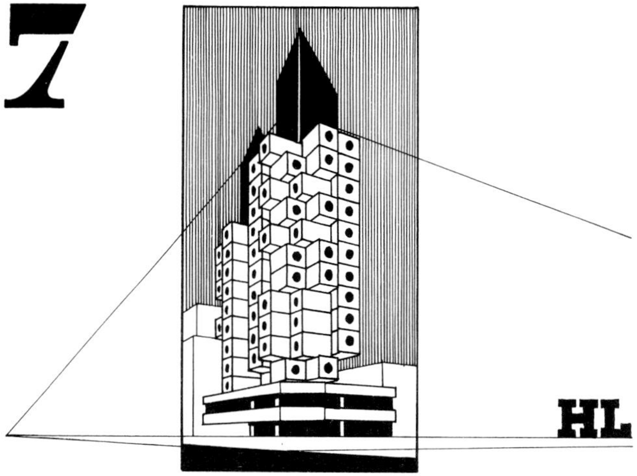

Remember that the nearer the station point, the greater the concentration on an individual form. Emphasis on an important face of a tall object will--together with a low horizon line--dramatize the object at the expense of ground features.

8

Conversely, by raising the horizon line, ground features are given a prominence which, if required, can be emphasized as a center of interest at the rendering stage.

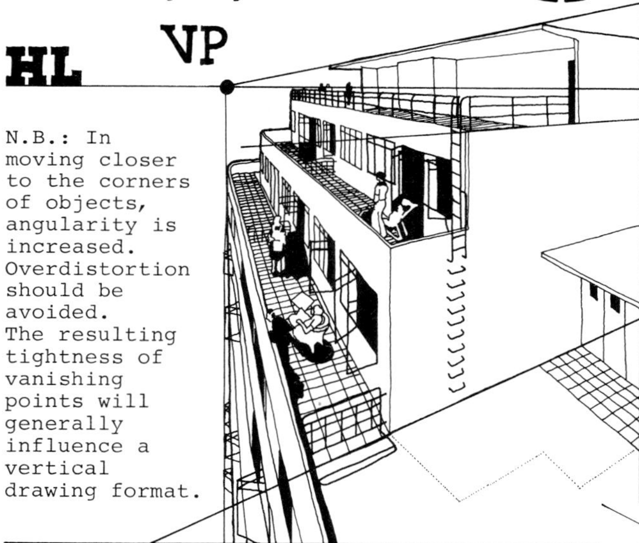

N.B.: In moving closer to the corners of objects, angularity is increased. Overdistortion should be avoided. The resulting tightness of vanishing points will generally influence a vertical drawing format.

9

In tending to flatten perspectives, the further station point spreads the center of interest. More widely spaced vanishing points result from horizontal forms and grouped elements, which naturally dictate landscape formats.

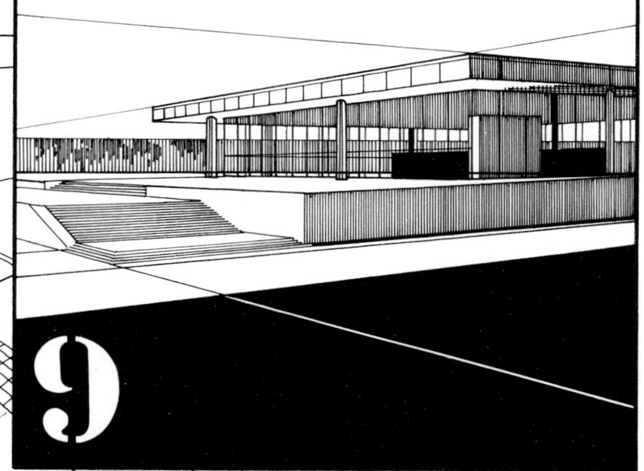

10

The basic plan-projection method for two-point perspective is readily applicable to the construction of more complex objects and grouped arrangements.

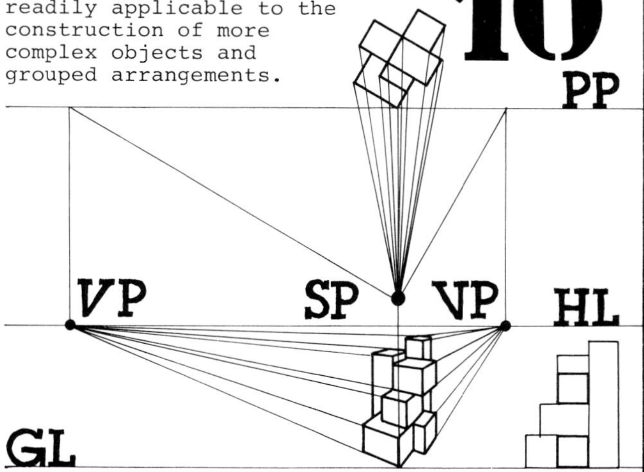

N.B.: Remember to make thumbnail diagrams prior to construction in order to predetermine the best viewpoint-composition-center of interest relationship.

11

At the later rendering stage, centers of interest can be reinforced with varying degrees of detail. For example, in this perspective the building is worked in fine detail while its subordinate elements are described more simply.

12

When drawing details of objects, make sure that the central reason for producing the graphic is evident. For example, the aim of this vignette is to illustrate "approach" and "entrance." Thus the door becomes the center of interest, the eye being led toward it via the structure of the drawing.

How to Construct One-Point Perspective

1

One-point perspective is much more employed for depicting interior spaces, but certain types of external views of objects and collections of forms can be constructed using the plan-projection method.

In one-point perspective a set of planes is parallel to the picture plane, i.e., located at right angles to the observer's line of sight, and the set retains its orientation and original shape. However, the horizontal edges of planes perpendicular to the picture plane converge on the single vanishing point. The method of construction in this drawing is that described for the two-point version.

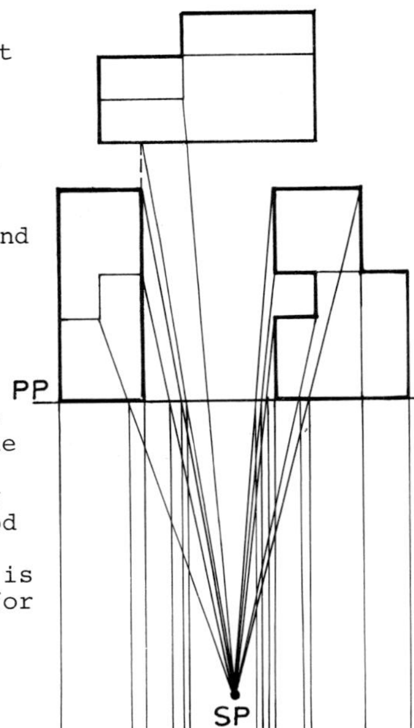

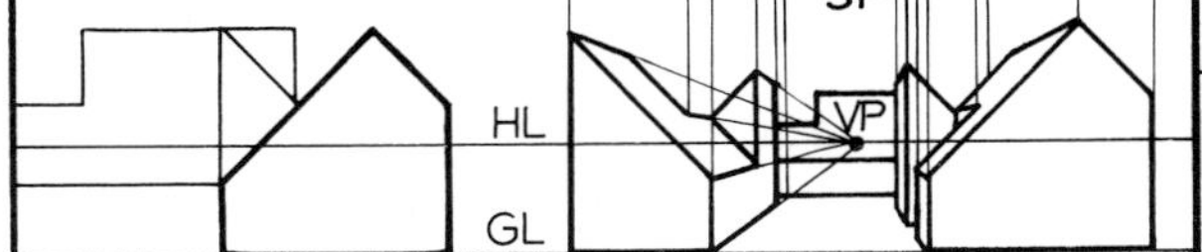

N.B.: The plan-projection method of perspective drawing essentially functions as a presentation device rather than a design tool because it relies upon the provision of accurate plan and elevation, in other words, a predesigned form.

The following system was devised in the fifteenth century by F. Brunelleschi and B. Alberti. Being an ingenuous application of the grid, it allows designers to quickly reconstruct a space that was previously only visualized in the mind's eye. This system, therefore, is particularly useful during the design process.

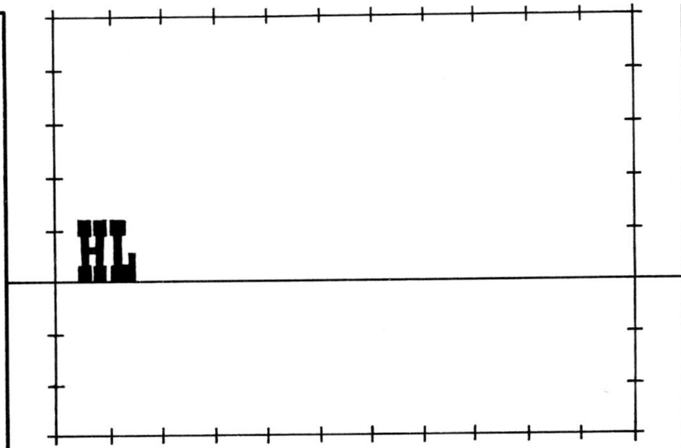

2

Select a scale and draw a "picture frame" (picture plane) on the drawing board. Mark off increments of equal measure around its edge. Next, draw in the horizon line (eye level), assumed to be 5'-3" (1600mm) above the ground line.

3

The vanishing point controls the direction of view. Position this on the horizon line to promote the best view--off center, if possible, to achieve a more dynamic drawing. Then, project radiating lines from the vanishing point through each of the ground line increments.

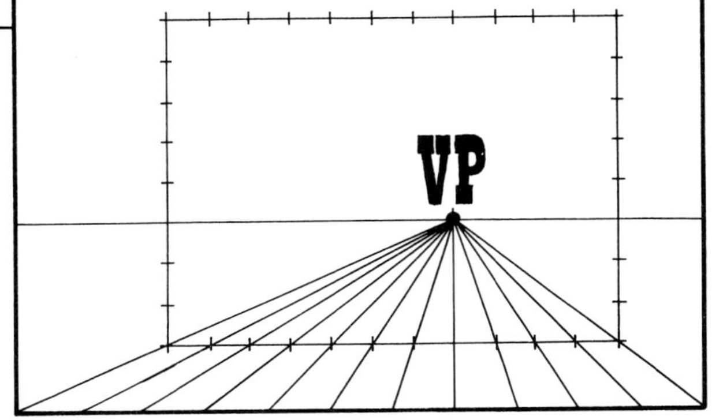

4

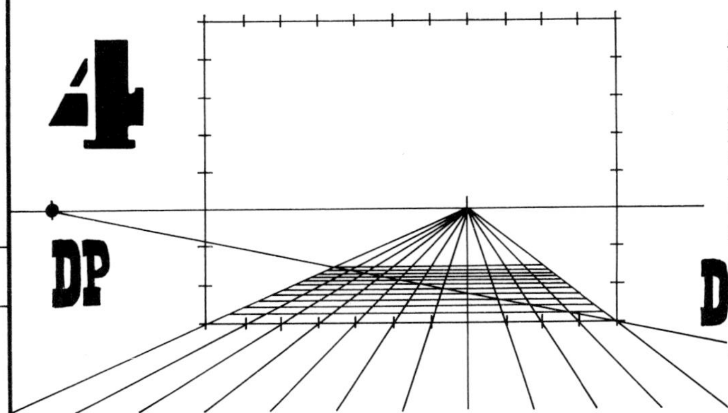

Locate a diagonal point outside the picture frame on the horizon line. Its distance from the vanishing point represents that of the observer from the picture frame plane--the nearer its position is to the vanishing point, the more acute the foreshortening. Next, project a line from the diagonal point to the farther, lower corner of the frame. Where this crosses the radiating lines it establishes the equal units of measure as diminishing in depth.

At this point it is worth pausing to examine the role of the diagonal point. This diagram demonstrates that it is, in fact, the station point found in the plan-projection method. However, in the grid method it has moved to the horizon line. Its distance from the vanishing point still represents that of the observer from the object but also acts as the point from which to measure degrees of depth.

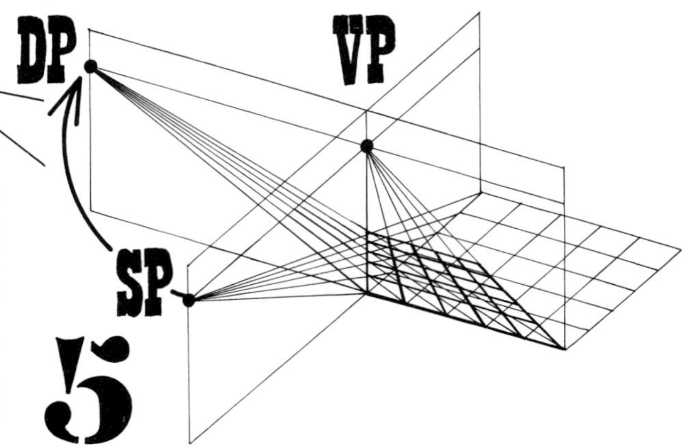

5

How to Construct One-Point Perspective

6

The units of equal measure can also be projected in front of the picture plane by taking a line from the diagonal point through the nearer, lower corner of the frame.

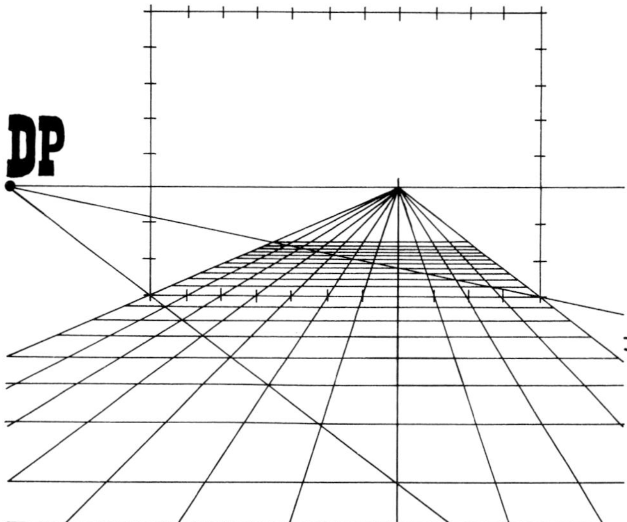

7

After connecting the upper corners of the frame to the vanishing point together with the radiating lines on the remaining three sides of the space, the horizontal depth measurements can be extended around the framework to complete the grid. This can now act as an underlay guide from which the size and location of the components of an interior or exterior can be scaled.

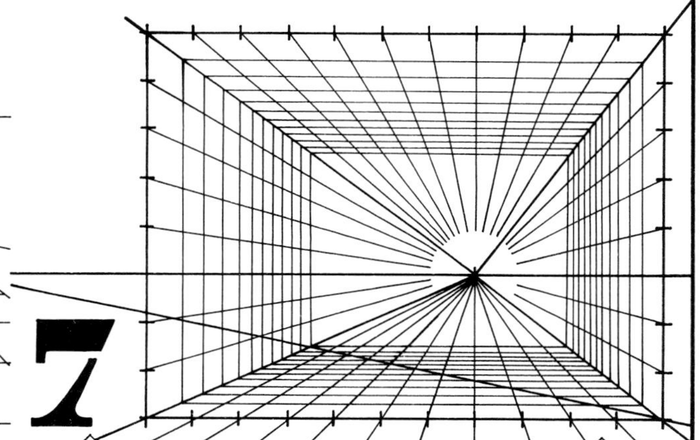

8

Perspective drawings worked from construction to final rendering on one drawing surface have to cope with the removal of initial and redundant construction lines. For this reason they often retain a constructed quality, appearing wooden and devoid of any atmosphere.

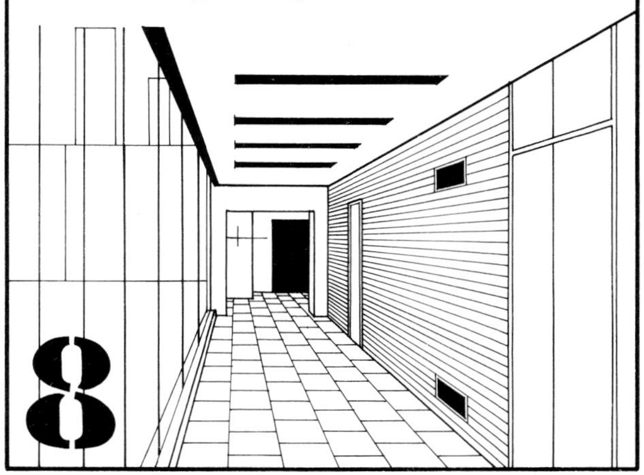

9

On the other hand, using an underlay separates the construction from the rendering stage, thus allowing concentration on the introduction of tone, texture, color, light and shadow, and so on.

10

Single-point grids can be quickly constructed for use as underlays to convert plans into aerial views of interior room spaces, bird's-eye views of the external appearance of individual or groups of buildings, and convert sections into sectional perspectives.

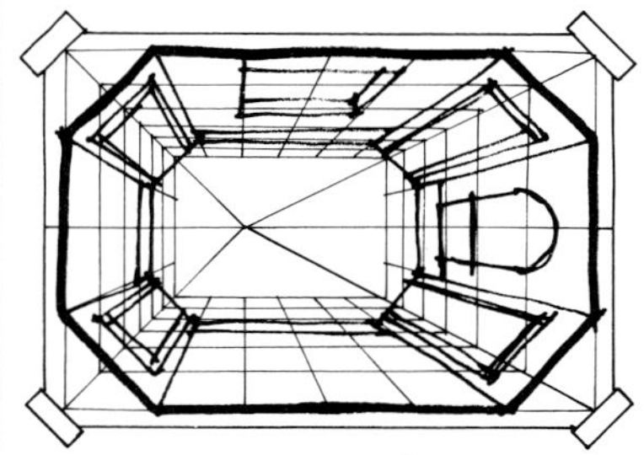

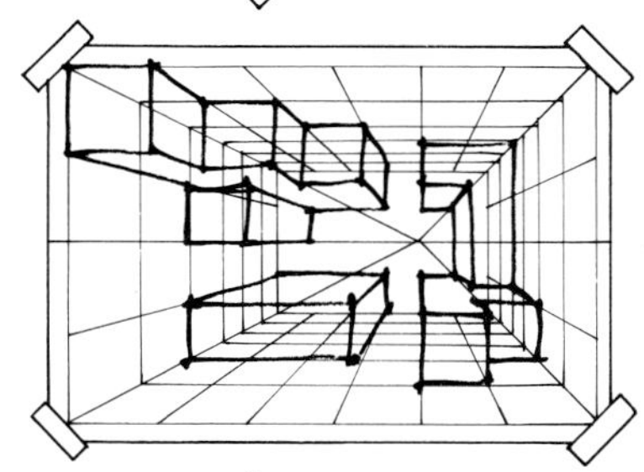

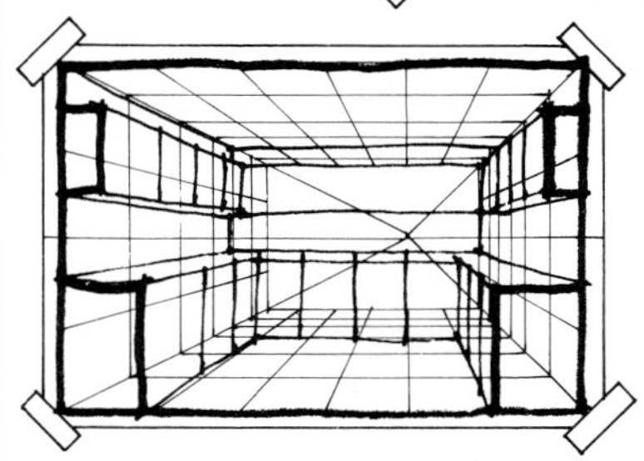

N.B.: Remember that, in representing the distance between observer and space in view, the degree of distance between diagonal point and vanishing point regulates the degree of depth in the illusion.

Do-It-Yourself Perspective Grids

A variety of perspective grids can be easily constructed for use as underlays when originating freehand or drafted perspective drawings on transparent materials. Each framework is extendable, allowing the position of those lines that do not coincide with the grid--together with curved lines--to be quickly plotted or estimated.

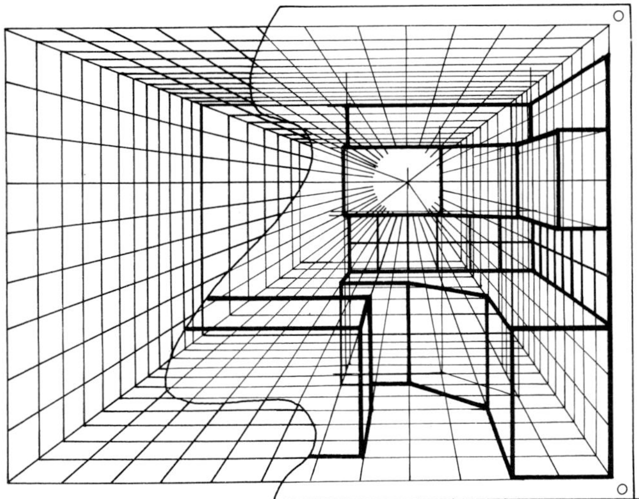

A basic one-point grid for use when generating all kinds of oblique perspectives, including bird's-eye views of plans, sectional perspectives, and head-on views of interiors, courtyards, and groups of buildings. Rotating and reversing the underlay provides different vanishing point positions.

1

2

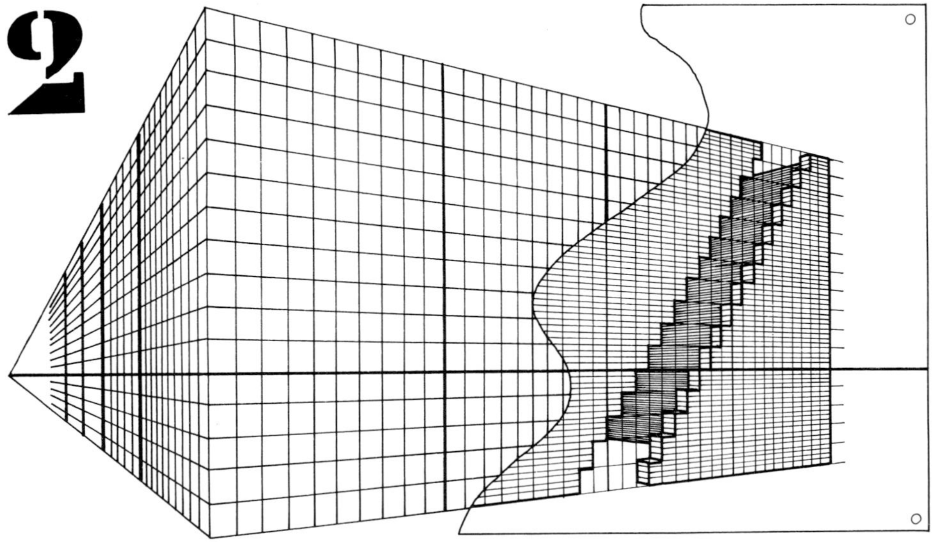

A basic two-point grid for use when producing the more common type of exterior view. It is also adaptable for sectional perspectives, which allow a simultaneous view of the side façade (see page 33).

3

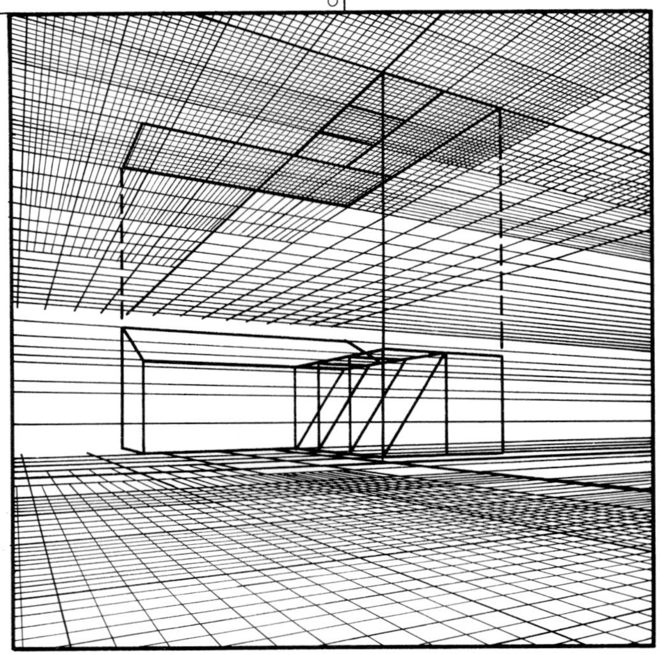

Another version of the two-point grid. For "normal" views, the plan can be projected vertically down to the base plane from the accessibility of the overhead plane. For aerial views, the grid can be turned upside down and buildings quickly extruded from their plans first plotted on the base plane.

4

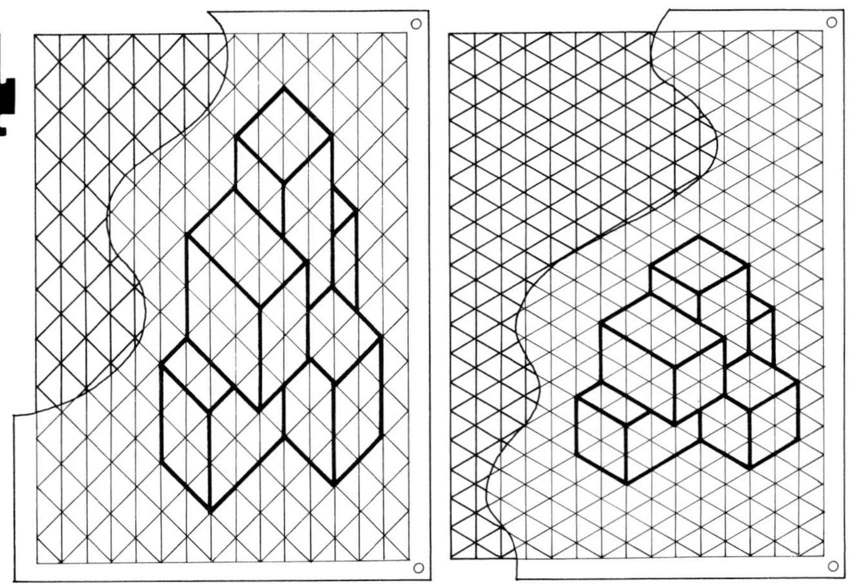

Grids can also be produced, in order to save time when drafting axonometric and isometric projections.

How to Eyeball Aerial Perspectives

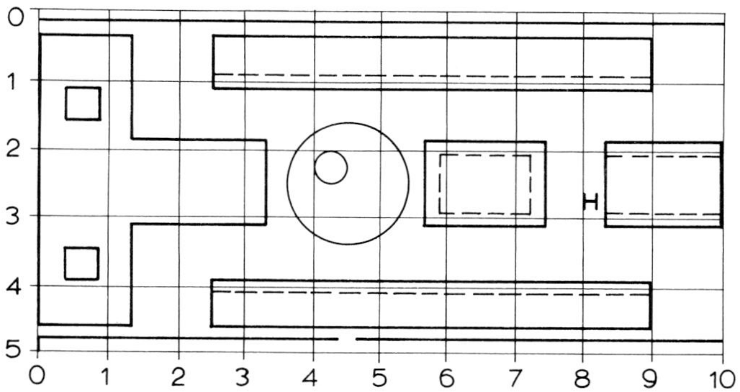

1

A speedy method of translating plans--particularly of large complexes or groups of buildings--into aerial perspectives is to superimpose a grid over the area to be transposed.

To aid converting it more accurately into perspective, number two sides of the grid and reduce the scale of the grid in more intricate areas.

Draft the same grid in perspective on the drawing board. To aid laying it out, first establish coordinates via a thumbnail sketch.

N.B.: If accuracy is required, the grid can be set up using the plan-projection method.

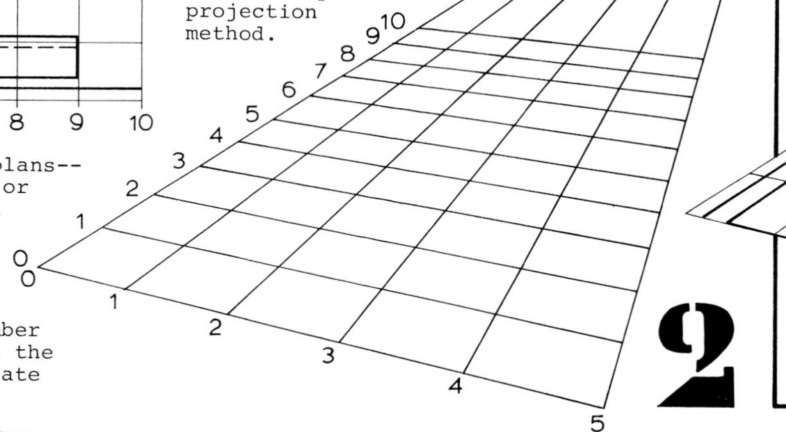

2

Transfer the floorplan into its appropriate location on the perspective grid. Make sure that each of its components is correctly positioned on the perspective grid in relation to the plan grid.

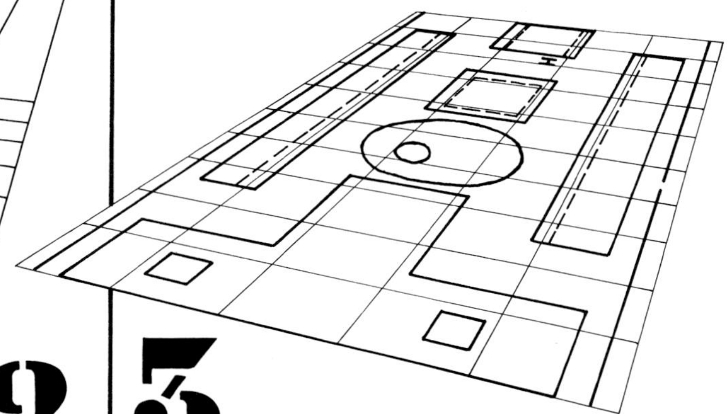

3

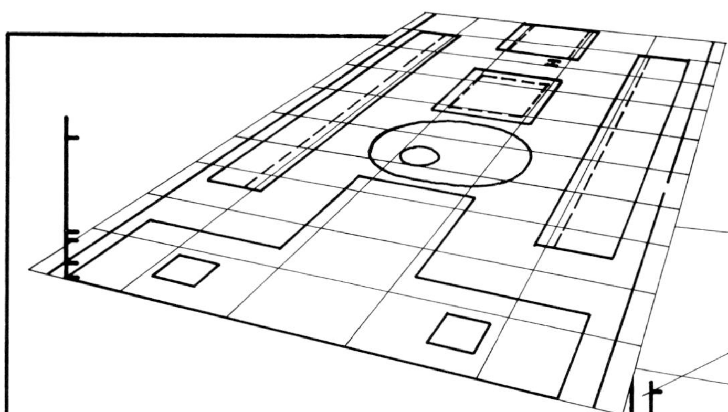

Introduce a "true height" scale high enough to accommodate all vertical features to be drawn. This is best located in the foreground, preferably coinciding with the near corner of a form.

4

Project vertically each corner of plan elements. Heights should be determined by reference to lines connecting the appropriate height on the vertical scale with the vanishing point.

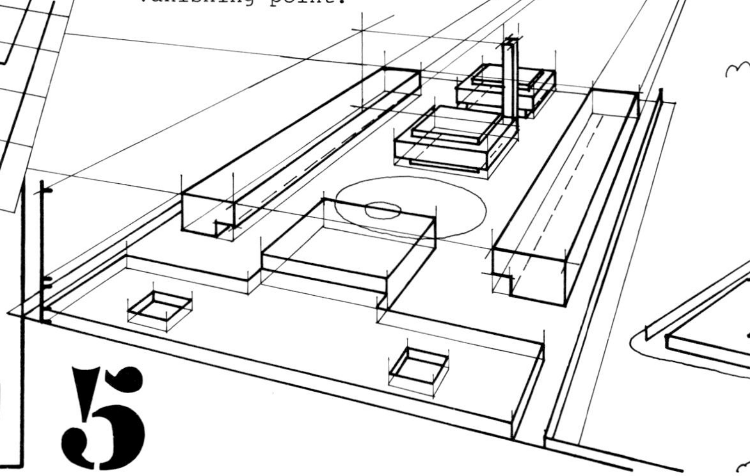

5

Finally, before rendering, add elevation details, landscape features, and other forms of interest.

6

How to Project Shadows in Elevations

1 By creating an illusion of solidity, the inclusion of shadows in architectural line drawings increases their readability. For this reason, shadow projections (sciagraphy) are especially useful in elevations because they describe the nature of surface and, together with the overlap cue, offer an additional means of indicating depth.

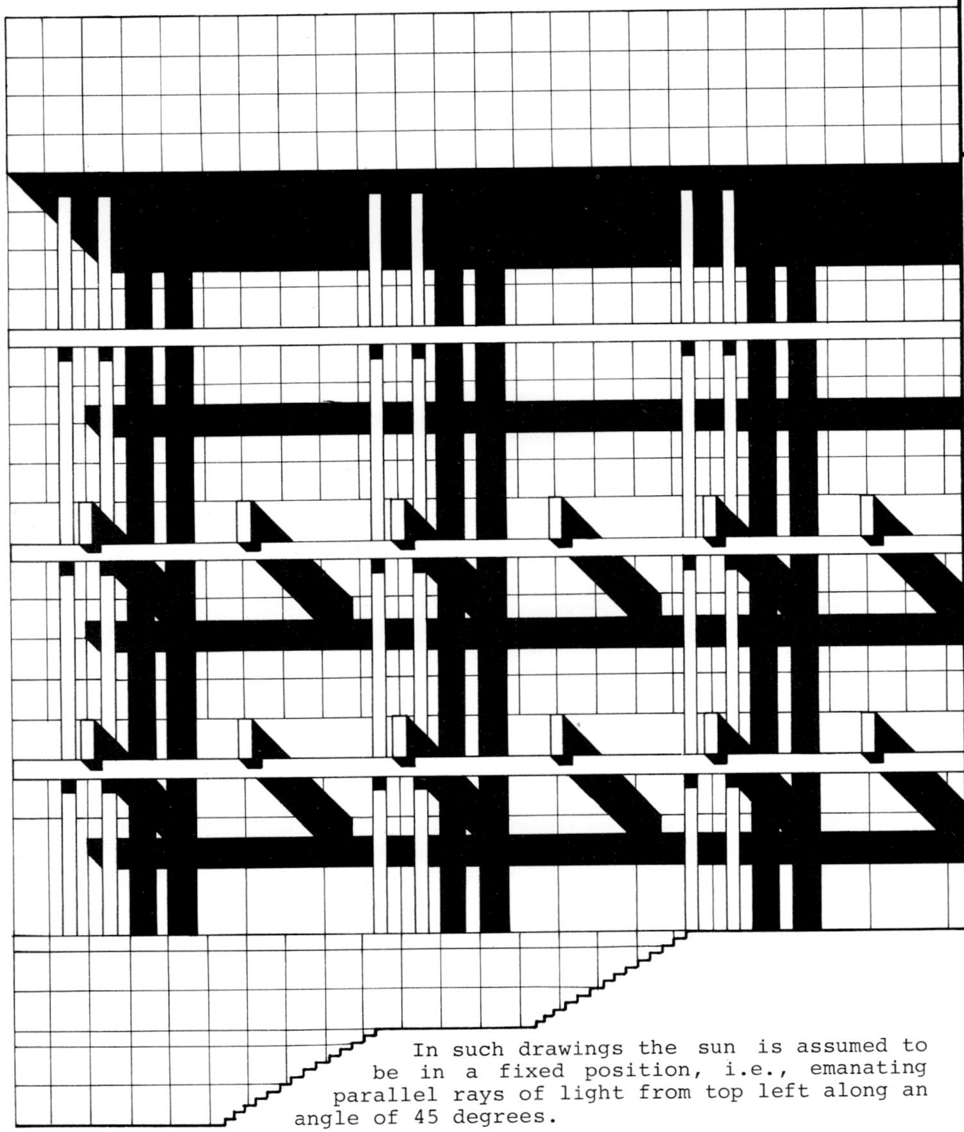

In such drawings the sun is assumed to be in a fixed position, i.e., emanating parallel rays of light from top left along an angle of 45 degrees.

2 Usually the projection of shadows in elevations is constructed from the plan, but occasionally the process is speeded up by reference to the section or side elevation.

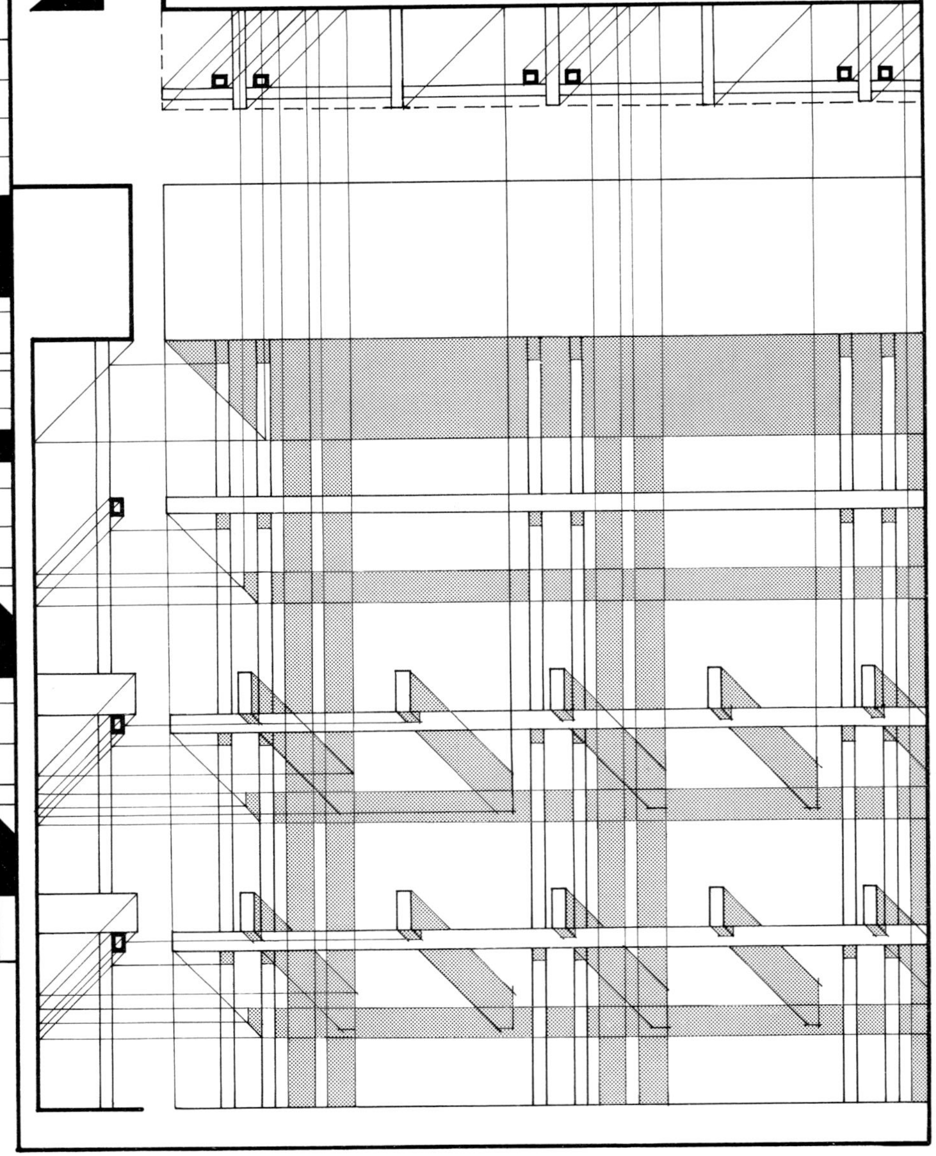

How to Project Shadows in Elevations

This basic construction is from the plan of shadows cast by rectangular and cylindrical forms projecting in front of the elevation plane.

N.B.: These are equivalent of shadows cast by objects seen in plan except that, when not inconvenient to the information being communicated, the convention for plans cast shadows diagonally upward from left to right.

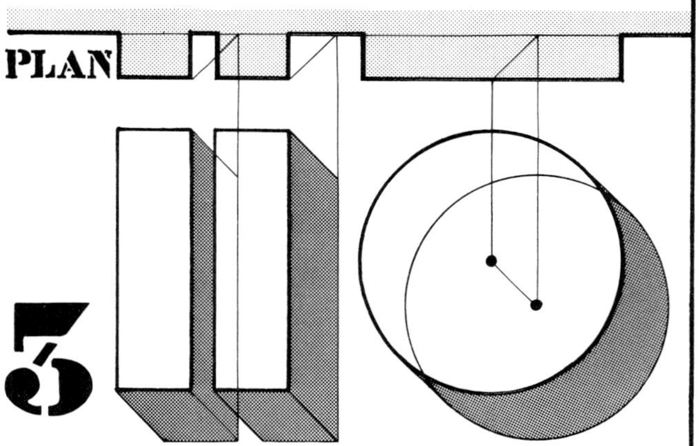

3

This basic construction is from the plan of shadows cast by rectangular and circular recesses in an elevation plane. At this scale the simplest method of plotting circular shadows is to find the center of the front edge of the recess, then mark the edge of the shadow from a 45-degree angle.

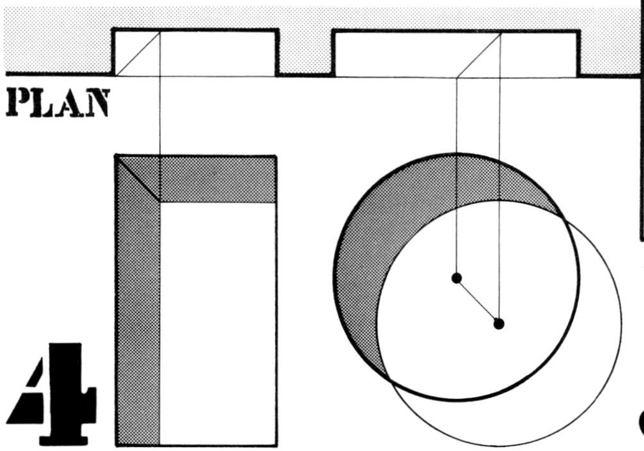

4

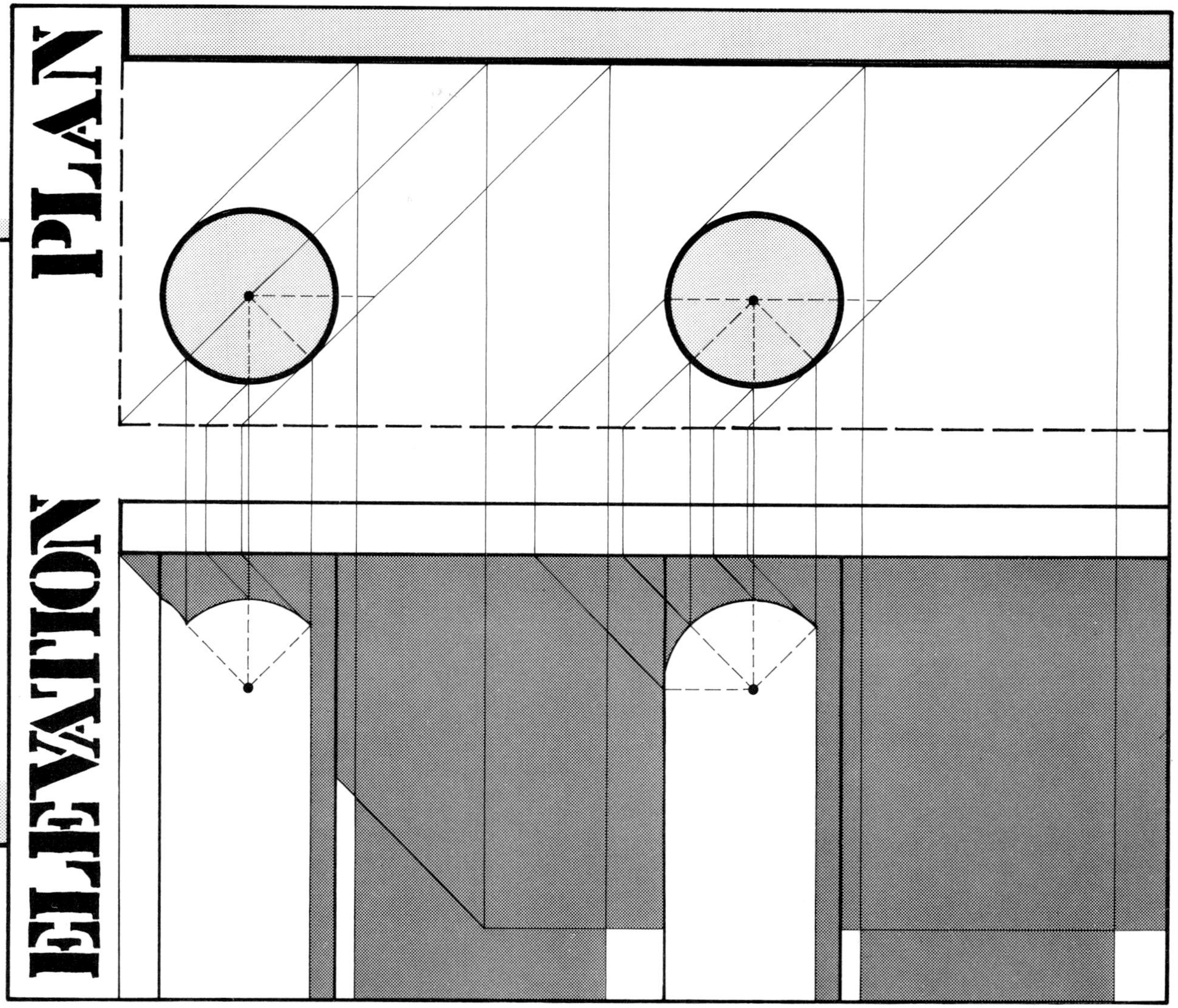

5

Here are some examples of shadows cast from a block on top of cylindrical columns. The shadow of the corner of the block is plotted on the surface of the cylinder, and a convenient number of points are similarly plotted along the lower, shadow-casting edge of the front of the block. A curve has then to be drawn by connecting these points. The shadow merges on the right with the shade of the cylinder. The shade is not really defined by a hard edge but gradually fades into the lighter portion of the surface.

N.B.: Notice the two different effects of the block's shadow on the two columns.

How to Cast Shadows in Perspective

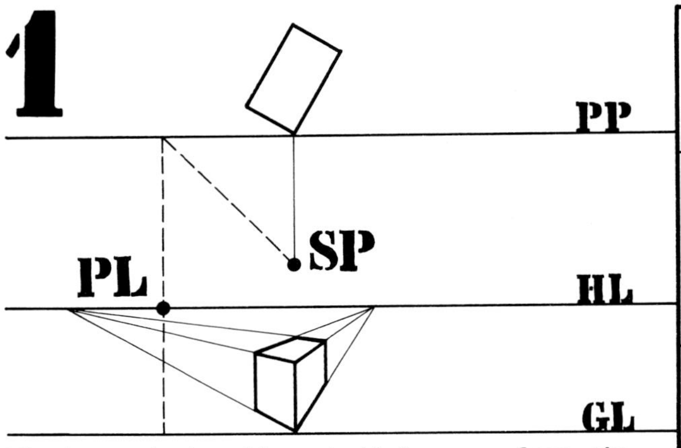

First, project a line at 45 degrees from the station point to the picture plane. From its point of intersection, drop a vertical line so that it bisects both horizon line and ground line.

N.B.: Its intersection on the horizon line represents the vanishing point for plan lines of light (PL).

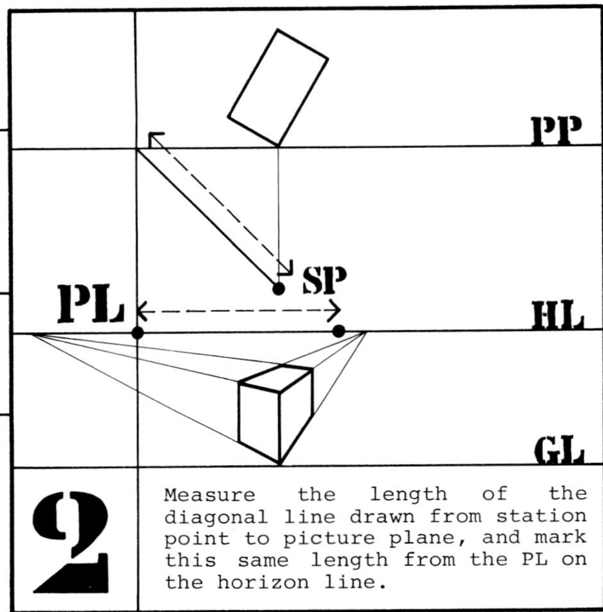

Measure the length of the diagonal line drawn from station point to picture plane, and mark this same length from the PL on the horizon line.

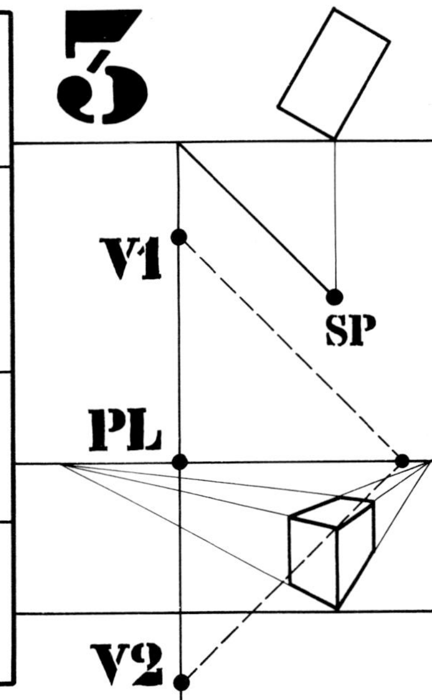

From this point, strike two 45-degree diagonals that intersect the vertical line.

The upper point of intersection (V1) represents the vanishing point for sunlight with lines of light occurring in front of the observer; the lower point (V2) represents the vanishing point for sunlight with lines of light emanating behind the observer.

Using either V1 or V2 plus PL, together with the original perspective drawing vanishing points, it becomes possible to cast accurate shadows.

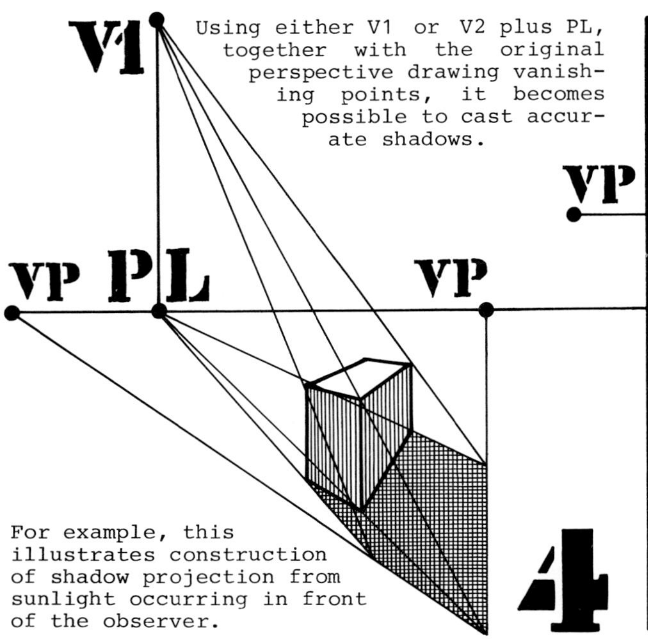

For example, this illustrates construction of shadow projection from sunlight occurring in front of the observer.

Conversely, shadows projected from sunlight occurring behind the observer are constructed from V2, PL, and original vanishing points.

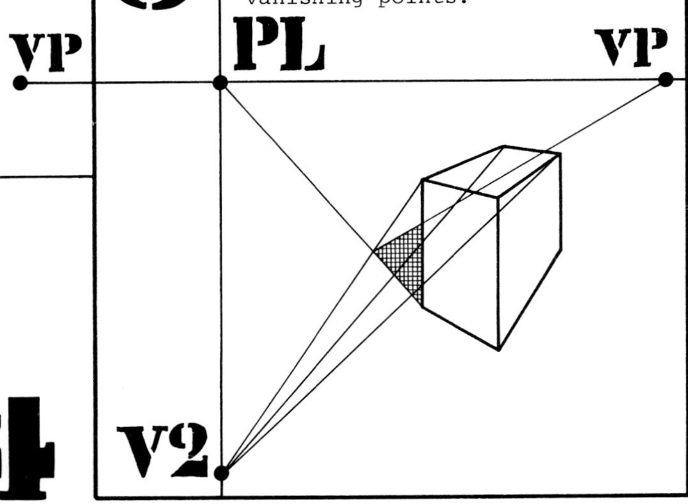

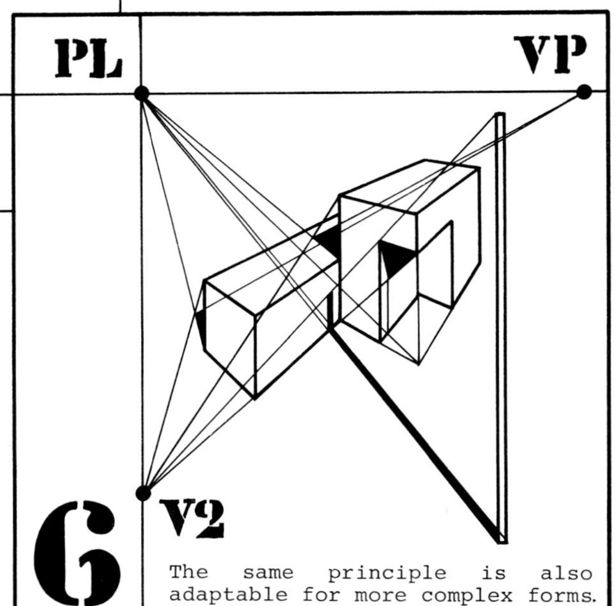

The same principle is also adaptable for more complex forms.

3 BASIC MARK-MAKING TECHNIQUES

Paper Surfaces and Mark-making Effects

Heavily textured papers, such as the rough watercolor papers and boards, exert a powerful influence over the quality of marks made by both broad and fine pigment applicators. Brushstrokes, chalk, and soft graphite marks become ragged and irregular, while hard pencil and pen lines become fragmented and difficult to apply.

Drawing and painting surfaces with a more pronounced "drag" should, therefore, be generally used with the broader mediums, for bolder effects, and in large images where suggestion rather than focal clarity is important. This occurs because the rougher surface textures can countermand attempts at illusion making by interfering with their pictorial credibility (see page 24).

1

When paper or artboard is smoother, such as cold pressed ("not" paper), or clay coated, a fine, textural grain allows the inherent nature of the medium to be expressed. The smoother surfaces afford the designer the freedom to invent and arrange textural zones within the format. They are more conducive to defining graphic detail by allowing the finely pointed applicators to respond to the user's intent. They accept liquid color more smoothly and take almost all mediums in the creation of all types of images--including illusions of realism. In fact, this is the surface for the beginner.

2

When the thinner, smoother papers are used, such as newsprint, layout, and detail paper, the surface quality of their support can be picked up and transferred into chalk and pencil artwork. If this frottage effect is not required, insert a sheet of vinyl, thick paper, or board between the drawing support and artwork. If the grain of timber drawing boards begins to make itself evident, its surface can be smoothed by a light sanding, using fine-grade glasspaper wrapped around a block of wood. To avoid buckling on the thinner papers, employ the drier mediums. Also, the more absorbent papers, such as newsprint, allow inks and paints to spread beyond their point of contact.

3

Extra-smooth surfaces, such as hot pressed papers, have little discernible tooth and therefore transfer the responsibility for textural mark-making and differential line quality firmly to the user. These surfaces are considered ideal for designers with complete control over mediums, especially pencil, pen and inks, watercolors, and dry-transfer materials, and for the creation of Super-Realist artwork. Other designers, however, find the shinier surfaces to be too slippery for brushwork, with liquid colors tending to run away from the brush. However, as experience is the only means of achieving ability in producing various forms of artwork, it is wise to attempt images on all types of paper surfaces.

4

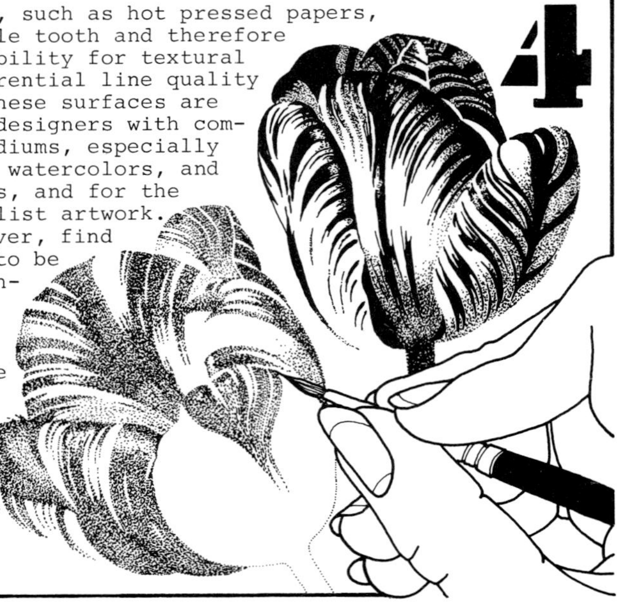

How to Use the Stippling Technique

Constructing images from dots can be laborious, as the regions of darker value require a heavy concentration of stippling. However, patience with this technique is often rewarded with an effective graphic.

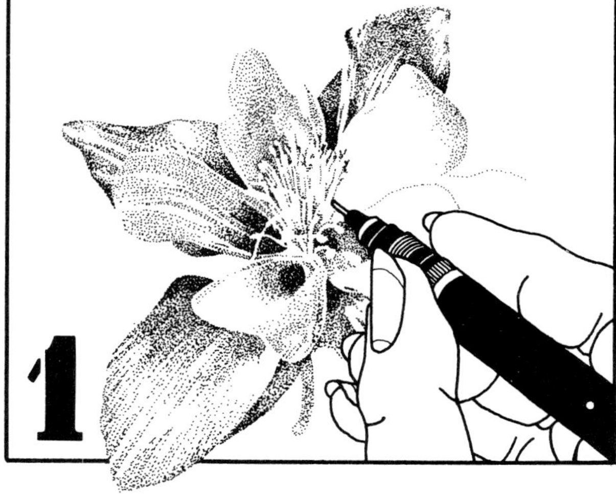

1

2

In large drawings, a variety of ink applicators such as nibs, brushes, match sticks, small doweling rods, etc., can combine a range of stippled scale in graphics--either exclusively assembled from dots or combined with line.

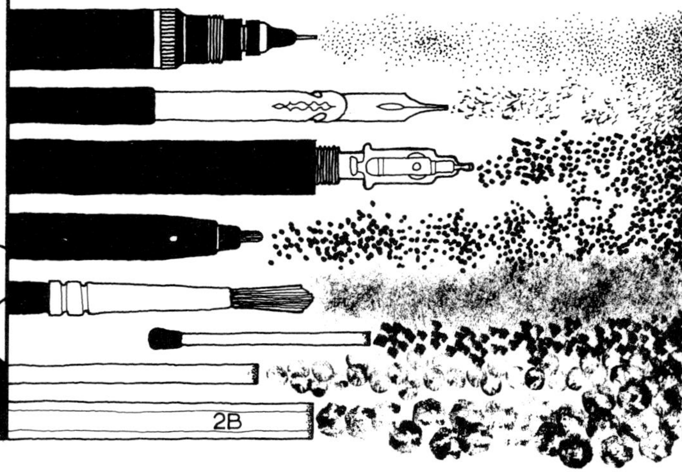

Stippling is useful in all kinds of artwork. It can be effective as a technique to suggest atmospheric haze in backgrounds of line drawings or, when stronger in impact and in contrast with other forms of rendering, it can attract the eye to an important middleground or foreground message area.

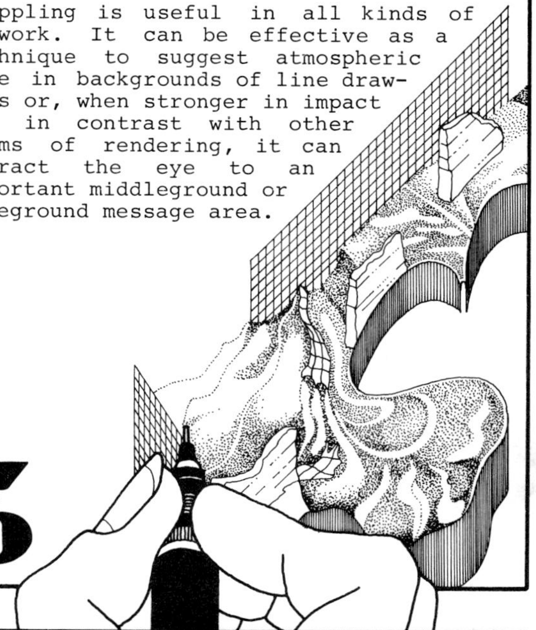

3

The use of a stencil brush will speed up the application process and introduce a much freer stippled effect. However, in order to retain control over more complex shapes in the artwork, the edges of the shapes should be masked prior to application. Always test the effect of a newly loaded stencil brush on a scrap of paper before applying it to the artwork.

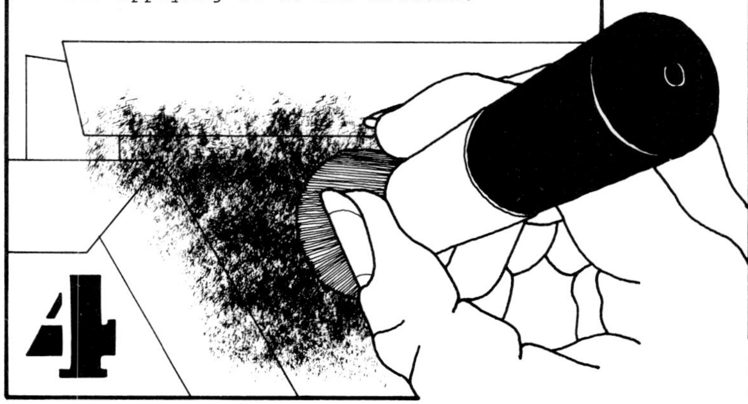

4

5

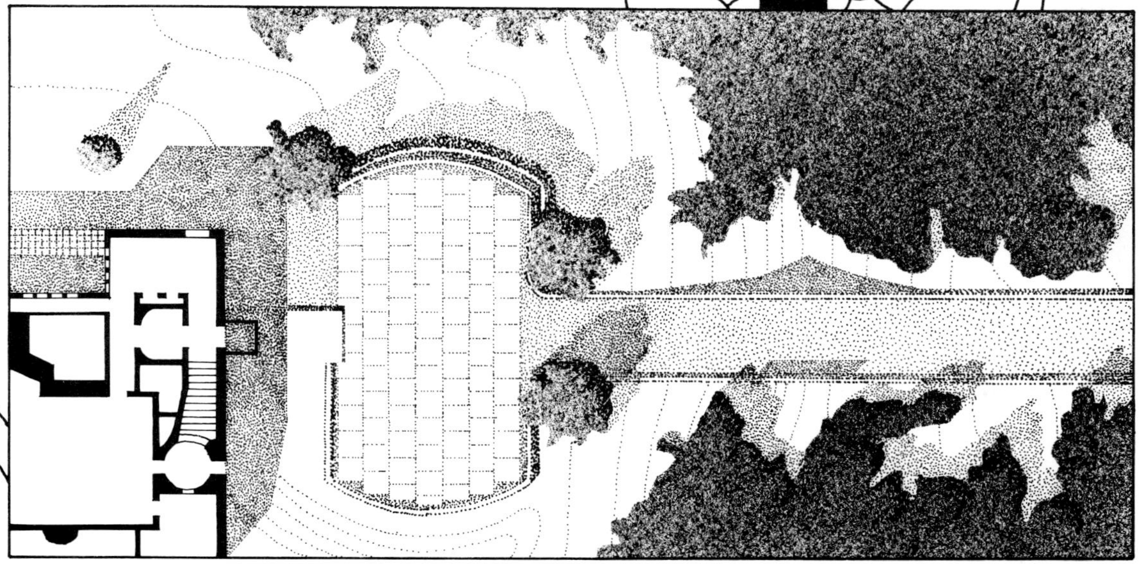

Here is part of a site plan employing various kinds of stippling effects, including a splattering technique using an old toothbrush (see page 63).

"Mechanical" Hatching Techniques

1 Hatching is a basic rendering technique that employs sets of parallel lines to create effects of value density, textural features, and solidity of form.

Usually associated with pen and pencil, hatching is much used in drawings destined for reproduction, such as those done by the diazo process.

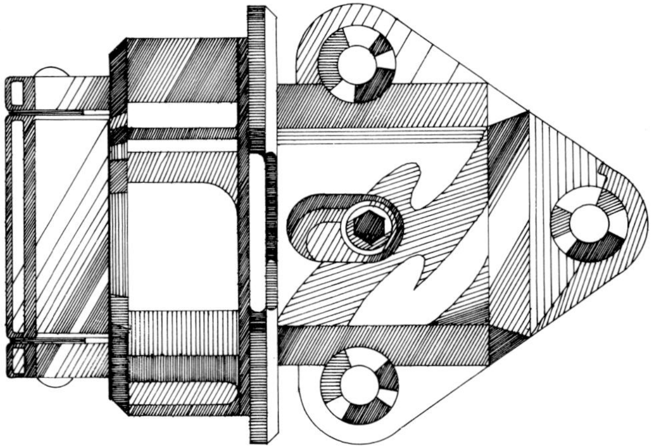

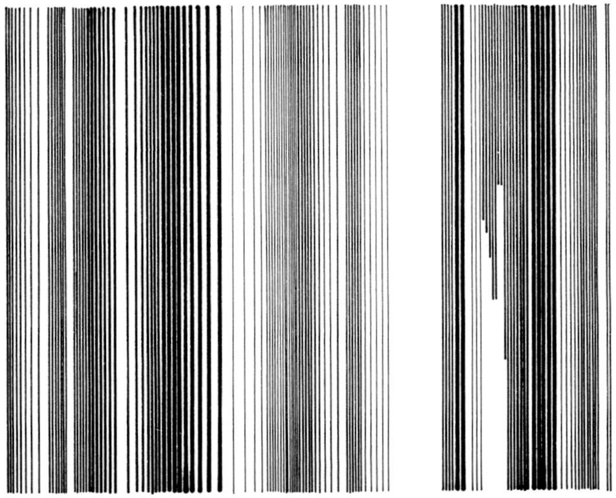

2 By using different nib sizes and graphite grades, together with ordered variations in line proximity, a wide range of value and surface simulation becomes possible.

3 A useful variation in hatching is the "hit or miss" effect. This is much used in orthographics to describe either rough textures or, paradoxically, surfaces that reflect light. This effect is created when ruled lines are allowed to break along their route. Some designers also create the same effect by deliberately using a clogged technical pen during application.

4 Complete drawings, which have no formal lines to contain them, can be constructed exclusively in single-directional "mechanical" hatching. In such drawings, the meeting of "open" and "closed" systems of parallel sets of lines creates an optical edge to their field, which is immediately recognized by the eye as a "line."

5

In this perspective detail, this optical effect is fully exploited in a single-directional hatching to depict a strong illusion of form in space.

"Mechanical" Cross-Hatching Techniques

1 Cross-hatching occurs when multi-directional sets of parallel lines are superimposed to extend the value range into its darker regions.

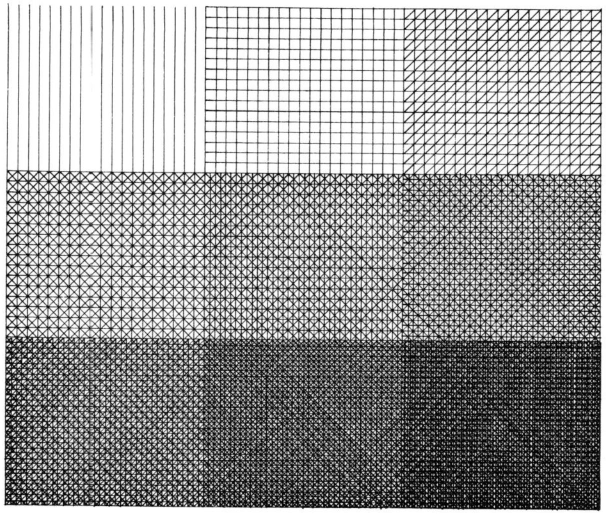

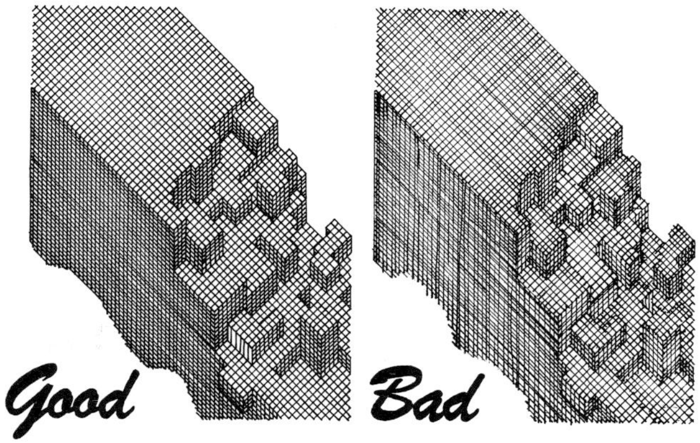

2 When a straightedge is used to achieve a mechanical appearance in hatching and cross-hatching, it is important to retain control over the regularity of line interval and to keep drawing equipment meticulously clean. Failure to do so can cause the rendering of arbitrary lines or smudging that will ruin the overall effect.

3 When required, highlights or softened areas in cross-hatched artwork can be easily "lifted" with an eraser or scraped away with a razor blade.

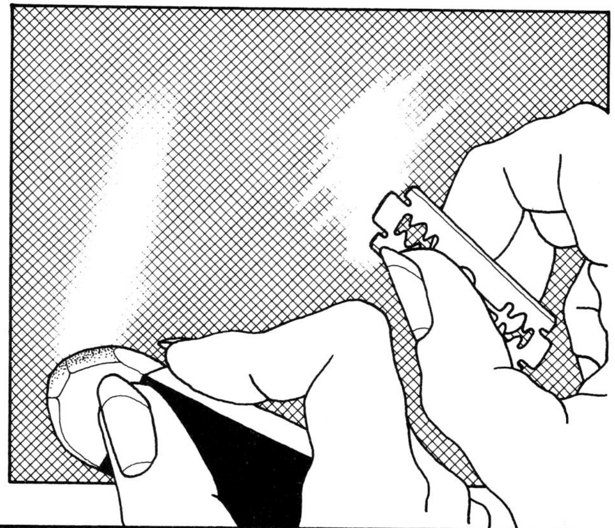

4 For special effects, a two-directional system of parallel lines can be decomposed for (depending on the scale of the cross-hatching) the depiction of textured surfaces or those receiving fragmented illumination or reflected light.

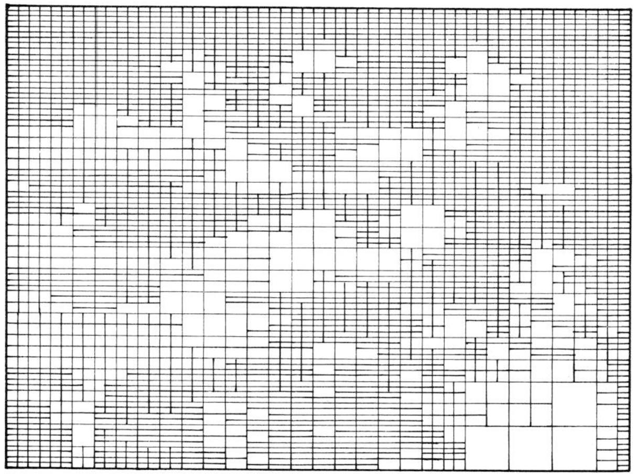

5

Hatching and cross-hatching are extremely effective when harnessed to the receding planes of perspective drawings. Used in this fashion, hatching increases illusions of depth by reinforcing plane inclinations and diminishing texture gradients.

Freehand Hatching Techniques

1 The potential of freehand pen and pencil techniques to achieve effects of space, surface, and value is limitless. The key to their success in graphics is their structure as controlled systems that rely upon one or a combination of techniques.

Structured "scribble"

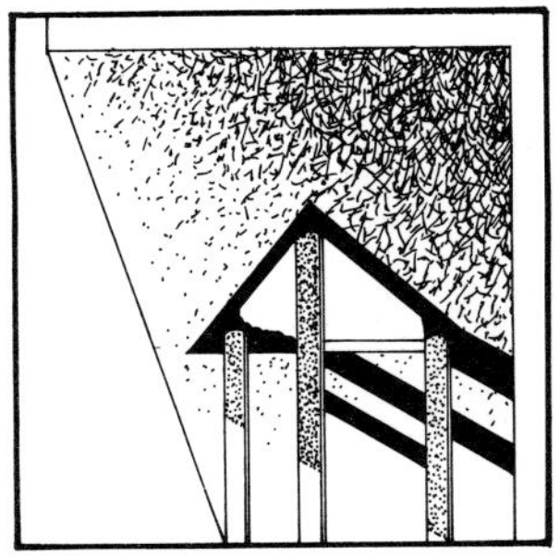

Dot-and-dash progression

Dash-to-"scribble" progression

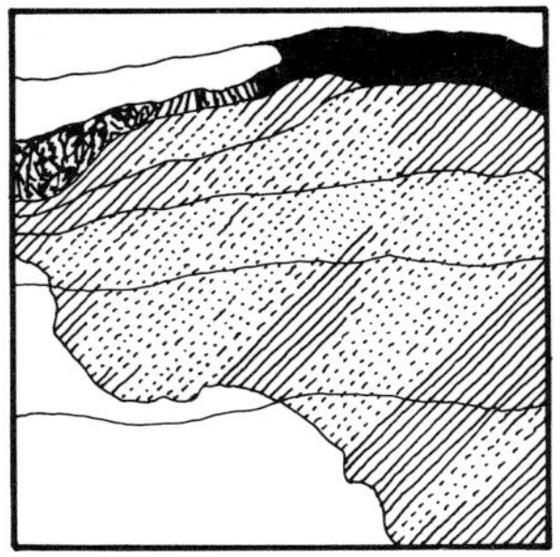

Line and dot

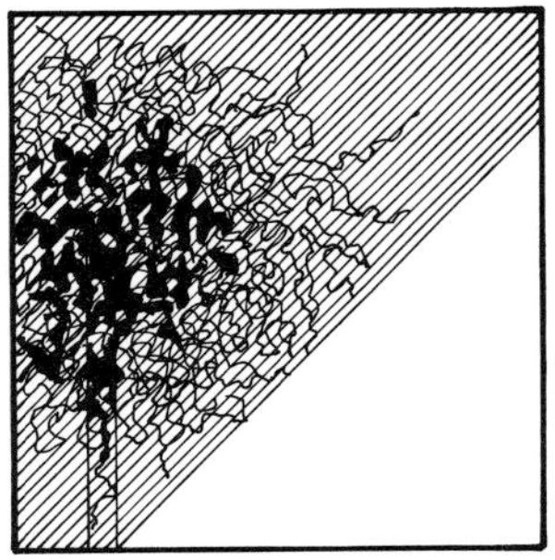

Hatched line over "scribble"

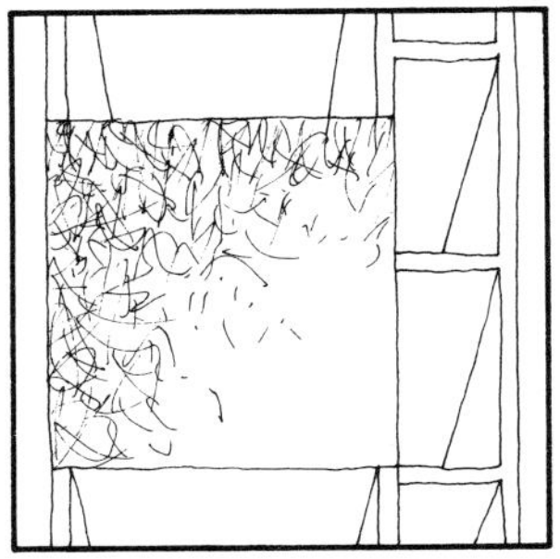

"Scribbled" dash

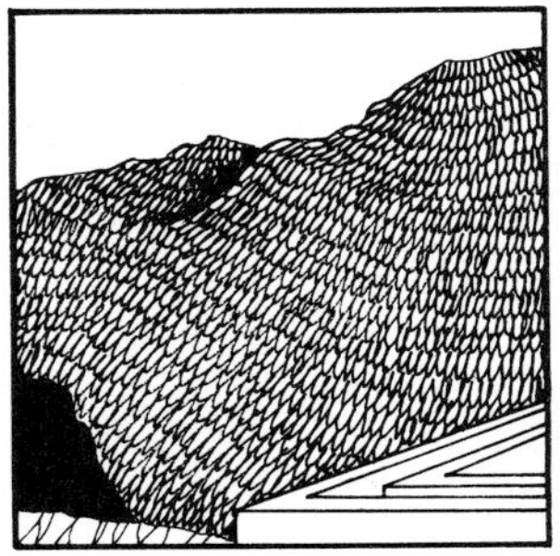

"Stitched" warp and weft

Freehand cross-hatch

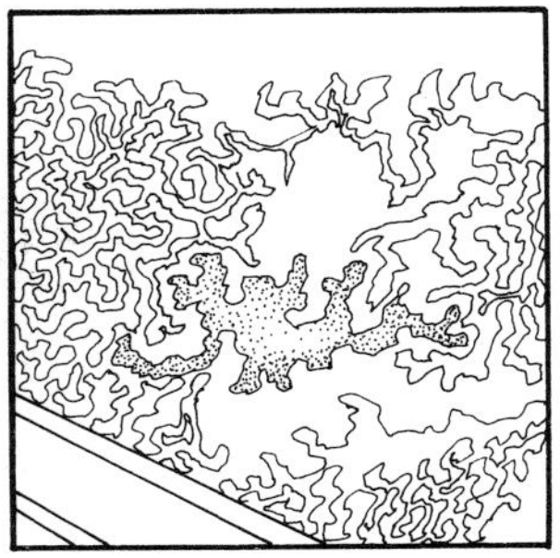

Continuous line "scribble"

2

When larger scale hatching techniques are developed, a more formal rendering of materials and surface textures becomes possible.

Hatching in Action

Mixed forms of freehand and ruled hatching techniques work well in all forms of drawing but are particularly useful in diazo-printed orthographics. Experience will develop a personal technique after experimentation with the more "closed" effects. These can later be allowed to become more "open" and relaxed during the production of increasingly confident artwork.

PLAN

ELEVATION

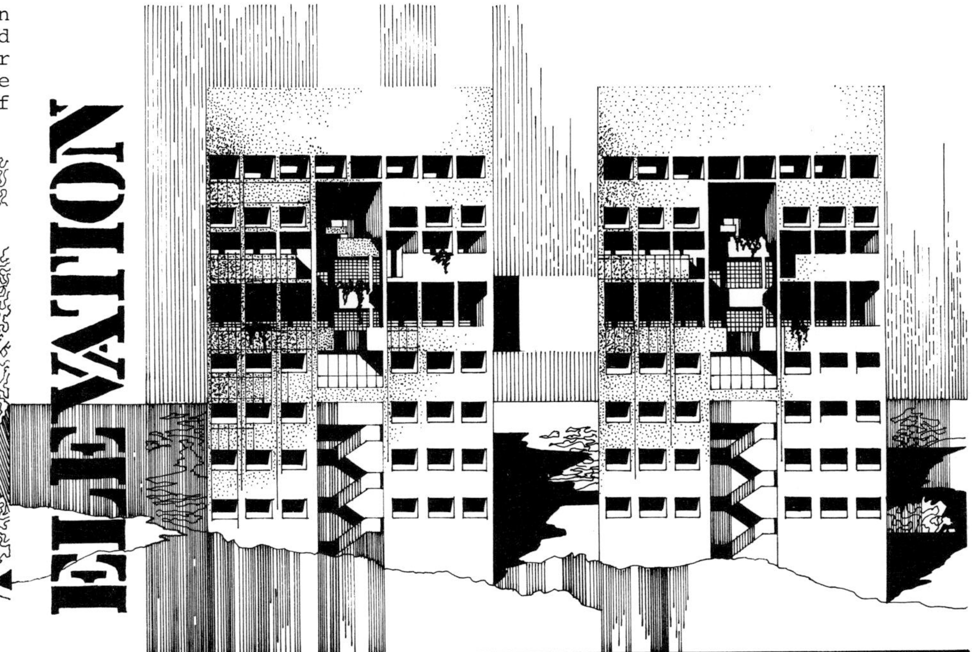

AXONOMETRIC PERSPECTIVE

Structured Graphite Shading Techniques

1

Badly rendered shading often leads to ruining pencil drawings. The simple rule is that shading should always bring surface information to forms and give visual cohesion to the overall image. For the beginner, it is a good idea to work graphite shading along the main surface inclination of form, as this reinforces the illusion of three dimensions.

N.B.: Always remember that shading describes surface and value. Therefore, the nature of the drawing will suggest the method best suited to render it.

2

Another basic method is to restrict hatching marks to single direction. In this instance, all marks describe a 45-degree angle. The various degrees of graphite value are achieved either by varying pressure on the pencil, or by being built up in superimposed layers.

3

Other forms of building cohesive shading are the structured "scribble" and freehand cross-hatch techniques.

4

Atmospheric shading is achieved by finger-rubbed or cotton wool-applied graphite dust collected from a pointer. This makes for very soft and subtle gradations of value, a "feathery" quality that works well with a sensuous line.

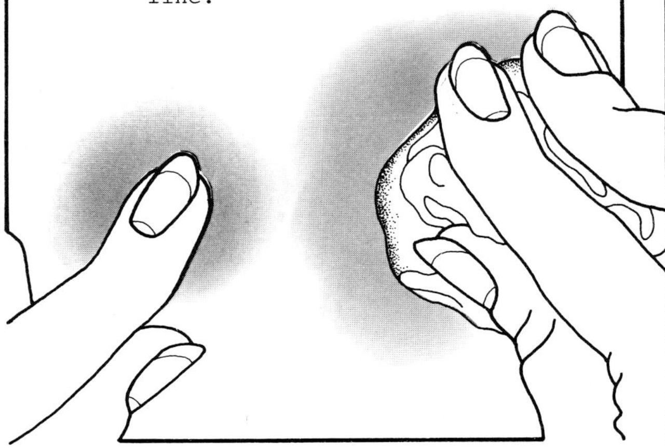

5

When shading hard-edged areas, avoid "woolly" scribble. Instead, concentrate upon defining a crisp edge for each value region in the tonal structure. This in itself will provide a structured basis for the drawing.

N.B.: Avoid working on paper supported on textured surfaces when attempting close-grained shading techniques.

6

When required, the transfer of textured surfaces can be successfully incorporated into shaded artwork. This technique, called frottage, is the process of making rubbings from variously grained or pitted surfaces. Once the frottage source has been removed, regular linework and shading techniques can be worked over it.

Frottage and Scoring in Action

1

All kinds of textured surfaces--such as different grades of glasspaper, cork, and the backs of linoleum and Masonite--can be transferred onto tracing-paper orthographics or perspectives via the frottage technique. Place a selected textured surface under the drawing and rub it over with a soft-grade graphite pencil or colored pencils. This method is especially useful for simulating grass, concrete, carpets, fabrics, and decorative finishes.

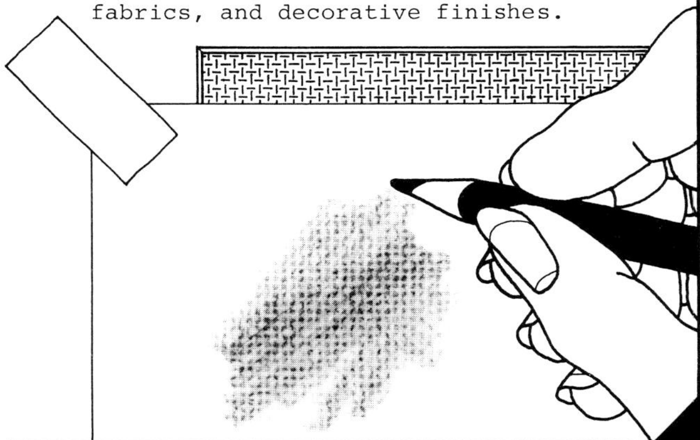

Textures for brickwork, blockwork, and other modular finishes can also be custom made to scale for use in plans and elevations destined for diazo reproduction.

First, make a template by scoring a sheet of card with the required pattern. This should use the metal stylus of a duplicator stencil cutter or the blunt side of a knife point against a straightedge.

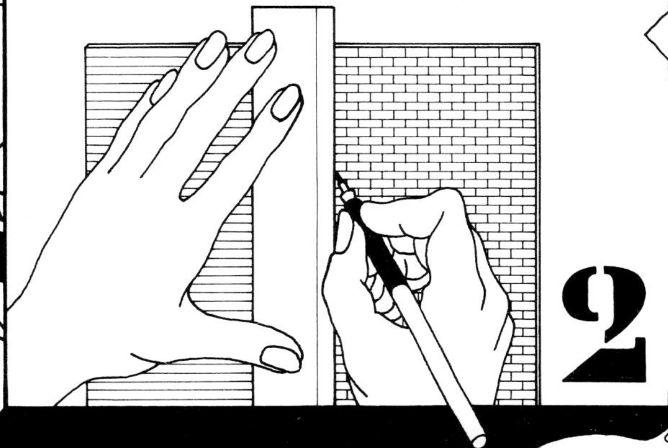

2

3

The completed template is then inserted under the tracing-paper drawing and positioned. Then its embossed image is transferred by frottage onto the appropriate part of the graphic.

1

Lines describing the modules of building finishes can also be scored directly into the surface of design drawings worked on the thicker, smoother drawing papers.

Again, using a duplicator stencil cutter or a knife point against a straightedge, score the required pattern while exerting enough pressure to achieve a fine, deep groove.

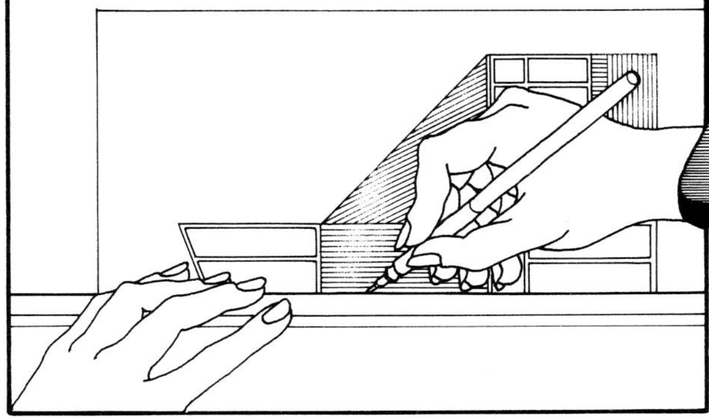

2

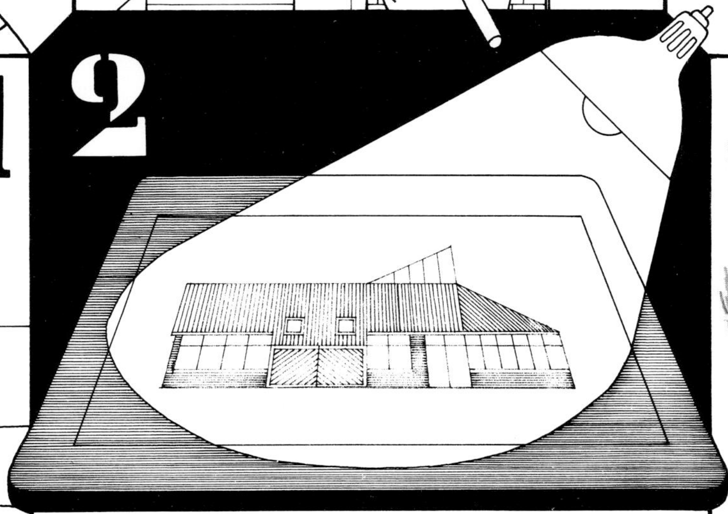

The scoring stage is best worked under side illumination so that its shadow pattern makes the operation more visible.

N.B.: Unlimited textures, including (when using the metal stylus) stencil-traced lettering can be achieved in this way.

Once the scoring operation is finished, the full effect is achieved when graphite or colored pencil is rendered over the textured drawing surface.

3

N.B.: In order to gain the full effect during this stage, aim for a tightly structured shading technique.

Black-on-White Reversal

The impact of a white ink line orthographic drawing on black paper can be quite dramatic, especially if displayed amid drawings of the more conventional black on white.

This reversal is also particularly useful when depicting night views exploring lighting effects in exterior perspectives and elevations or . . .

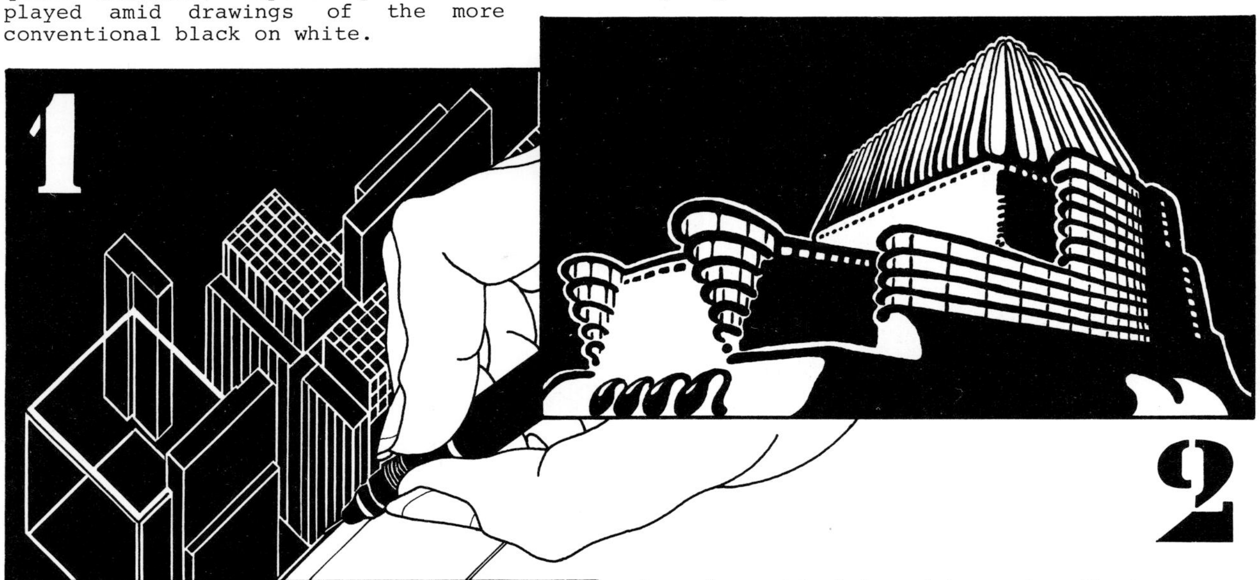

3

. . . large interior spaces such as auditoriums. In these perspectives, a concentration on the effects of light on objects and planes is central to the reversal technique, a technique that shifts emphasis from drawing the "positive" to a depiction of the "negative."

N.B.: Other mediums such as colored pastels can also be used to effect on black paper.

Another white-on-black medium is the scratch board (scraperboard) technique. Boards are coated with a black eggshell finish; scratching this surface with the custom metal stylus exposes the white underlayer. Drawings should be preplanned at same size and transferred to the scratch board via tracing paper. When transferring them to the board, make sure not to damage its brittle surface.

N.B.: White scratch boards are also available.

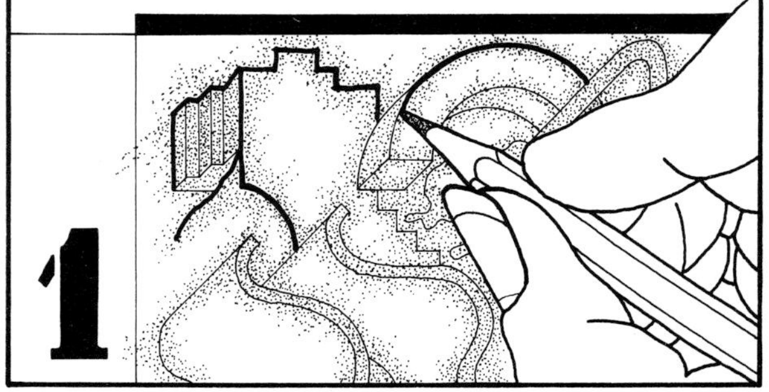

Assuming a black board is used, first scrape away all the main outlines of the transferred drawing with the metal stylus before exposing carefully any areas of solid white.

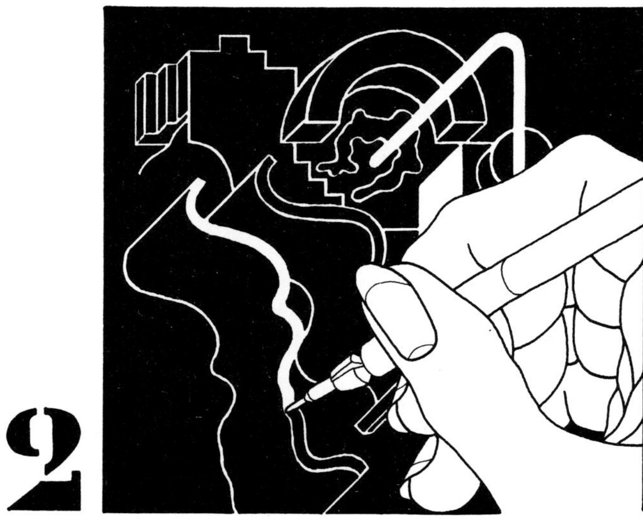

What remains can now be removed using any of the hatching techniques or their combination mentioned thus far. The difference in their rendering is, of course, that they appear in "negative" form.

N.B.: As the underlayer is unrelenting in its whiteness, value grades are achieved by a control of line thickness and proximity of scratched hatching.

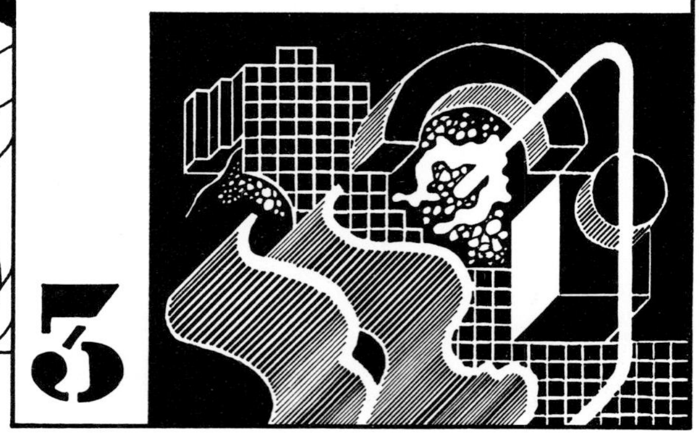

Black, White, and Color on a Stick

Pastel, chalk, Conté crayon, and charcoal are excellent mediums for spontaneous sketching and for rapid design perspectives. Their facility for creating atmospheric effects results from the softness of their composition in reaction to varying pressures during application, and the degree of tooth on the paper surface.

White chalk, pastel, and Conté crayon are available for the reversed, or "negative," drawing technique on black paper (see facing page).

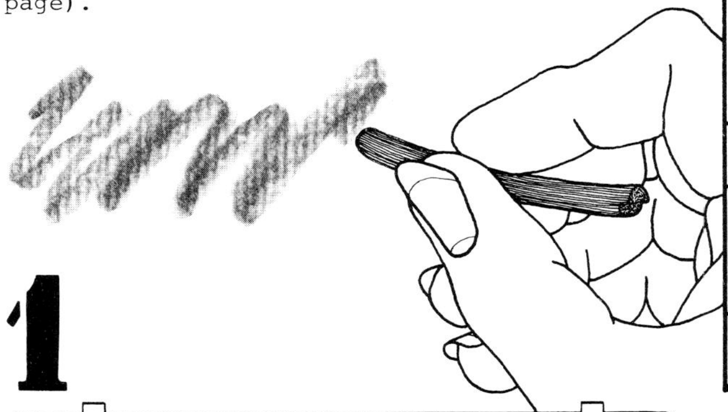

1

2

Stick mediums offer their sides for stroking broad areas of value, while their tips--or the edges of their ends--produce both fine lines and those of varying thickness.

N.B.: Apart from chalk, the other mediums are also available in wood-encased pencil form, allowing sharpened points.

Highlights and modifications in black-on-white drawings made in pastel, chalk, or Conté crayon can be effected by overworking with their white counterparts. Highlights and corrections made in the less stable drawings made of charcoal are removed by rubbing gently with a finger, dusting with tissue paper, erased with a kneaded "putty" rubber or a compressed ball of bread.

N.B.: All these mediums require stabilizing with fixative.

3

4

The spontaneity of stick color mediums such as pastels should be used to build up images as a whole rather than a "coloring by numbers" approach. By developing the total image in layers as opposed to a concentration on its parts, the designer has a better chance of retaining control over the structure of value and color.

One good method of building up the image in pastel is to apply strokes in open-mesh cross-hatched layers so that earlier strokes read through the upper layers.

N.B.: It is important to experience all mediums at their limits of graphic expression. With pastels, this arrives when the paper's surface grain becomes clogged with pigment.

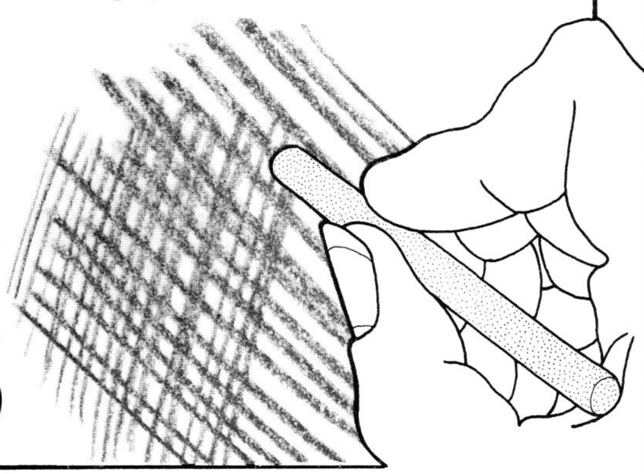

5

Colored pencils are similar in quality to pastels; together they have made a comeback, particularly in architectural graphics, for adding color details to wash drawings and pen-and-ink work. Colored pencils are a particularly useful medium; they are comparatively stable, color being rendered as flat areas, directionally, or cross-hatched using the technique described for pastels.

N.B.: When their graphic limits are reached, and surface clogging occurs, colored pencil deposits can be scraped away with a razor blade.

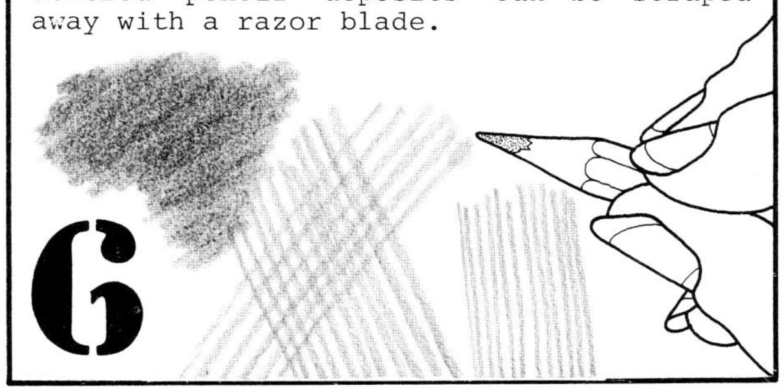

6

Adding Self-Adhesive Transfer Tone to Line Drawings

All kinds of line drawings, such as diagrams, illustrations, orthographics, and perspectives, can benefit from the added dimension of even a single tonal value. This can be quickly introduced using self-adhesive transfer sheets with tonal screens designed for drawings that are to be reproduced and therefore rescaled.

1

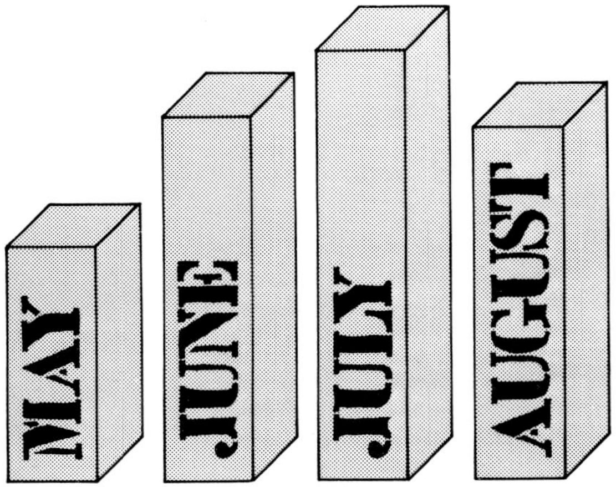

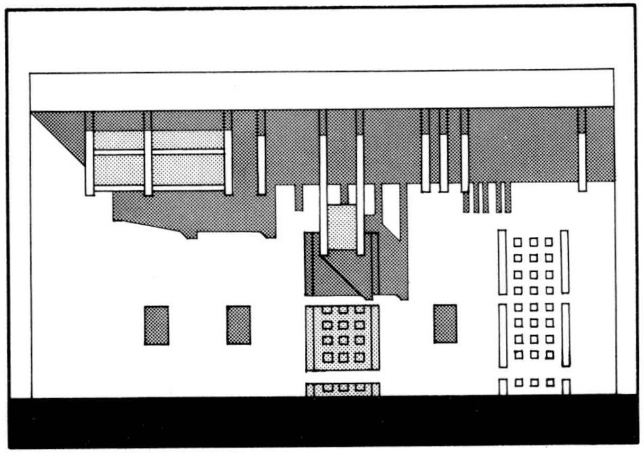

2

The effect works best if the initial drawing is executed in pen using single or multiple line weights. Depending on the type of drawing, the selection of areas for shading might be confined to the background, foreground, or, in orthographics, simply emphasize depth as shadows.

3

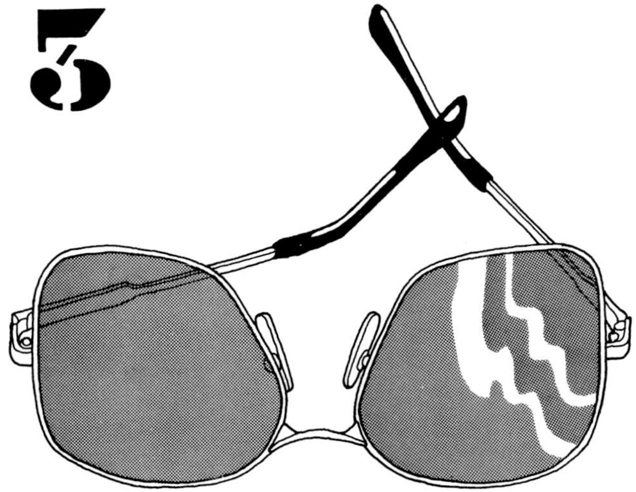

Two basic applications are worth consideration: shading that is completely contained by the line drawing, and shading that is independent of the drawing, which creates a freer effect.

Place the selected sheet of self-adhesive transfer tone over the area to be shaded and cut a piece of film slightly larger than the shape required. Use a sharp scalpel, but be careful not to cut through the backing sheet.

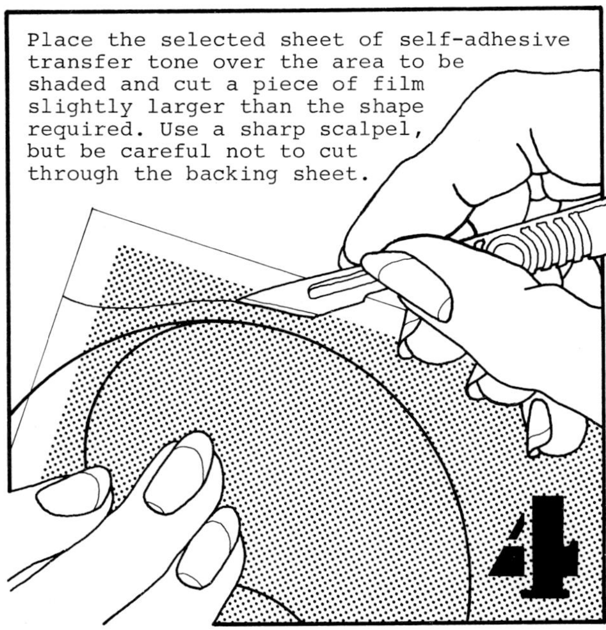

4

Lift the cut area from the backing sheet, position it on the artwork, and smooth it down with the heel of your hand.

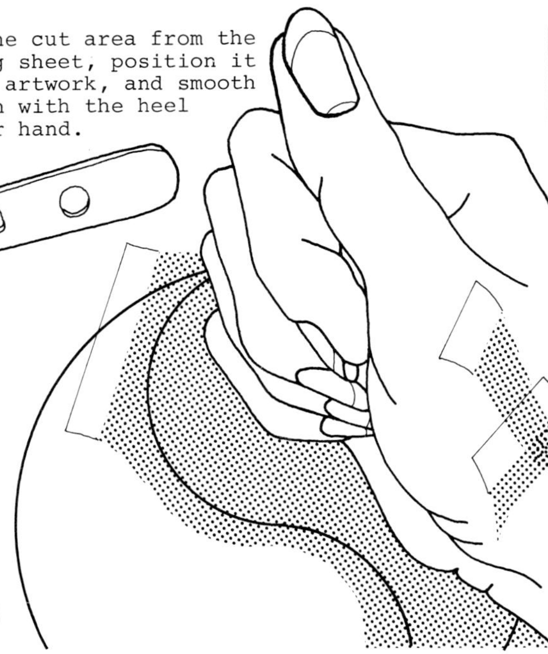

5

Trim away the excess tone, cover the transferred tone with clean paper, and burnish it firmly with a smooth, broad-ended burnishing tool.

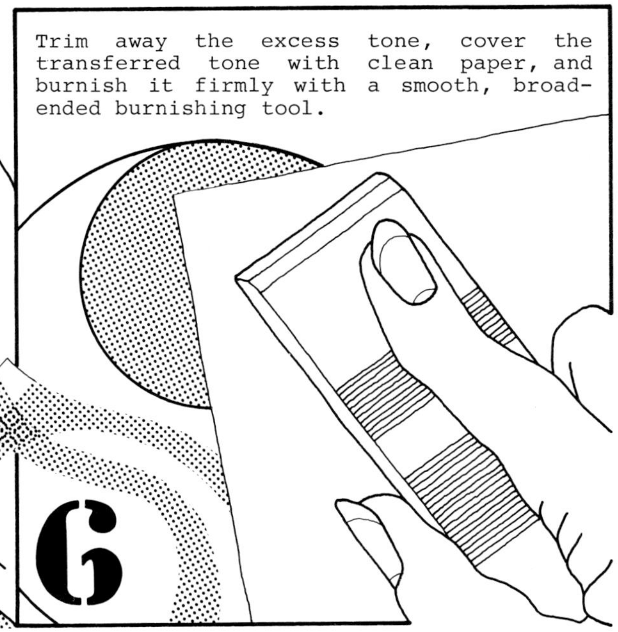

6

The Pen-and-Wash Technique

1

Draft the basic composition using a medium-grade pencil on a medium-rough-grain drawing paper. To avoid having the paper wrinkle during its later contact with water, it can be first stretched onto the drawing board (see page 67).

N.B.: Other points to avoid are the use of hard graphite, as this can irrevocably score the paper surface, and overworking the initial pencil draft.

2

Next, redraw the image, using a pen and waterproof ink. Depending upon the accuracy of the pencil draft, the image can be directly traced or, using the graphite as a guide, developed into more intricate levels of detail.

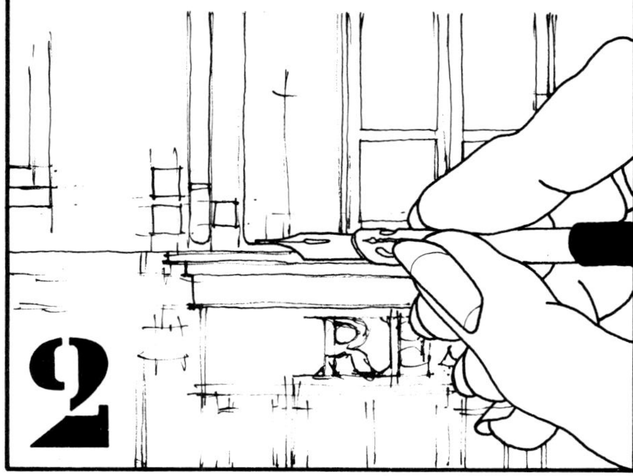

3

When the penwork is completed and the ink is dry, remove the pencil underdrawing with a soft eraser.

4

Various dilutions of the drawing ink or watercolors can now be introduced, using a brush size compatible with that of the areas to be washed. Edges of washes can be contained either by the lines or, for freer effects, be more loosely applied.

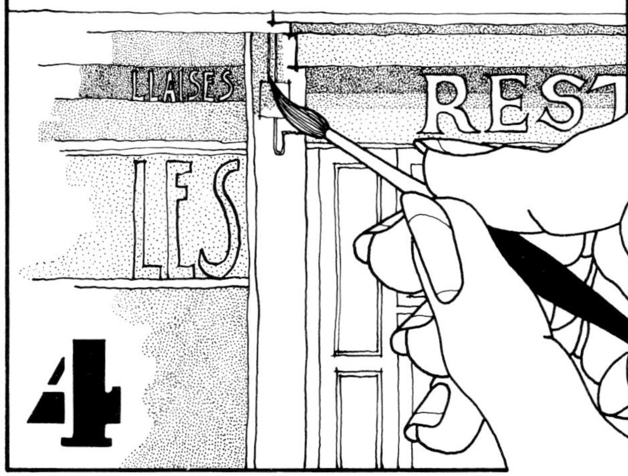

5

If required, excess amounts of wash can be removed from the drawing with a sheet of blotting paper.

N.B.: The use of blotting paper is itself a graphic technique, to lighten areas of a diluted wash by dabbing them with a piece of blotting paper while the areas are still damp.

6

When the wash application is finished and dry, adjustments to the line drawing, such as additional detail or emphasis, can finally be applied with the pen.

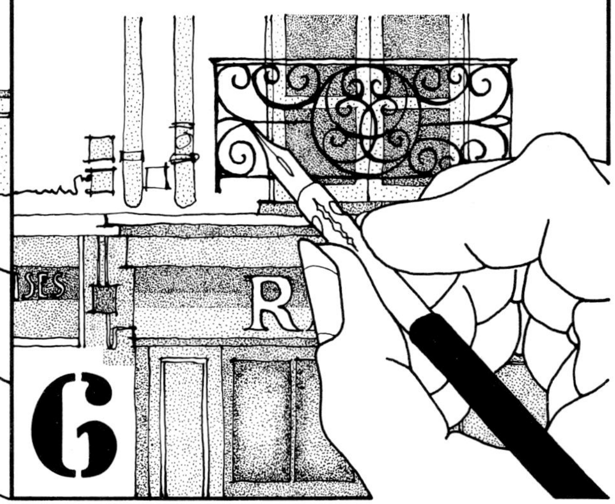

Rendering Hard Edges in Water-based Paints

Designer's color (gouache) can be applied in different consistencies. It can be diluted as with watercolor, used full-bodied and wet like oil color, or applied almost dry for dry brushwork effects.

Its main characteristic, however, is its opacity and resultant ability to produce flat or variegated washes in a consistency thick enough to obliterate the surface of paper together with dry, under-painted layers of another color.

1

The essence of the watercolor technique is achievement of a color transparency that utilizes both the colors of layers of diluted pigment and the tint of the paper.

To ensure accurate register of a watercolor wash with a complicated edge, first dampen the area along the edge with a brush charged with clean water.

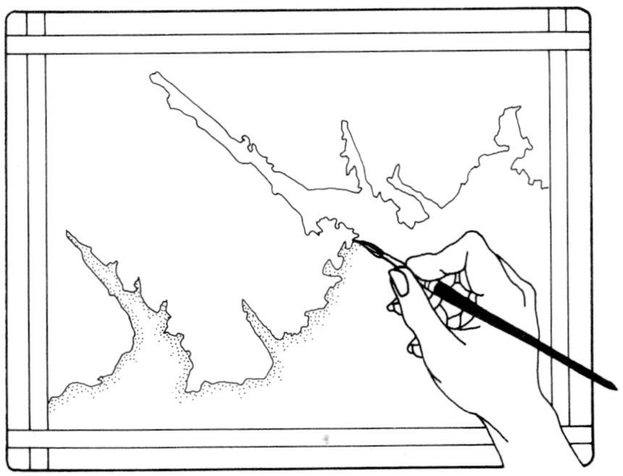

1

Hard-edge effects in this medium are achieved by first outlining the contours of a complicated shape with a fine-pointed brush before blocking in the main area with a larger brush.

Precision edges can also be obtained by first masking the shape with masking tape, or by trace-cutting more intricate contours from the tape with a sharp scalpel. After the application is dry, the tape is peeled carefully away to reveal a crisp, slightly raised edge with an "untouched-by-hand" appearance.

2

2

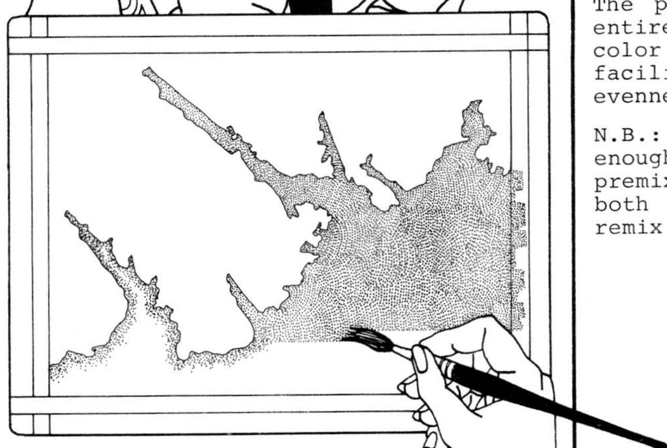

Next, recharge the brush with watercolor and apply over the dampened area before bringing the wash into the shape. Make sure that its leading edge is at the top of a slightly tilted drawing board. This allows gravity to play its part in pulling down smoothly the extending wash.

3

Flat washes are applied in parallel, overlapping bands that blend before drying. The delineated or masked edges of larger areas to be washed allow the more rapid application of a medium that tends to dry quickly.

N.B.: Never retouch newly rendered washes. These can be corrected by overpainting when dry.

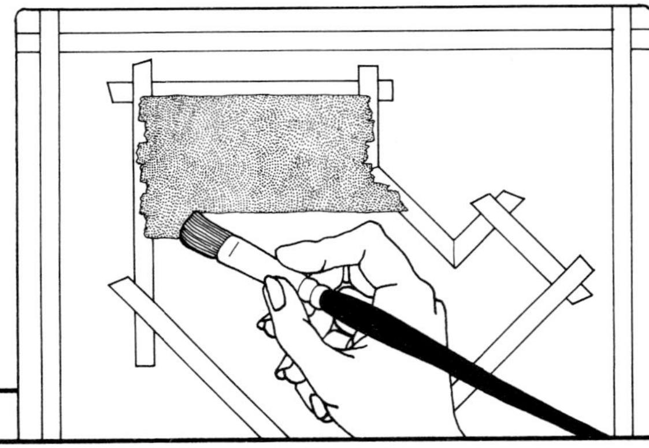

The predampening with clean water of an entire shape destined for a flat watercolor wash is a wet-in-wet technique that facilitates both crispness of edge and evenness of diluted pigment application.

N.B.: Always make sure that more than enough watercolor or designer's color is premixed before the rendering stage. In both cases, it is extremely difficult to remix an exact color match.

3

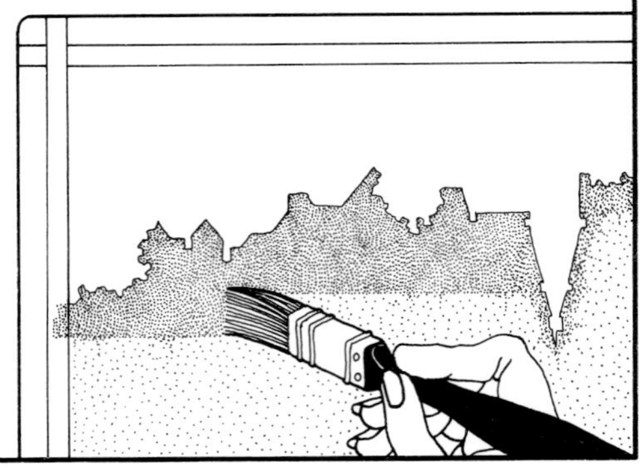

Ink and Watercolor Special Effects

1

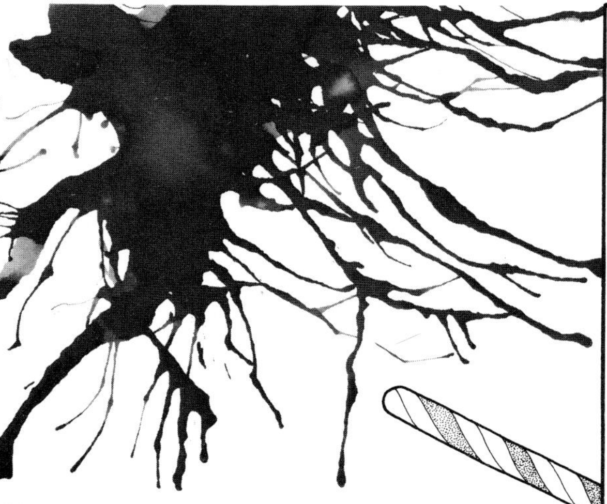

A delicate tracery effect can be achieved by blowing small pools of liquid pigment across areas of artwork.

N.B.: Using a plastic drinking straw offers more control over the effect.

2

Fabulous minimarbling effects can be produced when water-based pigment is mixed prior to application with pen-cleaning fluid or turpentine. This effect works best when one color is laid over an established, dry wash of another color.

N.B.: Thoroughly clean brush after use.

3

Splattering is another effect achievable in different ways: a blade can be drawn across toothbrush bristles heavily loaded with thickly mixed pigment, or a brush lightly loaded with diluted pigment can be directionally flicked over a masked or unmasked area of artwork.

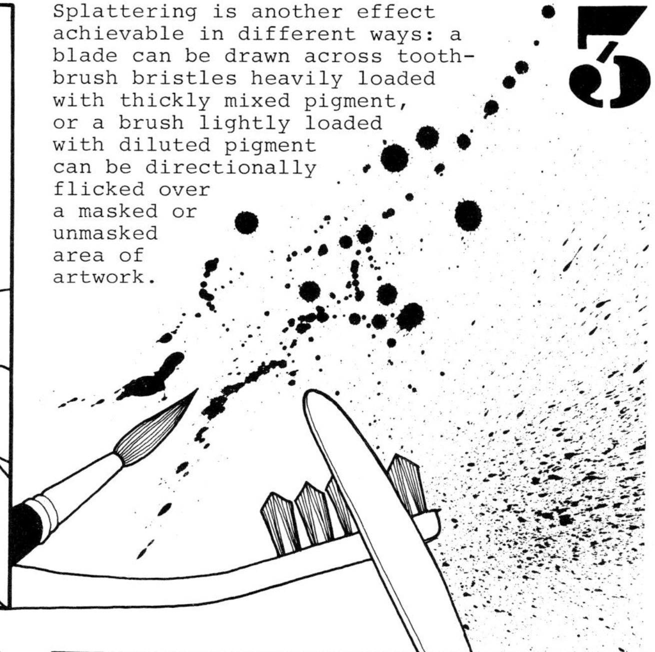

4

Zones of a picture can gain textural richness from imprinting. Printmakers include a well-crumpled wad of paper, wood end-grains, or a rough sponge. Experiment with ranges of unusual materials, and try printing one color over another.

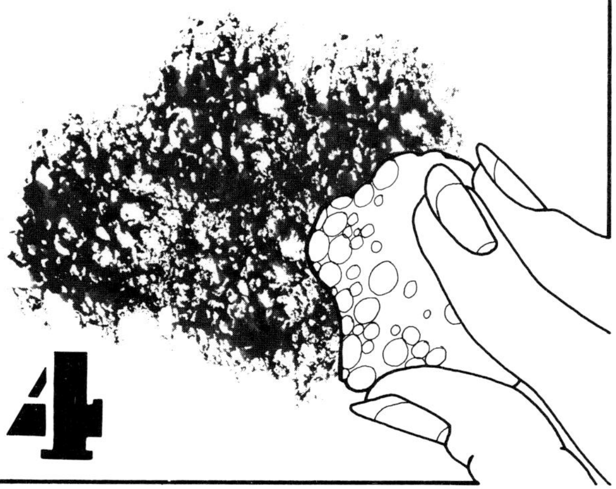

5

Apart from candle wax, another resist agent for watercolors is liquid masking fluid. First, brush-apply the fluid into the required area before thoroughly cleaning the brush. When the area is dry, apply the wash.

6

When the wash is dry, the areas with masking fluid can be finger-rubbed away to expose the effect.

Masking Tape and String Effects

1

Masking tape can be used with most pigments to produce either clean, straight edges for painting formats or to mask the perimeter of hard-edged shapes comprised of straight sides. When the full-bodied paints like gouache, tempera, or acrylic are used, the tape leaves a slightly raised but crisp edge when removed.

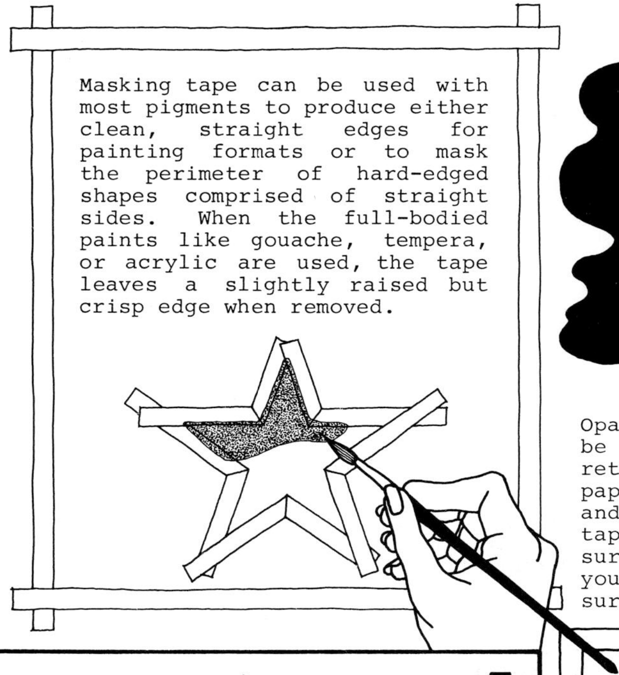

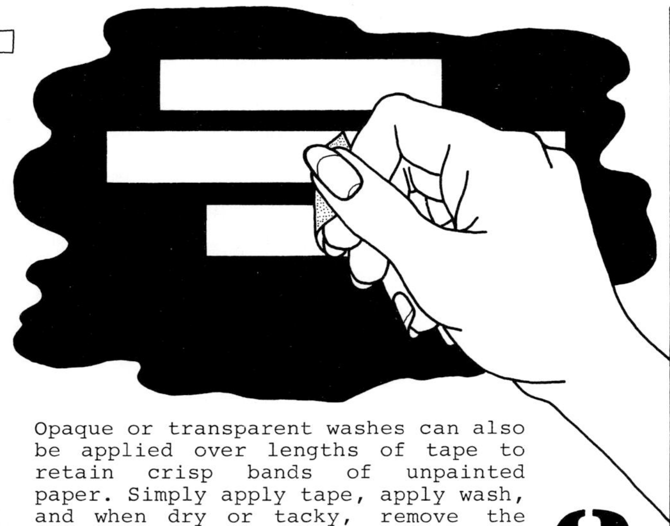

Opaque or transparent washes can also be applied over lengths of tape to retain crisp bands of unpainted paper. Simply apply tape, apply wash, and when dry or tacky, remove the tape. In order to preserve the paper surface, do this slowly, keeping your fingers close to the artwork's surface.

2

Cut or torn strips of tape can be arranged in required formations, overpainted and, when dry, removed. However, this effect works best when composing irregular patterns and when later subjected to the softening effect of transparent washes.

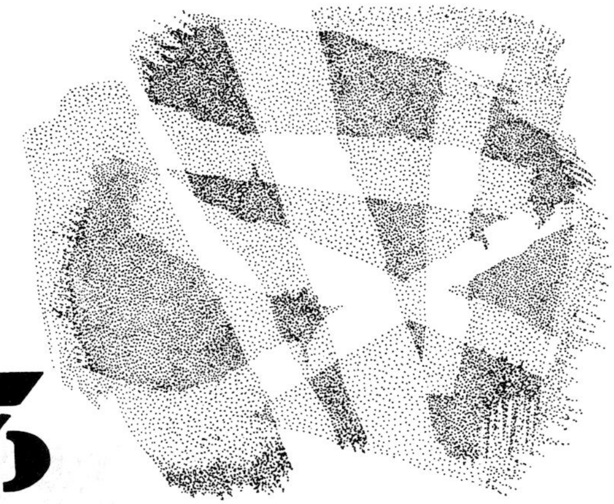

3

1

Load a length of string with ink or paint and, holding one end, lower it onto the artwork, allowing it to snake into a loosely coiled arrangement on the paper.

2

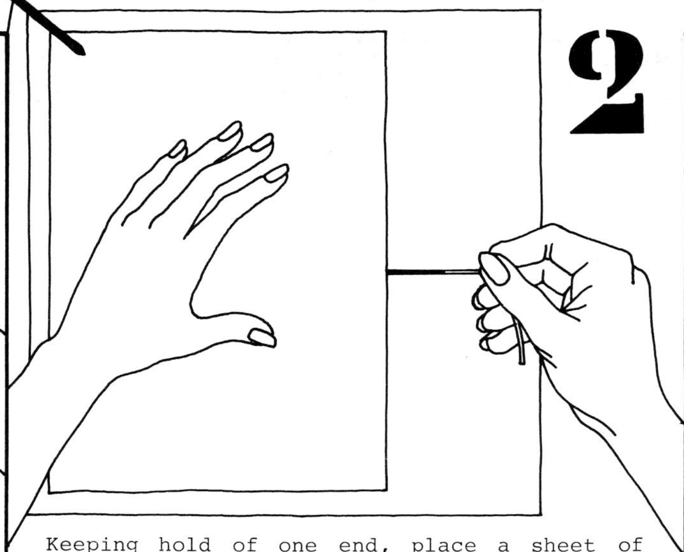

Keeping hold of one end, place a sheet of paper over the configuration of string. Hold this down gently with the flat of the other hand and slowly withdraw the string from its paper "sandwich," pulling from the side.

Although there is little control over this technique, it can create some interesting, if unpredictable, results when restricted to the edges of the artwork.

3

Unusual Techniques: Bleach and Shoe Polish

1 Regular household bleach can be worked into watercolor or colored ink washes as a correction medium (to bleach away errors), as a "whitening" agent for highlights, or to modify ink line drawings.

However, some fascinating effects can be achieved when bleach is worked into brush-applied washes of black or blue-black washable or "permanent" fountain-pen (not India) ink. Simply paint an area in undiluted ink and, when dry, draw into the wash using a strip of paper dipped in bleach. Never use brushes, as bleach will damage their bristles.

2

3 Intense lines can be obtained applying neat bleach with a pointed paper strip. Broad areas with tone can be achieved by "combing" the wash with the edge of a chisel-shaped paper applicator. A subtle gradation of a pinkish-yellow tone can be produced by increasingly diluting the bleach with water.

1

Another unusual medium is shoe polish, which offers a palette of subtle pigments, including blacks, grays, ochres, tans, and reds. These can produce attractive, atmospheric effects when combined with ink line drawings on white paper.

2 Always apply the polish after the drawing stage. Work the pigment into the drawing with a soft cloth or cotton wool, superimposing one color over another for color mixes or building up layers of one pigment for deeper values of a single hue.

3 Because of the way it is applied, shoe polish pigment is only loosely related to the drawing. This freedom of technique adds to its attractive quality.

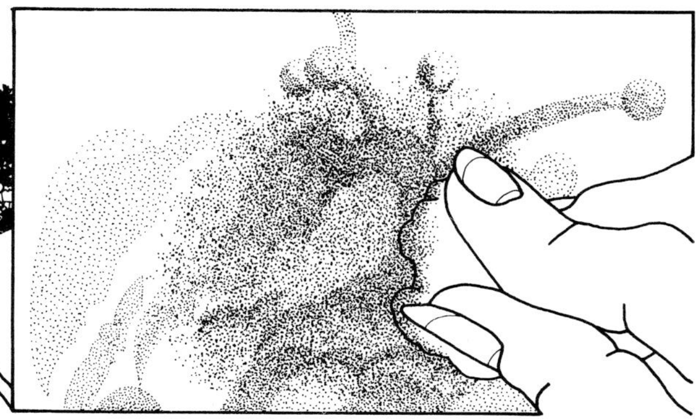

If used sparingly, the staining effect of shoe polish is also useful to modify colors in dry gouache and poster color artwork, with the polish acting as a color film through which dissonant hues can be modified.

Some Quick Aerosol Spray Color Effects

1

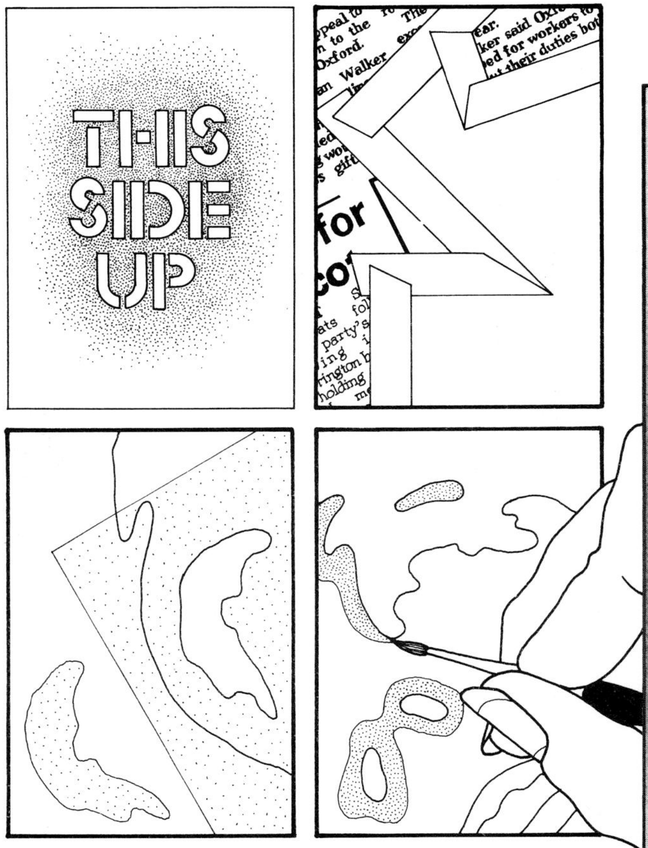

Being quick drying and quick to apply, the aerosol spray method represents a fast medium for rendering color or value on artwork. Color effects can be rapidly built up using a series of oversprayed layers comprising different hues, the edges of areas receiving color being first protected by a mask. Masking methods include the use of cut card templates, masking tape with newsprint, and frisket film. Two paint-on masking methods are liquid frisket and rubber cement, both being finger rubbed away after the spray application has dried.

2

"Found" stencils can also be introduced as a means of creating patterned or textured spray washes. The "stencil" is placed onto the artwork before spraying or--for effects relying upon interaction among several colors--between spray applications.

3

A variety of objects, such as open-weave fabrics, netting, lace, expanded metal sheeting, string, cut paper strips, confetti, gravel, pressed leaves, ferns, etc. can function as stencils for simulating a wealth of visual texture in spray-color artwork.

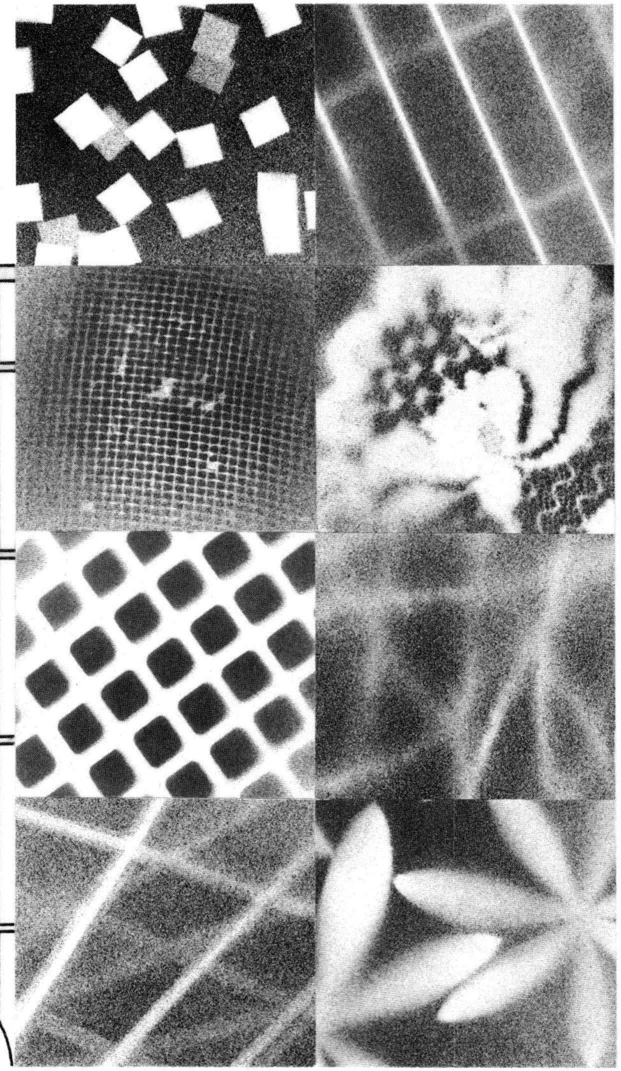

How to Stretch Drawing Paper

1

In order to avoid wrinkling paper, it is advisable to stretch lighter-weight paper intended for important artwork in watercolor, inks, pen and wash, or gouache. Apart from boards, all kinds of paper can be stretched. Some designers even prefer to stretch heavy-duty tracing papers.

One of two methods of soaking paper is to immerse the sheet in a sink of water for a few minutes. Then carefully remove it, allowing all excess water to drain off before placing it on the drawing board.

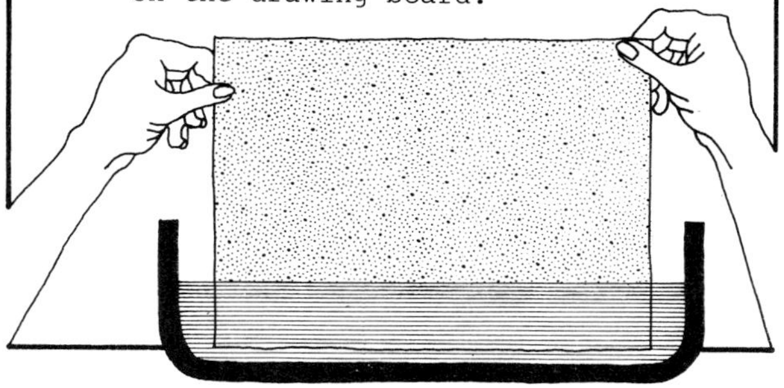

2

The other method is to carry out the soaking operation on the drawing board, using clean water and a sponge. Both sides should be saturated by first working the sponge around the edges and then in a star-shaped configuration before covering the entire sheet.

N.B.: The presence of a water-mark, seen right way round, indicates the correct side of the paper.

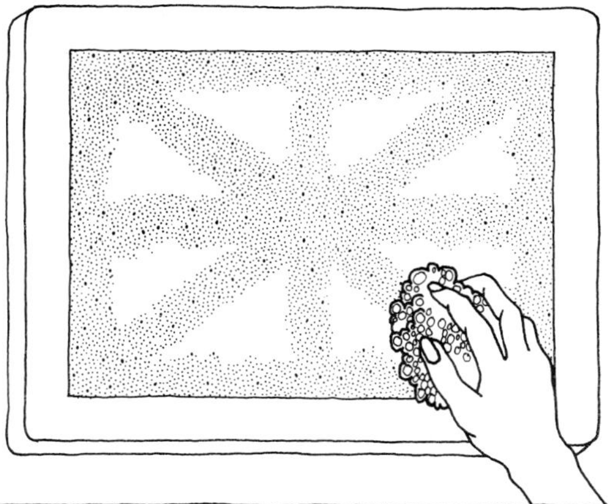

3

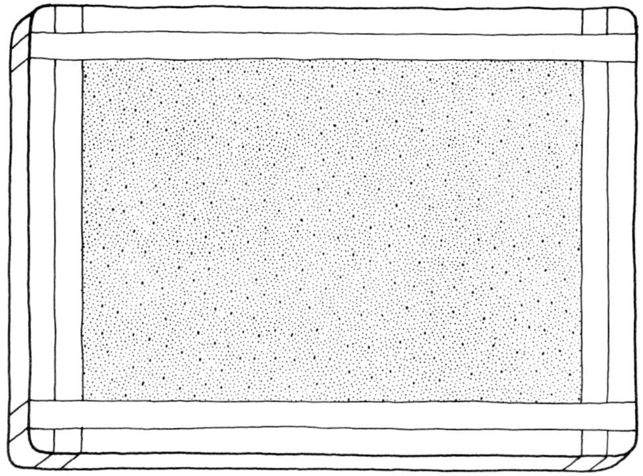

After making sure that the saturated sheet is as flat as possible, attach it to the board, using a two-inch gum strip and applying half to the edges of the paper, half to the surface of the board.

4

Make sure that the tape--especially at overlapped corners--is properly stuck down, by burnishing it with a finger. When the paper is dry the artwork can begin.

N.B.: Keep the board flat and away from direct sunlight. Resist the temptation to accelerate the drying process artificially.

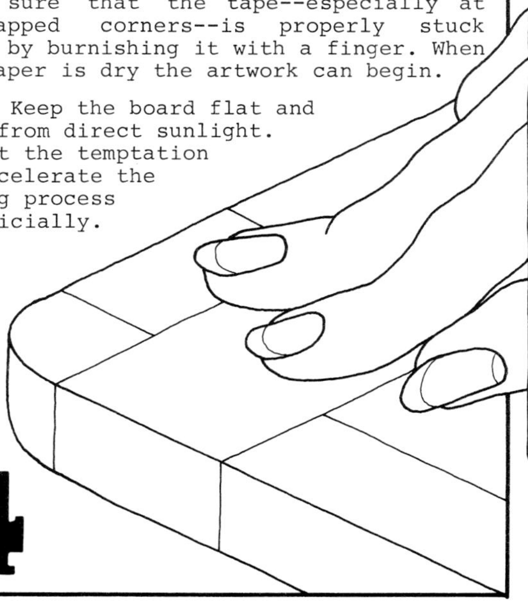

5

When the artwork is completed and dry, it should be carefully removed with a sharp scalpel, cutting in one continuous direction along the center of the tape.

6

When several stretched sheets are required, these can be stretched one on top of another on the same board. After one layer of artwork is finished, it is carefully removed--making sure that only one layer of tape is cut--to expose the next sheet.

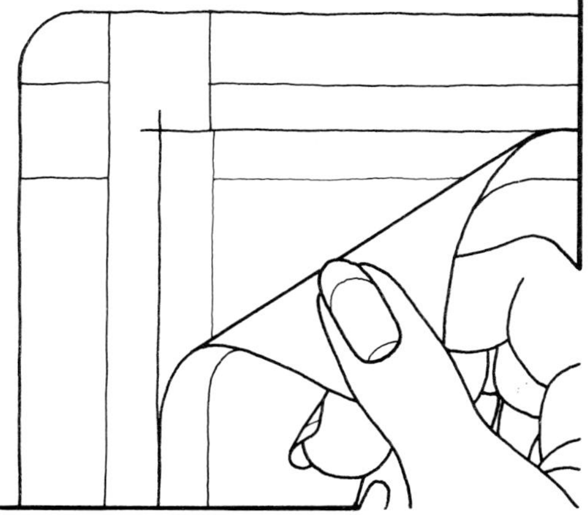

How to Pre-Plan Artwork

Many design students make the mistake of attempting artwork without the aid of preparatory guidance graphics. This impulsiveness often leads to frustration when an image distorts or to time wasted in redrawing artwork that has accidentally turned out to be either too large or too small. Other students, however, can literally be terrorized into timidity when confronted with large, blank sheets of paper.

These common frustrations can easily be short-circuited by an initial linear planning or a preparatory underpainting, which predict the compositional layouts of both subjective and objective artwork directly on the sheet.

1

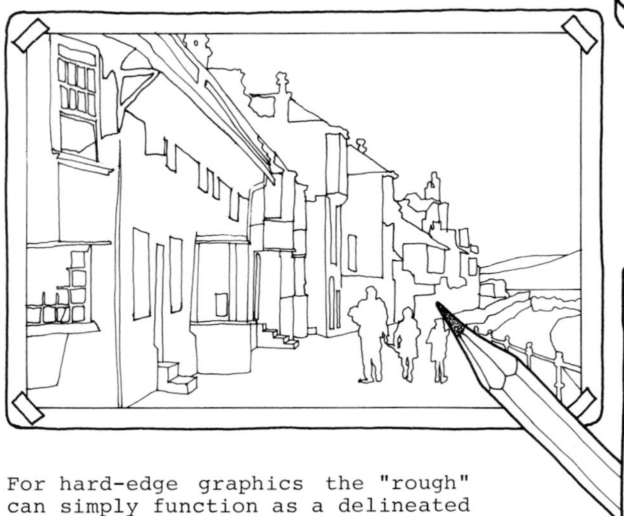

2

Generally, the use of pencil for preparatory compositional drafting is recommended for all kinds of artwork. In order to provide an unscarred surface for ensuing mediums, the following basic rules apply: employ medium-grade graphite (e.g. H.B.) and refrain from using erasers; exert little pressure when drawing so that initial planning remains faint.

3

When using pencil to prepare for ink drawings, keep initial graphite work to a minimum and refrain from shading. As the two techniques are subtly different in character, this restraint makes sure that a pencil technique does not unduly influence the penwork of the ultimate drawing.

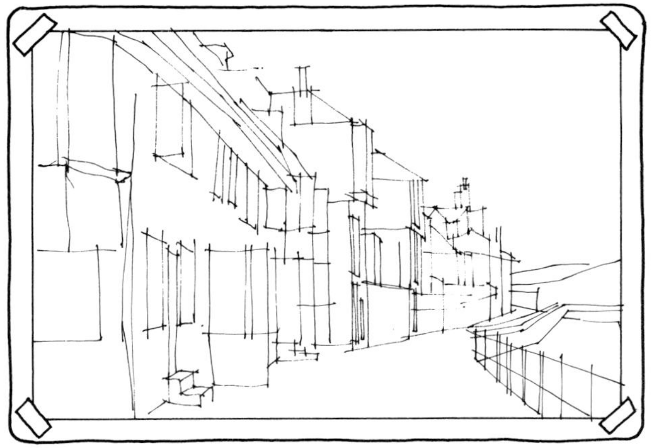

4

For hard-edge graphics the "rough" can simply function as a delineated structure of the "painting by numbers" type, or, in other words, as container shapes, which await occupation by the medium of your choice.

5

When making objective paintings, preparatory "roughs" can be established rapidly in charcoal or Conté crayon. However, to prevent ultimate washes or color mixes being contaminated by excess dust, these can be gently wiped over with a cloth without removing the image, or be stabilized with aerosol fixative prior to applications of liquid color.

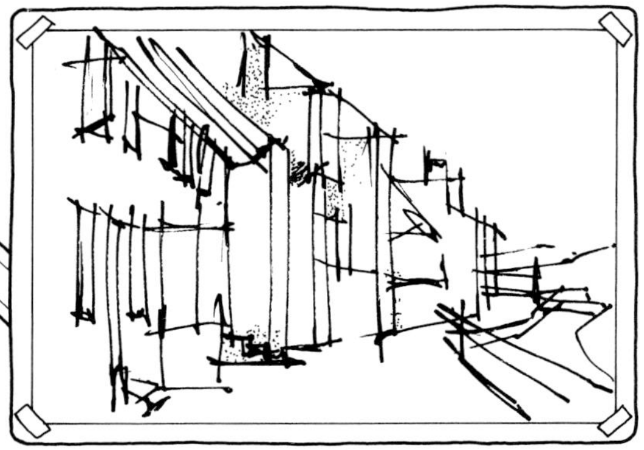

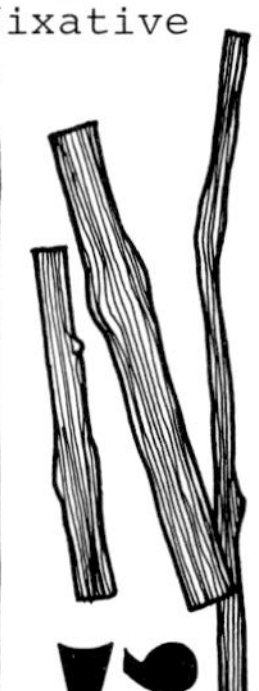

6

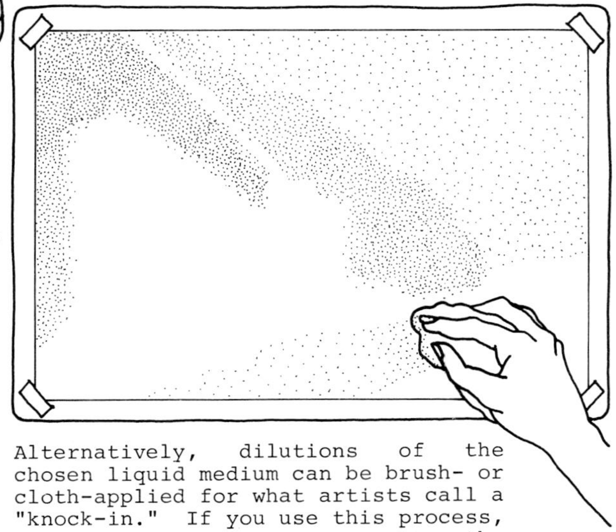

Alternatively, dilutions of the chosen liquid medium can be brush- or cloth-applied for what artists call a "knock-in." If you use this process, be sure not to oversaturate the paper. Instead, adopt almost the dry-brush technique of application so that the next painting stage can proceed immediately.

How to Stretch Canvas

1

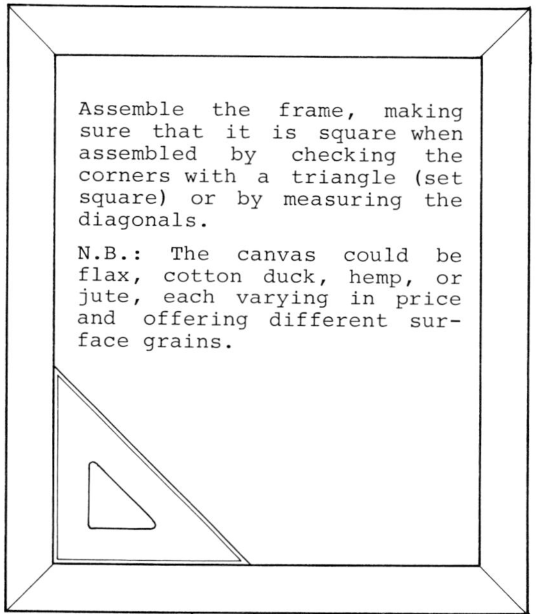

Assemble the frame, making sure that it is square when assembled by checking the corners with a triangle (set square) or by measuring the diagonals.

N.B.: The canvas could be flax, cotton duck, hemp, or jute, each varying in price and offering different surface grains.

2

Place the frame over the canvas with its primed side down on a flat surface. Cut the canvas to size allowing 1" (25mm) to 1 1/2" (38mm) surplus all around, plus the frame thickness.

3

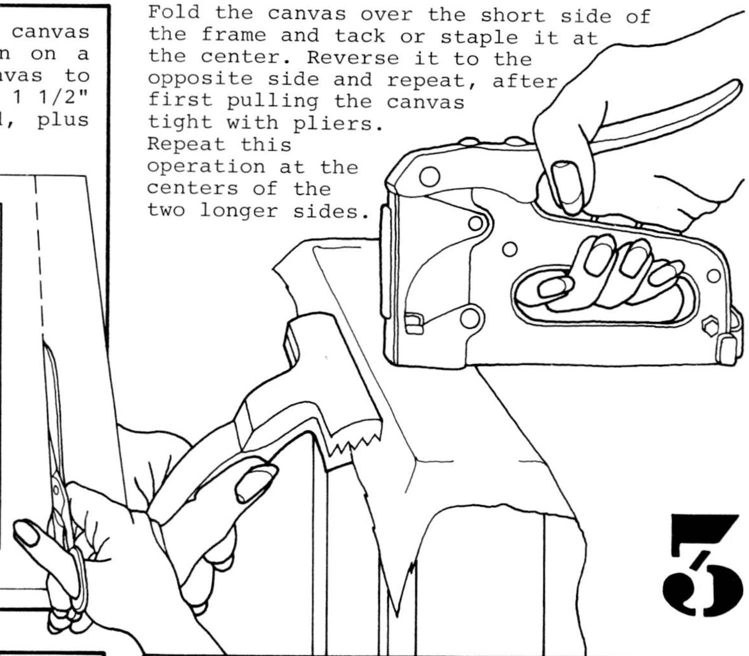

Fold the canvas over the short side of the frame and tack or staple it at the center. Reverse it to the opposite side and repeat, after first pulling the canvas tight with pliers. Repeat this operation at the centers of the two longer sides.

4

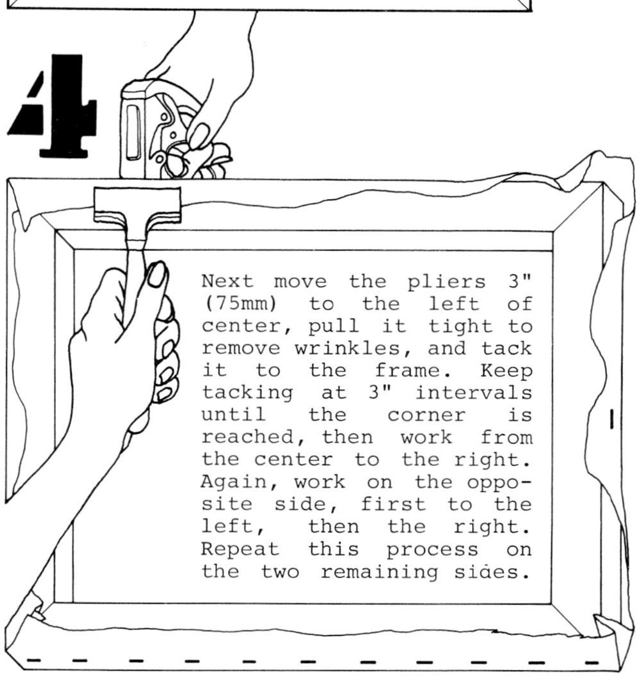

Next move the pliers 3" (75mm) to the left of center, pull it tight to remove wrinkles, and tack it to the frame. Keep tacking at 3" intervals until the corner is reached, then work from the center to the right. Again, work on the opposite side, first to the left, then the right. Repeat this process on the two remaining sides.

5

To tidy the corners, fold back one part of the corner under the other and tack.

N.B.: If further stretching is required, wedges can now be inserted into the corners at the back of the frame.

6

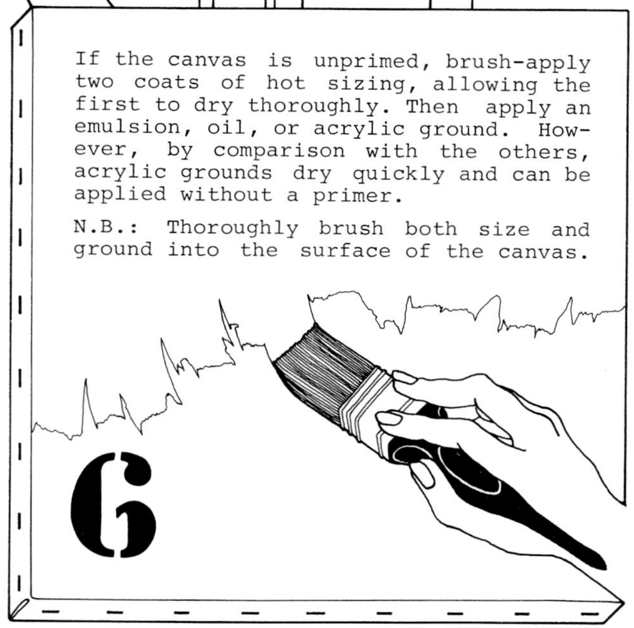

If the canvas is unprimed, brush-apply two coats of hot sizing, allowing the first to dry thoroughly. Then apply an emulsion, oil, or acrylic ground. However, by comparison with the others, acrylic grounds dry quickly and can be applied without a primer.

N.B.: Thoroughly brush both size and ground into the surface of the canvas.

How to Structure Painted Artwork Tonally

1

Many artists make occasional checks on the tonal structure of their paintings by peering through half-closed eyes or through sun-glasses. By thus screening daylight, the perception of color is reduced to an impression of value. Another method is to study reflections of paintings in progress within the color-reducing surface of a tinted mirror. However, even before color decisions are made, it is good strategy to structure initially the tonal value of polychromatic artwork, as value orchestration is central to the color rhythm and composition of images.

First determine a range of value that will usefully operate in the ultimate picture. At this stage, the range could utilize between three and seven tones, including the white of the paper.

2

Using the medium to be employed in the final artwork, mix a progression of increasingly darkening values of one color, such as black, brown, or blue. These can be achieved either by dilution with water (white spirit, if using oils) or by mixture with white pigment.

3

Using a fairly large, flat brush (a cloth or sponge can also be used), apply the lighter background tones. Resist the temptation to overwork; simply establish the main areas of tonal value in a broad manner.

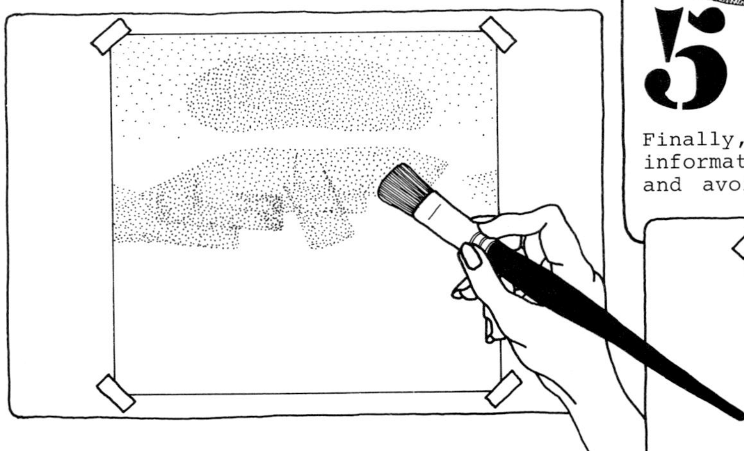

4

Next, introduce the middle values for middleground areas. Remember to apply pigment smoothly, keeping the brush or cloth as dry as possible.

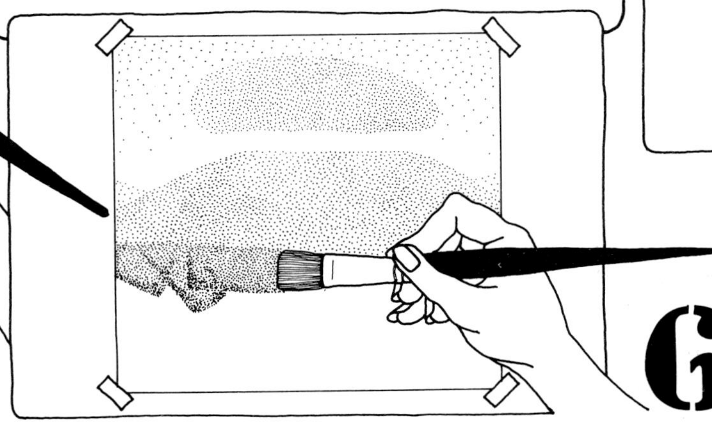

5

Finally, establish the darker foreground information. Again, keep detail to a minimum and avoid any textural buildup of pigment.

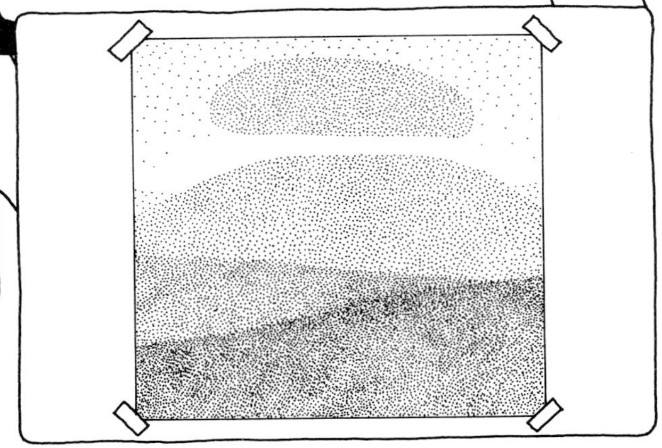

6

Beyond any final modification, you now have a conventional underpainting--a guide for organizing the ensuing paintwork. When dry, it will inform both the location of detailed brush-work and guide the tonal value of subsequent color mixes. When the painting is completed the underpainting disappears, but not without playing its important role in the structuring of the ultimate picture.

4 GRAPHICS WITHOUT TEARS

Drawing for Diazo: Line

In diazo printing, different graphite grades print as different values. Hard grades become lighter than softer grades, the latter requiring stabilizing with fixative before printing. Combinations of graphite grades, together with the range of technical pen point sizes, offer a variety of mark-making abilities, emphasis occurring when differences in line weight and quality are exploited. At a basic level, contrast between the clarity of an ink line used for written notes and indicating important zones in pencil drawings aids communication in tracing paper drawings.

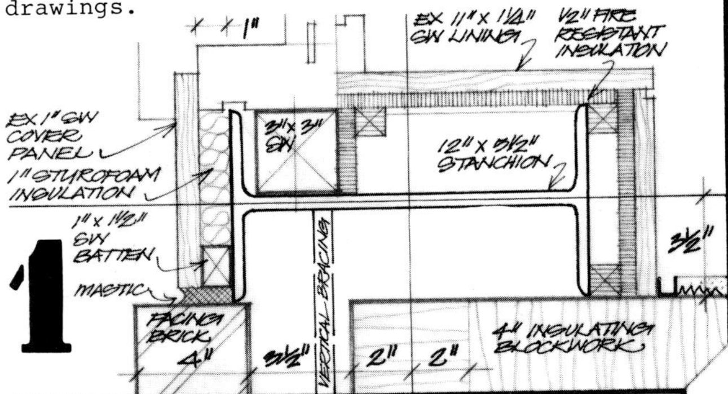

1

2

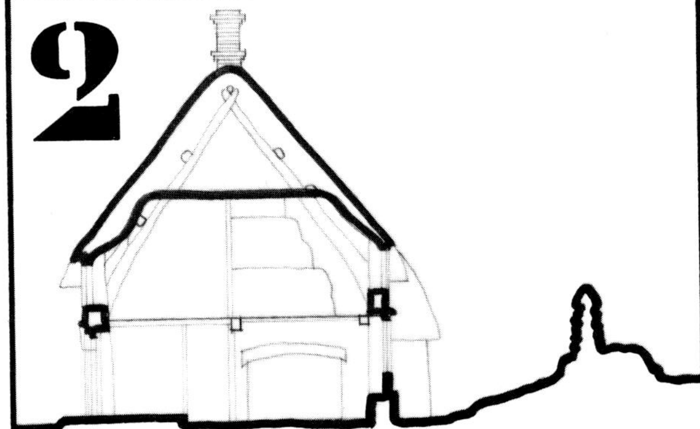

Similarly, areas of emphasis (such as the fixed structural points in pencil-drawn plans and sections) will benefit from a change in medium. These could be added as a ruled or freehand fiber-tip-pen line. Its thicker, softer quality brings an added dimension to the drawing. Red is a good choice for this purpose for, in diazo, it prints as a dark gray.

The visually refreshing quality of freehand drawing can be used to modify the often sterile appearance of exclusively ruled orthographics. The process of converting them is easy. First, draft the complete image in ruled pencil work. This is then ghosted in freehand using a technical pen, exploiting line weights.

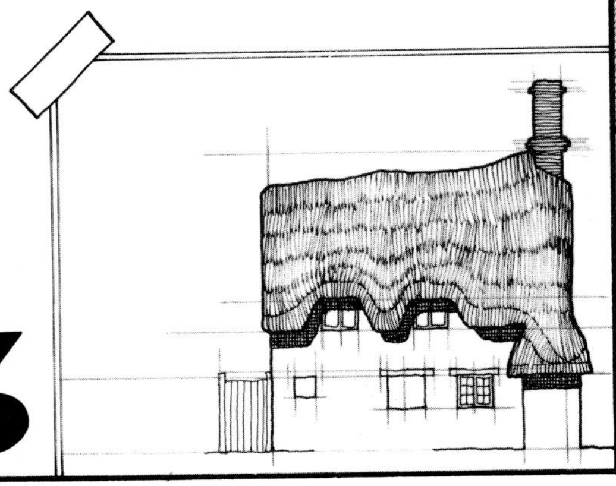

3

4

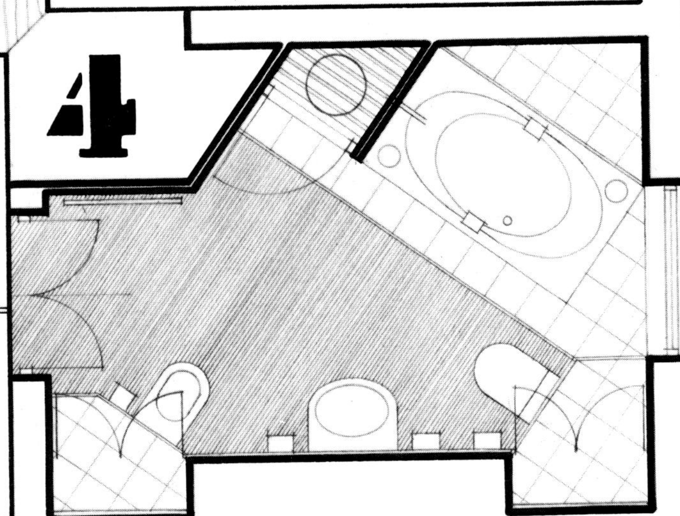

The reproduction requirements of diazo tend to encourage a graphic simplicity. However, in all forms of line-drawn orthographics, the addition of even a solitary area of value will become a center of interest or at least impart a little drama.

5

The convention of the heavy groundline functions as a visual ledge on which to view sections and elevations. This can be simply elaborated for added visual interest using any one of a series of pen or pencil hatching techniques.

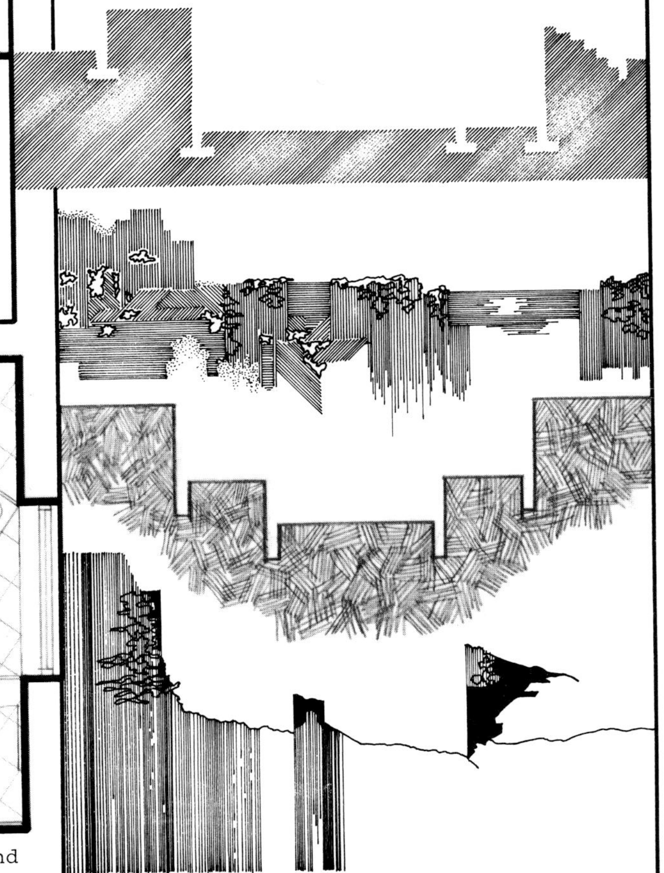

N.B.: Make sure that the textural grain of groundline elaborations does not overpower the main body of the drawing.

Drawing for Diazo: Value

The main reason for adding value to drawings destined for diazo is to emphasize an element or an area of importance in the drawing.

1 When areas of lighter value are required in tracing-paper drawings, the quickest method is to trace the required shapes on a second, same-size tracing paper sheet. Next, remove the shape with a scalpel, place it as a "stencil" over the original drawing, locate it with "invisible tape," and print.

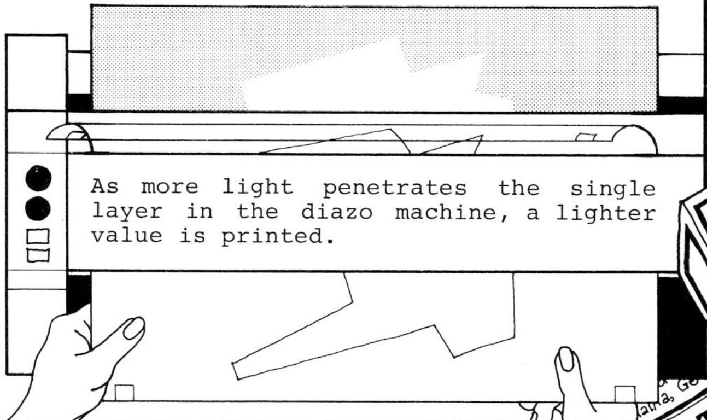

As more light penetrates the single layer in the diazo machine, a lighter value is printed.

2 Conversely, when isolated areas of a darker value are required, precision-cut shapes of tracing paper fixed in position over the drawing with "invisible tape" will print as a deep contrasting value.

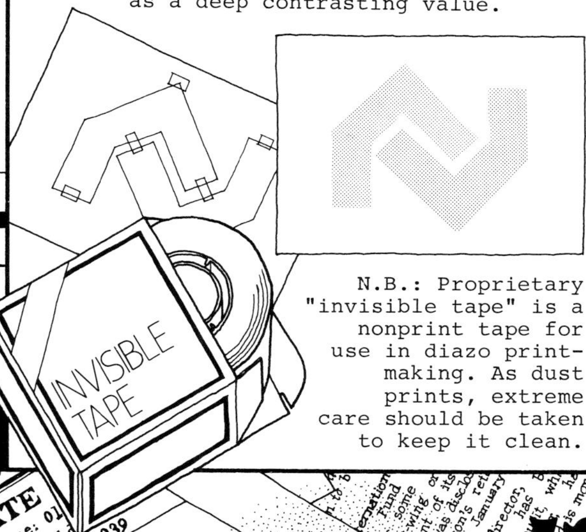

N.B.: Proprietary "invisible tape" is a nonprint tape for use in diazo printmaking. As dust prints, extreme care should be taken to keep it clean.

3 Graphite dust makes an excellent medium for achieving large areas of even values on tracing paper. Simply collect it from a pointer and, using tissue paper, apply evenly to the premasked shape on the back of the drawing. Stabilize with spray fixative before printing.

N.B.: It is recommended that this and the following techniques be applied to the backs of drawings, to allow an unimpeded drawing surface.

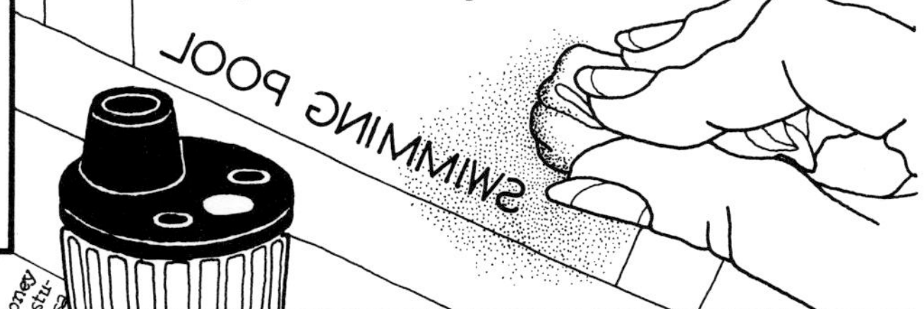

4 The extensive range of values and patterns offered by self-adhesive dry-transfer tones is ideal for small areas of value in drawings for diazo. After removing it from its backing sheet, apply the selected film to the shape and trim away surplus with a sharp scalpel, making sure not to damage the tracing paper.

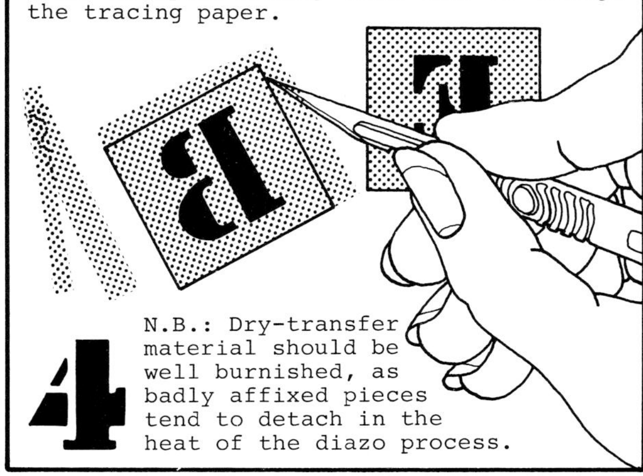

N.B.: Dry-transfer material should be well burnished, as badly affixed pieces tend to detach in the heat of the diazo process.

5

Aerosol spray colors can also be used to effect. After masking the edges of the area to be rendered, apply in even strokes, working approximately twelve inches from the surface. Remember that colors produce different values in diazo prints; e.g., yellow becomes black, and blue becomes almost invisible.

6 Boot polish is an unusually good medium for rendering large areas because it produces a fine, even range of values. Mask around the required shape and, using tissue paper as an applicator, build up to the required degree of value.

N.B.: Brown polish prints as a mid-gray value.

How to Render Shade and Shadows

1

Apart from areas of overlapping shadow, it is inadvisable in other areas to render shadows in a dense medium in architectural drawings, because solid tonal areas obliterate detail and tend to overpower a drawing. For this reason transparent liquid color washes, self-adhesive film tones, graphite shading, and pen or pencil hatching are conventional ways of rendering shadows in plans and elevations.

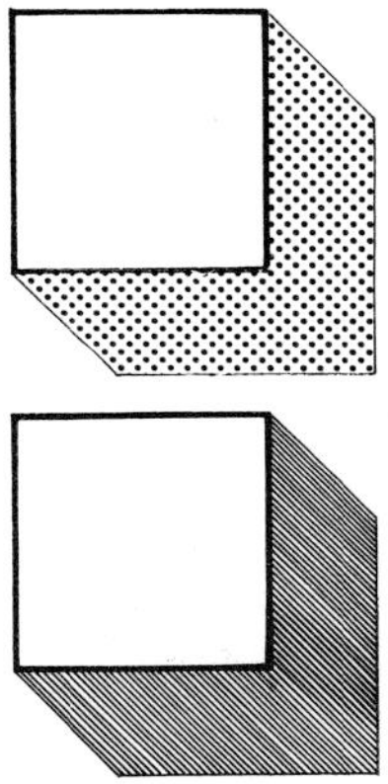

2

It is also important to indicate graphically the difference between the surface condition of shade and shadow, with shade being frequently shown as less dark than shadow.

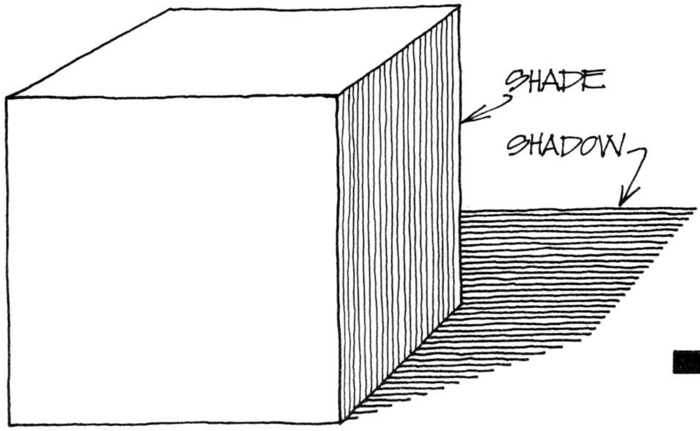

N.B.: Shadows are projected onto another surface from an object that intercepts light, whereas shade represents the unlit areas of the surface of an illuminated object.

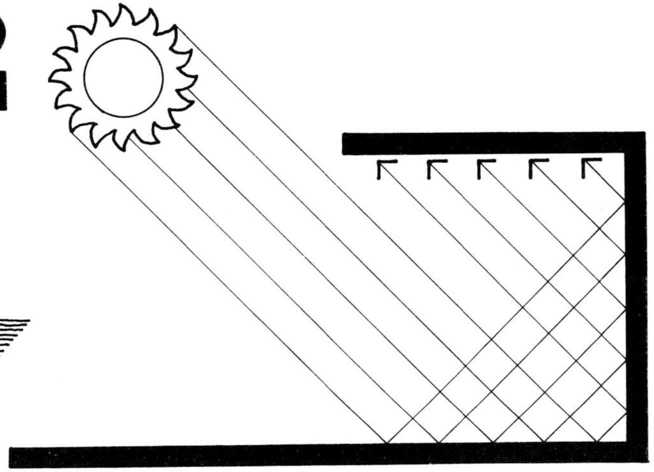

3

A further aspect of shade and shadow rendition is a graphic acknowledgment of the modifying effect of reflected light, i.e., a secondary light source caused by indirect illumination.

4

This rendition, however, is only worthy of attention in larger-scale drawings containing significant expanses of shadowed or shaded planes.

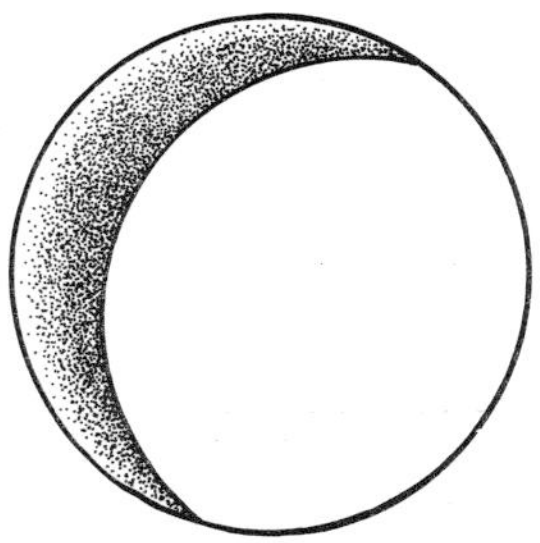

The effect of reflected light in the shadow of an elevation recess.

The effect of reflected light from the ground plane in a shadowed elevation recess.

5

It is always worth making a thumbnail sketch to predict the configuration of lit, shaded, and shadowed areas on an object prior to rendering.

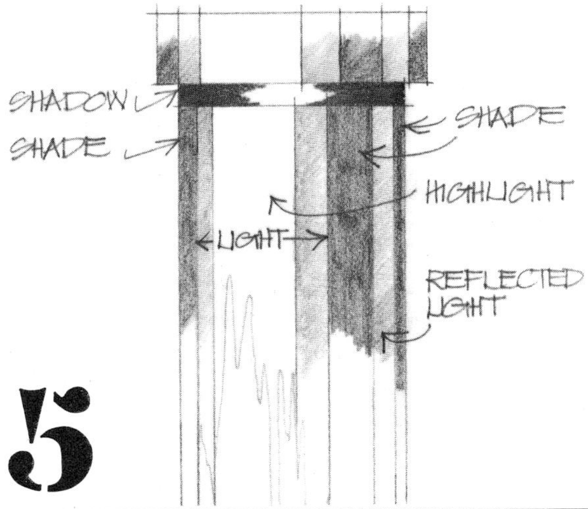

6

Decisions concerning the medium and rendering technique will relate to the size and surface quality of the object and to the kind and, of course, the scale of the drawing.

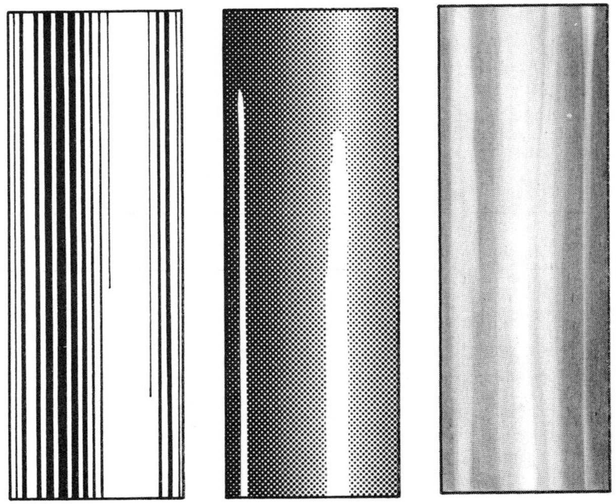

How to Render Reflective Surfaces

1 The rendering of glass in elevations is, as a general rule, depicted as a dark architectural element--since this is how it tends to appear in reality. However, the scale of a technique to render glazing should always be compatible with the scale of the drawing and the size of the glazing.

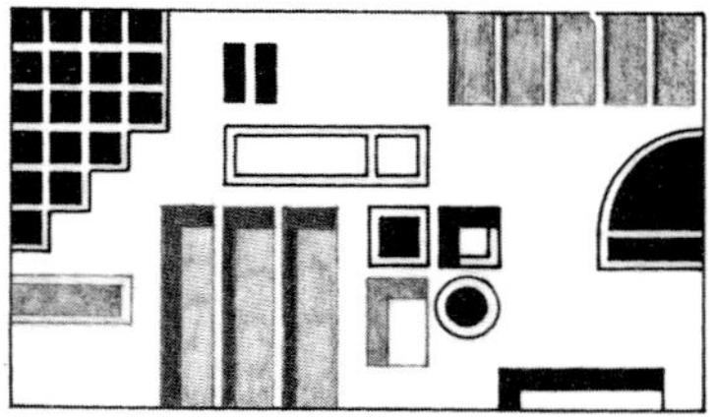

Individual windows and glass façades in small-scale elevations are usually picked out in a flat technique. Variants include the line drawing, with or without recess shadows.

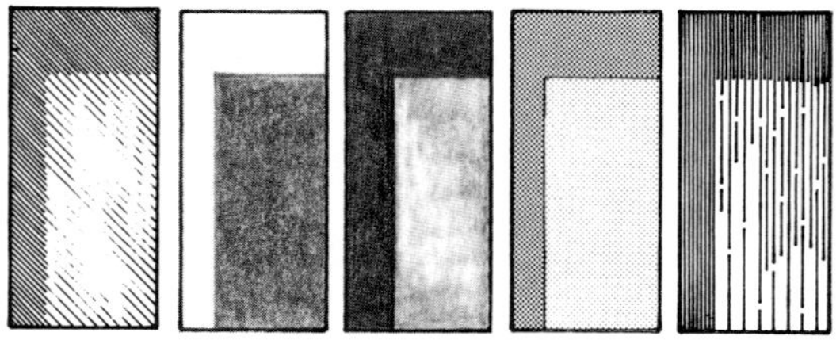

When windows appear larger in drawings, there are various hatching techniques to exploit the contrast between shadow and glass. Others include contrasting values of dry-transfer tone, liquid washes, structured graphite shading, and so on. Highlights can sometimes be removed using erasers or a razor blade.

In façade-sized glazing, "out-of-focus" freehand techniques can suggest the presence of objects reflected in its surface. Sizes of reflected objects are modified by distance; i.e., they reflect at the same size they would appear if seen from the window.

Sharper "in-focus" graphic techniques are especially effective when depicting mirror glass façades. These can be derived from appropriate photographic sources.

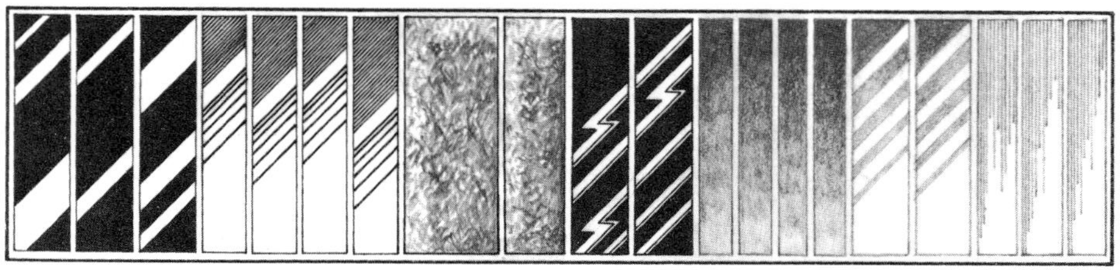

More decorative techniques can be invented but, when doing so, care should be taken not to allow the excesses of these treatments to detract from the façade design.

2 Sir Basil Spence described his love of surrounding his architecture with water as a means of giving clients "two buildings for the price of one." When designing for waterside and seaside sites, do not miss the opportunity to present elevations or perspectives together with their reflections. Unlike vertical reflections, their horizontal counterparts reflect an inverted, same-size image of their original. Various techniques are in use, and many others await invention.

A A mirror image broken by a secondary surface pattern of water movement.

B A shimmering effect in horizontal freehand lines.

C The disturbed-water technique using vertical and horizontal bands.

D A simplified reflection using freehand line and silhouettes, suitable for water and wet street effects.

The Importance of Sky in Elevations

1 The inclusion of sky in design drawings can make the difference between an image appearing unfinished . . .

. . . and one that is more compelling because by helping to define the upper portion of the "picture frame" it projects a sense of completeness. Skies can be quickly added to drawings by working in pencil with reference to appropriate magazine photographs.

2 When an elevation contains a building that is light in value, the darkening of its skyline--especially around its corners--will strengthen its visual impact. Reversing this contrast will project buildings of darker value.

3 If the tone of an elevation skyline varies dramatically in value, a counterchanging contrast in the value of its sky can also help to counterbalance the composition.

4 In hatched ink drawings, the usual sky convention is a ruled or free-hand line series that increases in proximity as it nears the upper edge of the picture.

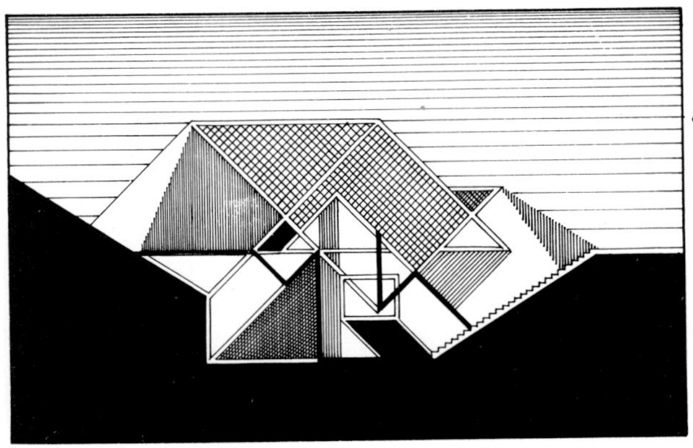

While the darkening value at the top of the image attempts the illusion of placing the sky "overhead," the fading lower section simulates the "graying" of atmospheric haze.

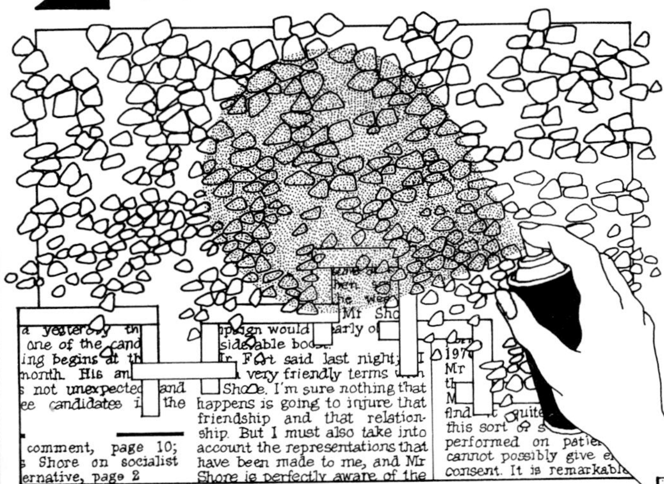

5 A great and fast way of creating interesting skies in aerosol spray or mixed-medium elevations is to first scatter various grades of gravel over a masked-off sky area.

Then lightly spray the area with one or two aerosol spray colors.

6 The gravel is then tipped away to reveal one of many potential effects using various arrangements and densities of the gravel "stencil."

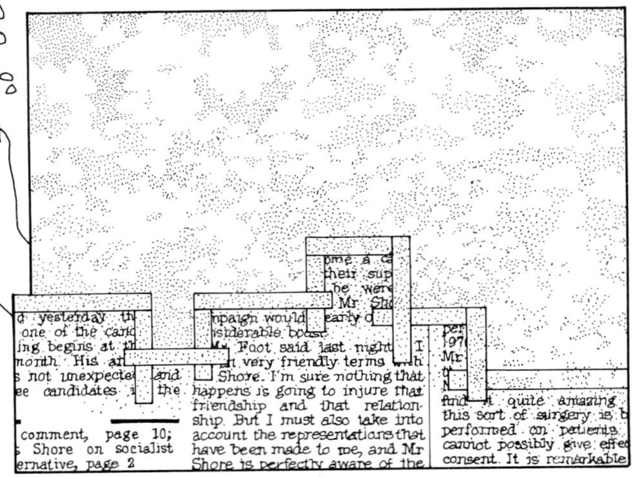

Color in a Hurry

1

There is no doubt that color can help to sell ideas. A test using a questionnaire printed on different-colored papers found more responses to those on red and green than on white or russet. Similarly, in design presentations even a small amount of color can attract attention and aid communication.

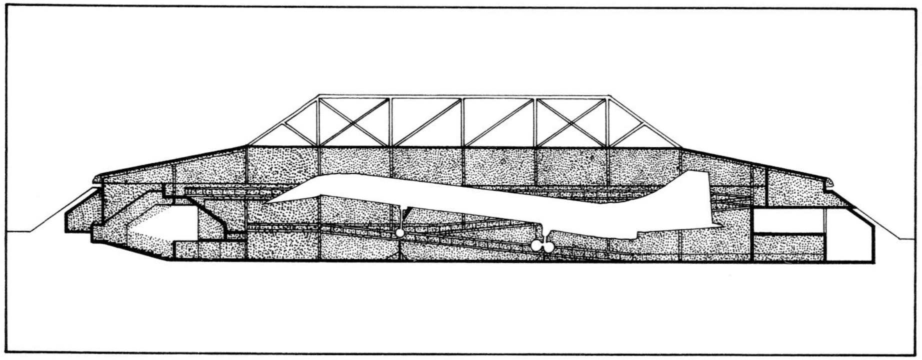

Even when deadlines are imminent, color can be quickly introduced into displays via the hues of mat boards, backing sheets, colored titles and labels and the like. In the blandest displays a splash of liquid color or an area of dry color will emphasize an important zone in the graphic.

2

When time does not allow for completely coloring artwork and orthographics, a vertical section of the format can be selected for color treatment. The panel should be located at a point that will convey a representative area of the colors to be used, with its size reflecting the amount of time at hand. Obviously, in multiple-image displays its position could vary from one drawing to another.

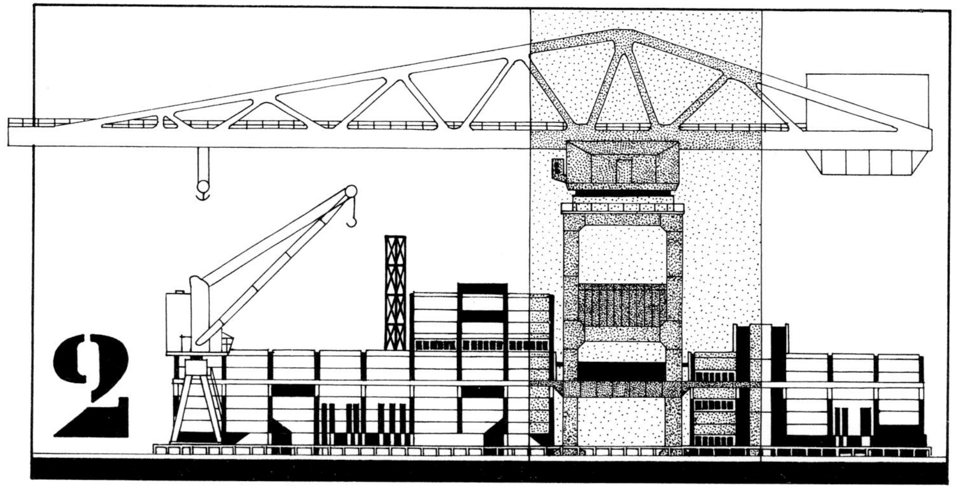

3

When presenting interior perspectives in pencil or ink line, quickly indicate color intentions by inserting a legend alongside the drawing. This can be assembled from:

A

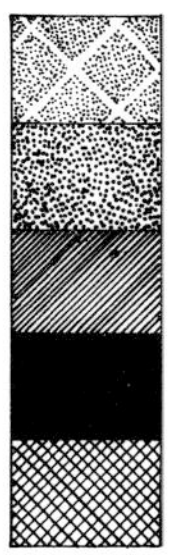

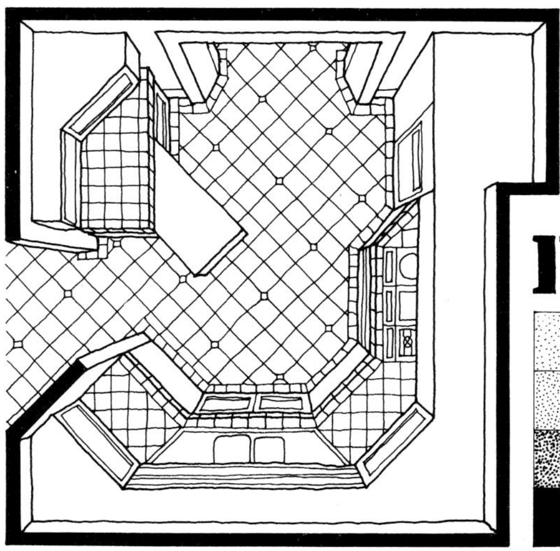

A "found" colors cut from magazines.

B colors painted in gouache or watercolor.

C paint swatches and actual samples of fabrics, finishes, etc.

B

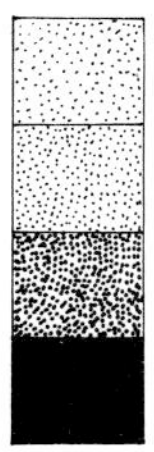

C

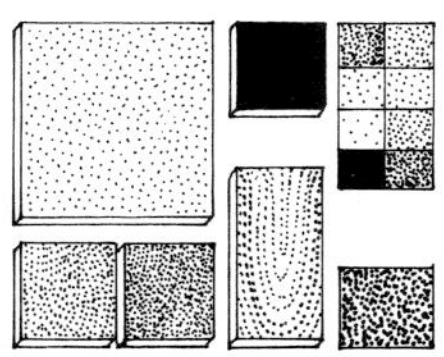

4

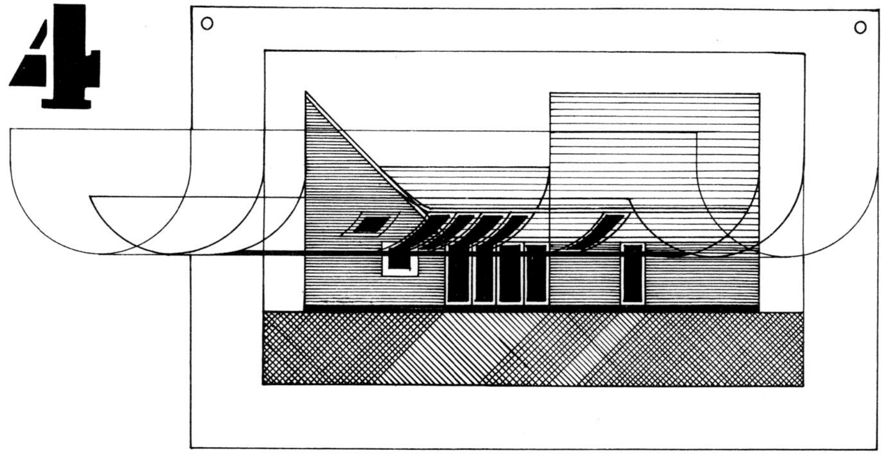

In order not to ruin drawings on tracing paper when working under extreme pressure, take a diazo print and work this in color using markers, colored pencils, dry color, or whatever. This can then function as an underlay to the tracing paper image, with its colors viewed through the overmounted original.

Figure-Ground Relationships in Plans

1

Le Corbusier described the plan as the "generator" of architectural design ideas, but writers such as Bruno Zevi question its real value as an adequate graphic container for spatial ideas.

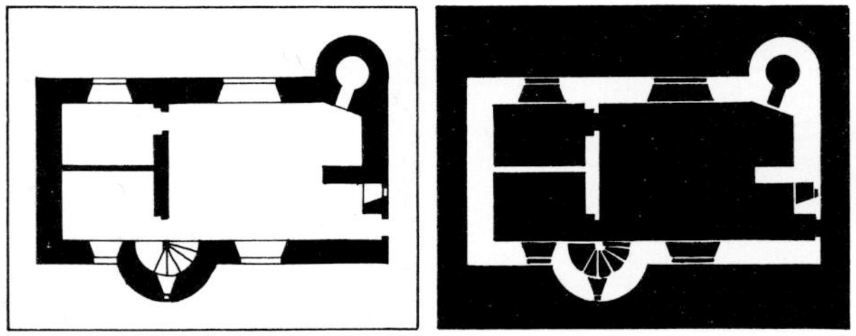

Zevi suggests that, at an analytical level, the plan's usefulness is increased when the roles of medium and paper are reversed; i.e., when white represents "positive" or "solid" and black represents "negative" or "void."

2

This graphic approach has been used to effect by contextualist designers who find that the figure-ground reversal communicates a more profound sensation of urban space, especially when presented together with conventional line drawn plans.

The exploitation of line weights, value, and color ranges, together with their axonometric or perspective conversion into aerial views, will extend the spatial legibility of building plans. However, when scale permits, shadow projection introduces an important visual cue because it describes both the height of the form and something of the nature of the ground plane.

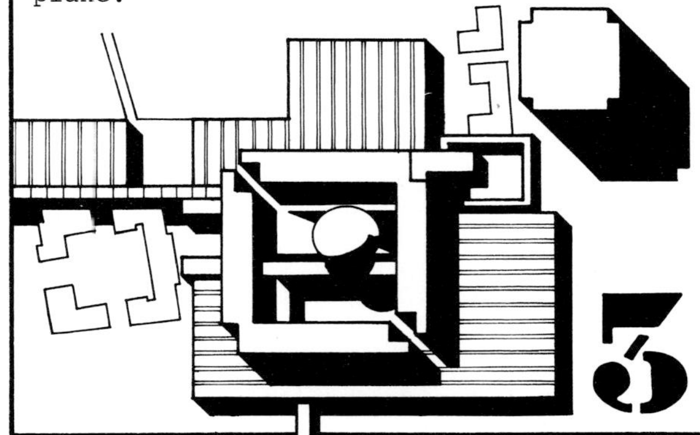

3

4

The principle of plotting shadows of buildings with known heights is easy to apply.

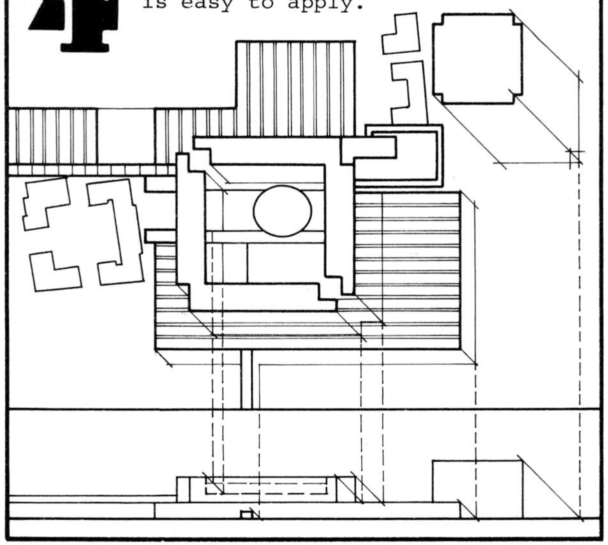

Further intensification of the third dimension can be achieved in the roof plans of gabled buildings simply by including a shaded plane.

5

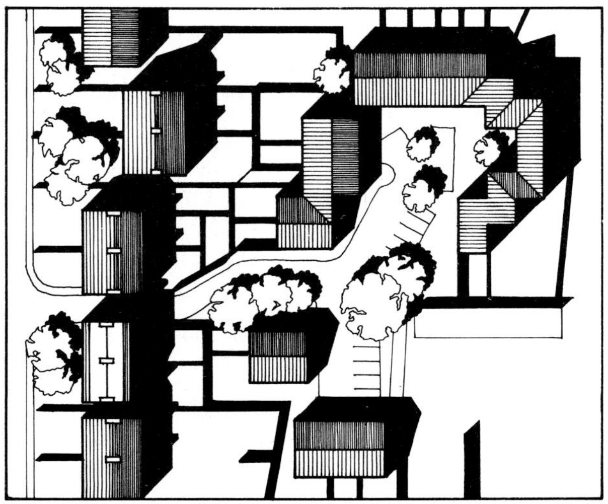

6

Extreme contrast between "hard" and "soft" areas in site plans is another method to increase figure-ground legibility. In this example, a hatched aerial view of landscape elements intensifies the building plan by using a form-following technique plus shadows.

Pinpointing Message Areas in Site Plans

Depending upon the nature of the site, the design proposal, the degree of information to be conveyed, the scale of the drawing, and the time available, there are a variety of methods that can be effectively employed to concentrate the observer's eye on site-plan message areas.

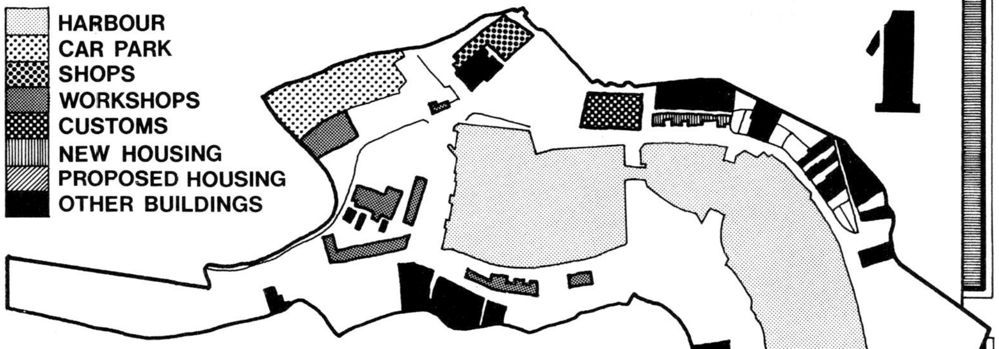

The quickest method is pen hatching or dry-transfer tones applied to determine physical or spatial design components. Areas of different hatching techniques should be bounded by strong lines of containment. Changes in patterns are useful (especially when annotated with legends) to communicate various design aspects.

2

Contrast between the projection of a design proposal into an axonometric format against the flatness of its plan surround will also draw immediate attention. This contrast can be simply extended by the addition of heavier line weights, shadowed planes, or shadow casting.

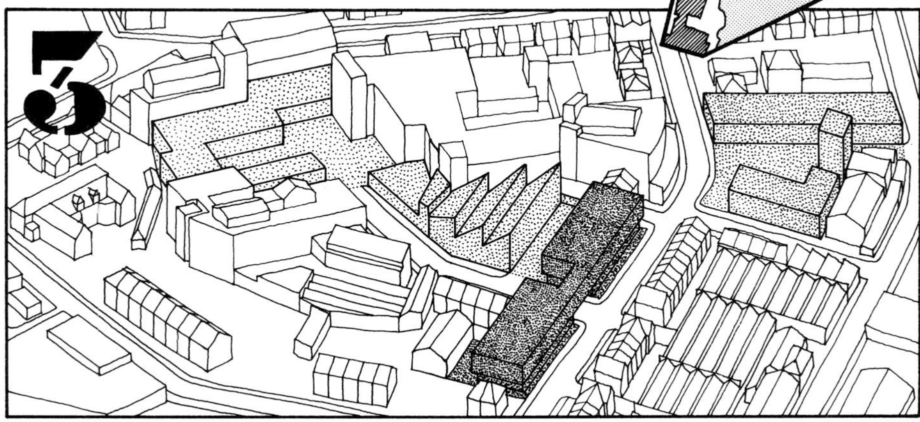

Alternatively, site plans that have been extruded into a linear axonometric format can have their design proposals targeted by the addition of pen hatching or dry-transfer tones to describe light and shade or, if scale allows, surface elaboration in paint or dry-transfer color film to describe objective or schematic colors.

N.B.: The designer should distinguish between a naturalistic and schematic color use. The former describes the perceived hues of objects, whereas schematic color is arbitrary color use to code or zone design concepts.

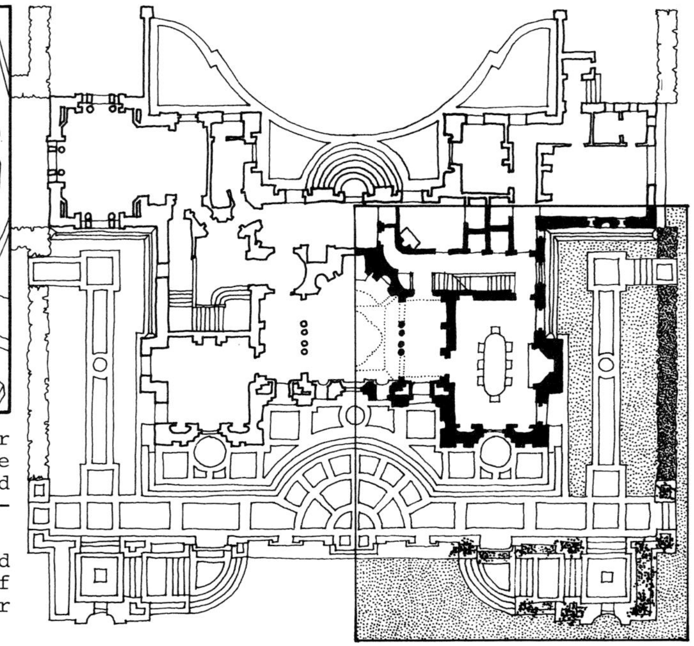

4

Another method is to isolate the message area within the site plan by superimposing a secondary frame of reference within which the design idea is contained. This can be applied as an overlay or worked directly on the plan.

Information within this subframework is then treated in greater detail than its surround, using a high intensity of line activity or color techniques to project design intentions.

How to Aerosol Fast Site Contours

A speedy method of producing tonal progressions for contours in presentation site plans and small-scale site models is the aerosol color-spray technique. As the precision of this graphic technique relies on trace cutting rather than masking, it short-circuits similar and more time-consuming methods.

1

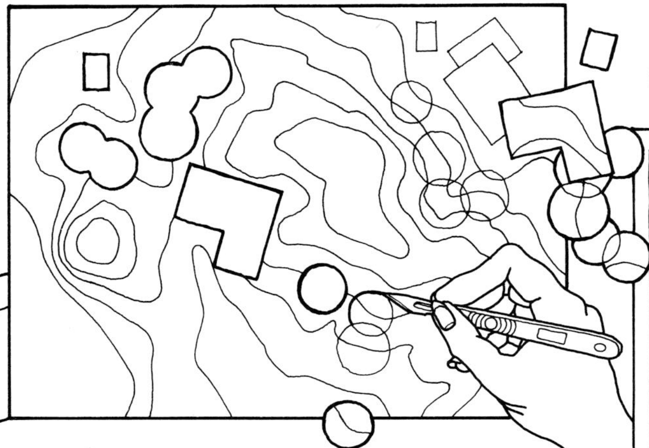

Redraw the contours of the plan or model on a separate sheet of paper to same size using pencil or pen. Then cut away any elements such as existing trees and buildings, a proposed building plan, and so on, which may be worked later.

2

3

Lightly color-spray the entire sheet in a hue of your choice, and leave it to dry. This initial wash represents the uppermost level on the site.

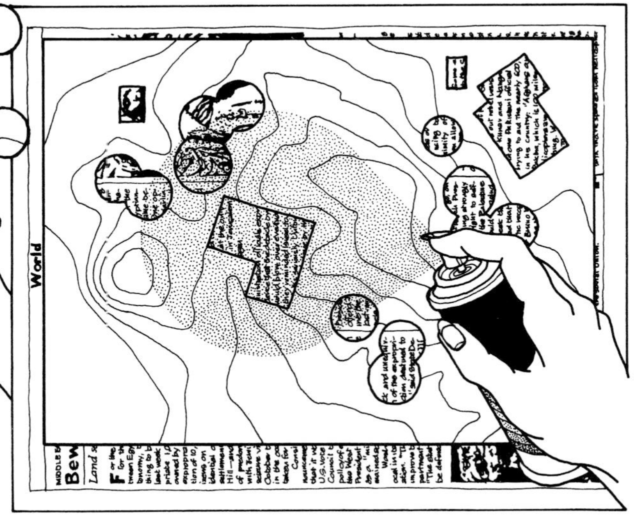

4

Cut away the highest contours with a sharp scalpel or scissors and, using aerosol-spray adhesive, mount them into their appropriate locations on the plan or model.

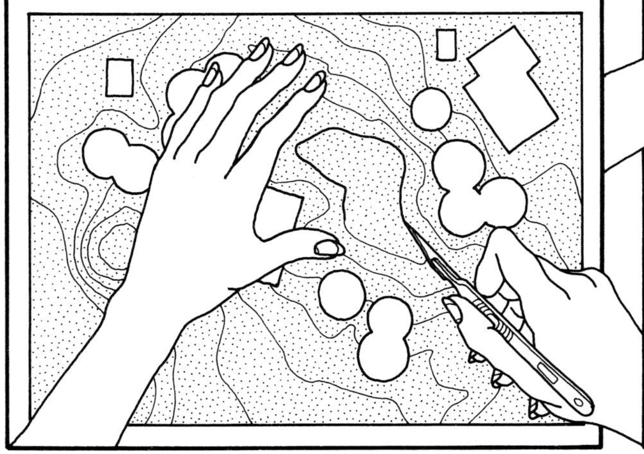

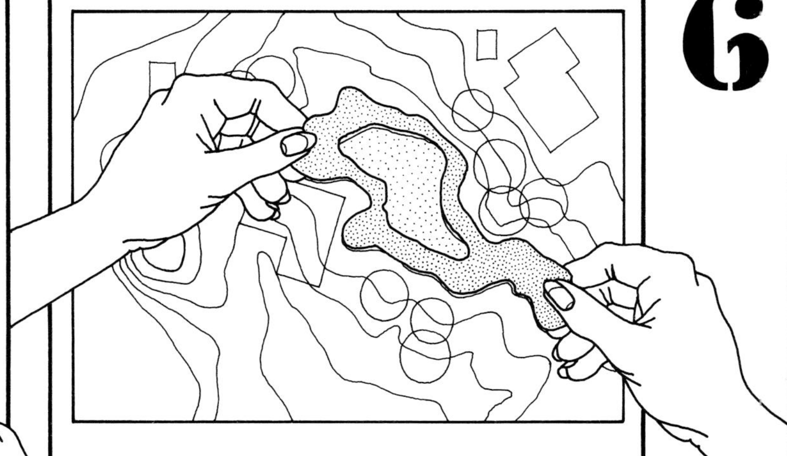

5

Maintaining the same intensity as the initial color wash, respray the remaining area of the sheet and remove the next level for mounting into the site.

6

Simply repeat the process for each subsequent level until all contours are transferred. The act of respraying between each level will establish a descending value scale, with the total number of applications representing the lowest level.

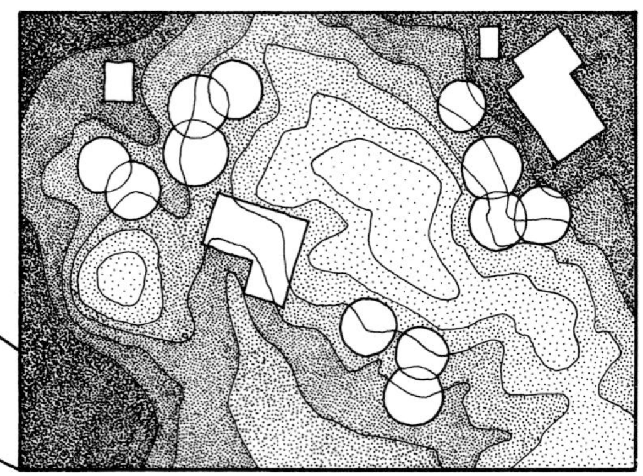

The ccmpleted transfer of contours provides a tonal topography on which to draw or laminate further information.

How to Aerosol Fast Design Plans

1

Many beginners to design presentation find problems when tackling orthographics. Sometimes it is the challenge of the sheet with its sheer size and intimidating blankness, or even the inhibiting effect of a high-quality paper or board. This causes a hiatus in the design process that can often lead to frustrations when working against deadlines.

One valid method around this problem for graphics not destined for diazo reproduction is the composite image: constructing a graphic from separately worked paper components. This is a flexible process allowing experimentation with different color mediums in one graphic and the easy replacement of malfunctioning parts.

2

First, decide upon a structure of tonal value that will establish some organizational control over the total composition.

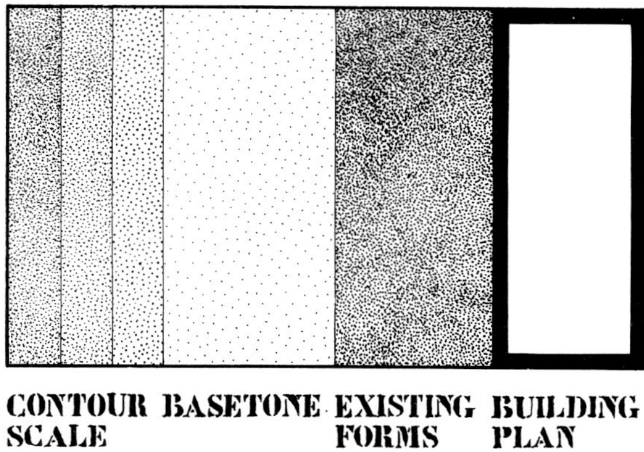

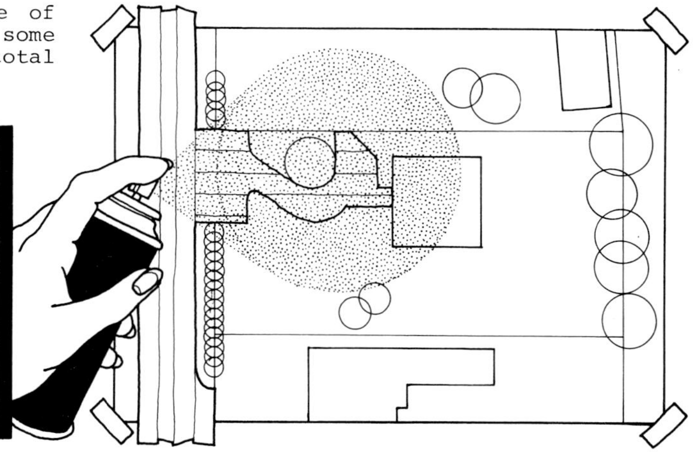

Within each value range, any color medium may be employed, provided the scale of its mark-making ability fits within the overall textural grain.

3

Next, carefully outline the elements of the site in ink or graphite on a base sheet. Then, using any wash medium, apply the ground value. Road systems and the like can be established in a slightly lighter version of this value.

4

If contours are to be described, these should employ a closely related range of value descending a scale from lighter to darker.

A fast method is aerosol spray color (see page 66).

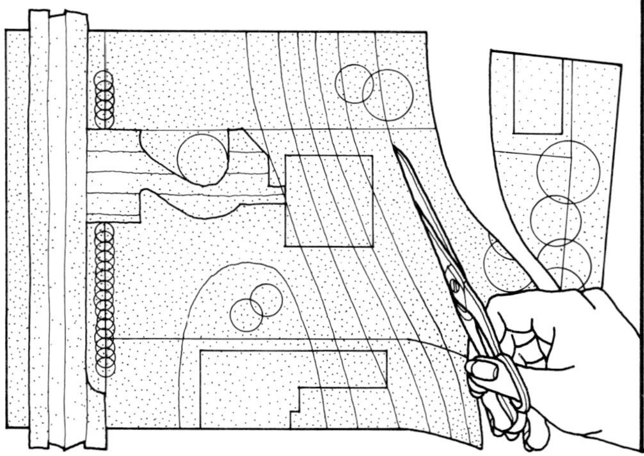

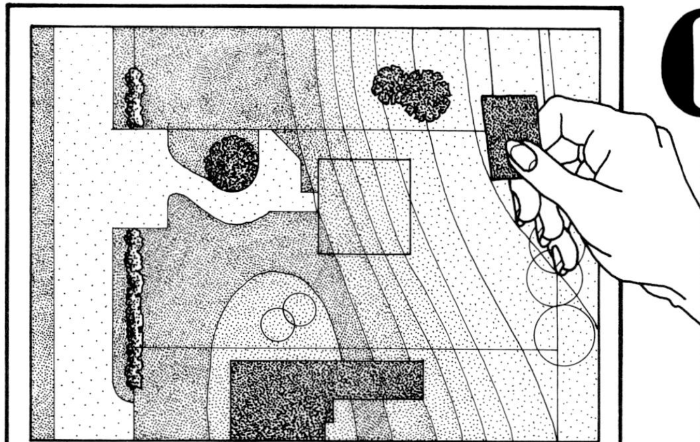

5

Darker forms such as existing buildings, vegetation, trees, and so on can now be worked in any medium but within their allocated values on separate paper. When dry, cut out and spray mount each element into the support sheet.

6

Drawing the building plan in technical pen on a sheet of white or light-colored paper will maintain a contrast between interior and exterior planning when mounted into position.

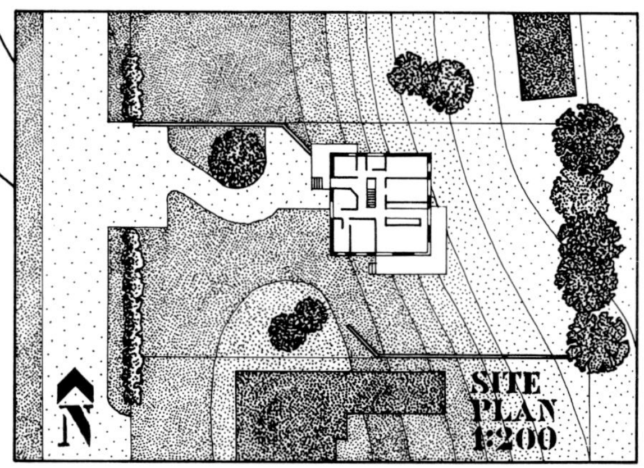

Finally, insert hand-written, stenciled, or dry-transfer labels, plus the north point.

How to Produce Composite Elevations

1

When making composite orthographics, any variation in paper or card thickness will not detract from the ultimate visual effect. On the contrary, precision-cut edges of component parts add a pleasing marquetry effect. When producing elevations using this technique, first set out their outlines in ink or graphite on the drawing board to guide their reception during the image-building phase. If a diazo print of the elevation exists, it can also be used, after heat mounting it on a card support.

A separate tracing (or the diazo negative) of the elevation will also be required as a template, because much of the artwork will be produced independently.

After being traced from the template, the design elevation can now be cut from thick paper or card to receive artwork--either directly or indirectly via lamination--in mediums sympathetic to the building's surface finishes.

For example, brickwork, blockwork, cladding, and so on are easily shown in fine-line waterproof inkwork under transparent washes of watercolor, ink, aerosol-spray color, or the subtlety of colored pencils.

2

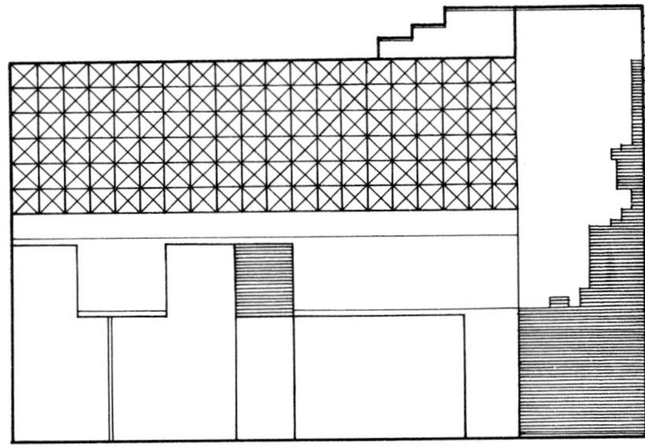

3

An alternative method is the superficial incision of the artwork surface with a scalpel against a straight-edge. The incisions expose the paper fiber which, by attracting more pigment during subsequent color washes, causes them to appear as darker lines.

4

A further method of representing vertical or horizontal emphasis using either dry mediums such as graphite and colored pencils, or dried ink and watercolor washes, is to score the rendered artwork surface with the back of a cutting blade against a straightedge. This exposes a subtle structure of white lines.

5

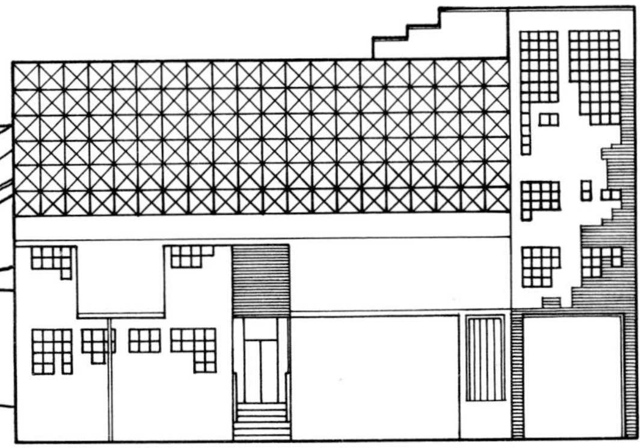

Façade openings present various opportunities. Doors and windows can be drawn directly on the card elevation, laminated as independent graphics, or applied to the artwork after removal from a second diazo print. Alternatively, physical openings can be cut into the elevation to expose windows and doors on a diazo support print, or a premounted artwork, revealed by simulated recesses.

6

Also, projections such as balconies, canopies, and walls before the main plane of the image can be worked on thin card, cut to shape, and laminated onto the façade as a three-dimensional illusion in relief.

How to Produce Composite Elevations

7

Further modeling of the elevation can be achieved using shadow rendering. This can be introduced as pen hatching or applied in dry-transfer tones.

N.B.: Avoid adding graphite shadows; if badly rendered they will undermine the overall effect.

8

The sky mass will be the first element to be introduced to the support sheet. This can be a transparent watercolor or aerosol spray color wash, worked either directly on the support or on a separate sheet. Otherwise, self-colored paper, magazine photographs, or a proprietary "sky paper" can be shaped and spray mounted into its location.

N.B.: By allowing a margin of overlap into the skyline and elevation outline, time spent in precision-cutting edges will be saved.

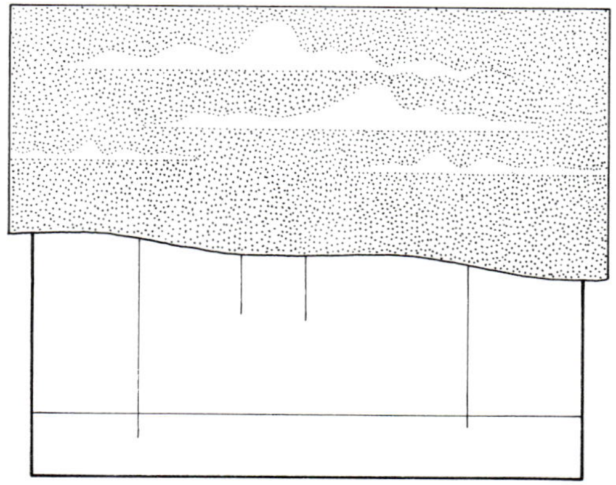

9

Background mass such as existing skyline (i.e., landscape or townscape occurring either side of and behind the elevation area) can now be originated on separate sheets in a medium of your choice. These can then be cut out and mounted on the support, allowing a margin of overlap at the groundline.

10

At this stage, the elevation artwork should be carefully glued into its position on the support sheet. If required, foreground trees, shrubs, and figures can now be added. In-scale dry-transfer figures and silhouette-type foliage are fine for smaller-scale elevations, while drawn or "found" versions cut from magazines can be used to effect in large-scale artwork.

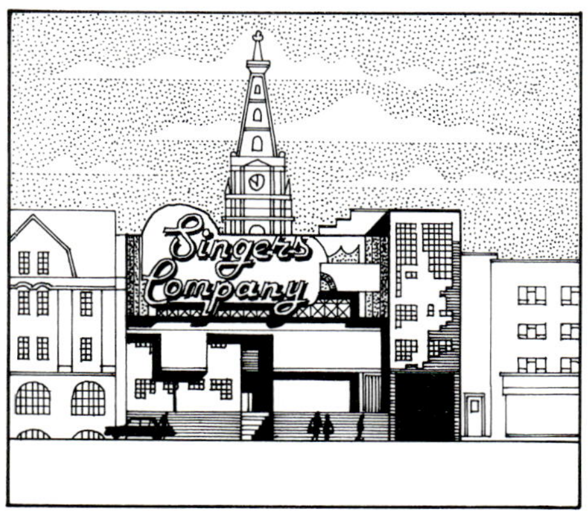

11

Finally, the groundline section can be added. Being cut from card as thick as that used for the elevation, it will function as a graphic "plinth." For the same reason, this component should be among the darkest values in the completed artwork, utilizing a self-colored surface, or being presprayed with aerosol color.

12

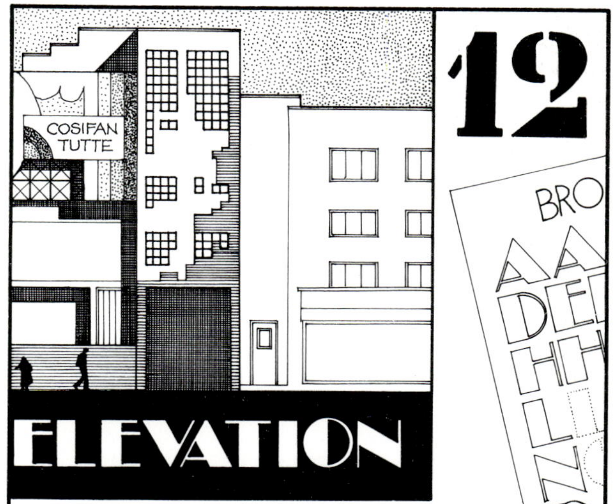

To complete the composite elevation, the groundline "plinth" can now receive white or colored titles using stenciled or dry-transfer lettering.

"Three-Dimensional" Orthographics

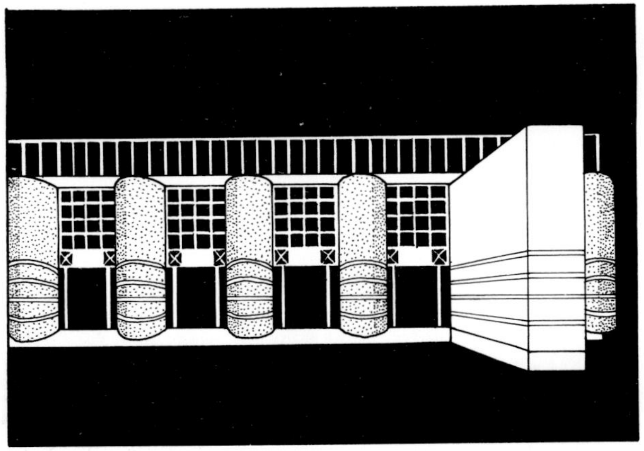

1

Beyond the construction of presentation orthographics using various thicknesses of paper and board to imply depth is the simple process of projecting selected elements in a design before an elevation graphic. This works best if the projected element is unusual or unique to the design.

2

Projections are quickly assembled in paper or board using simple model-making techniques. The forms can be cut out and have artwork applied before glue assembly and final gluing into the drawing.

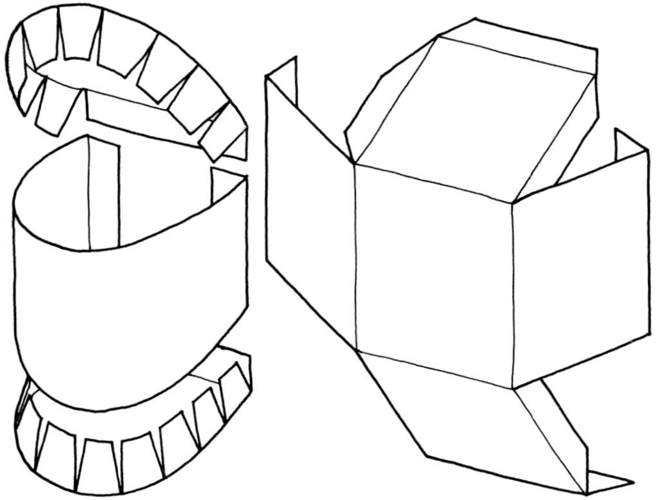

3

Three-dimensional sections in card can also be quickly assembled in "stage-set" fashion to convey convincing impressions of depth in both interior and exterior spaces. First, cut out the selected sections, apply artwork, and glue assemble them within an open-ended card box or a balsa-wood space frame.

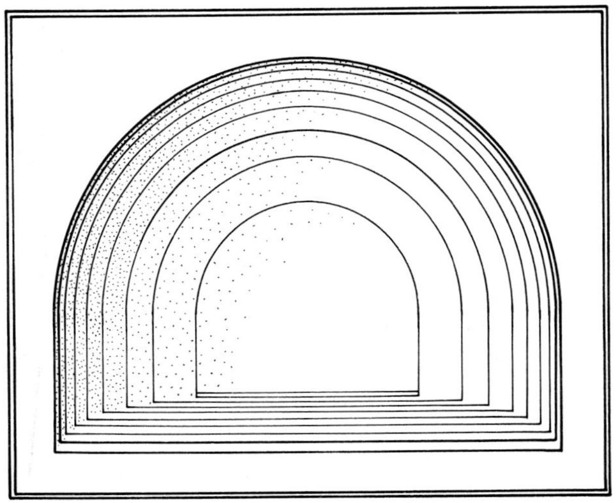

4

Forms such as domes that are difficult to draw and build are easily constructed using the stage-set method.

5

A sophisticated version is the assembly of a series of clear acetate layers which, in carrying ink , dry color, or collage artwork simulate realistic sections at progressive points through an interior or exterior volume. The sections can then be glued into position within an open-ended card box and mounted at eye level for viewing in wall presentations.

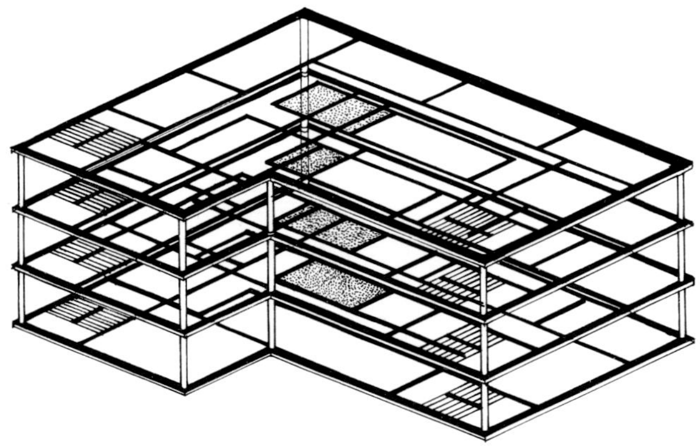

6

Multilevel plans can also be represented with this method. Each plan is worked in ink on acetate or in dry-transfer medium on acrylic or glass sheets, then stacked on support rods and separated by spacer tubes. During critiques they can be reassembled in upward sequences to explain the progression of floors.

Converting Elevations into Pseudo-Perspectives

One of the quickest methods of creating convincing presentation graphics (especially when working against looming deadlines) is to combine two drawing systems--the elevation and the perspective.

1

After setting up the elevation, introduce background information. This can be worked from site photographs or from other photographic sources offering elements appropriate to the nature of a visualized setting.

2

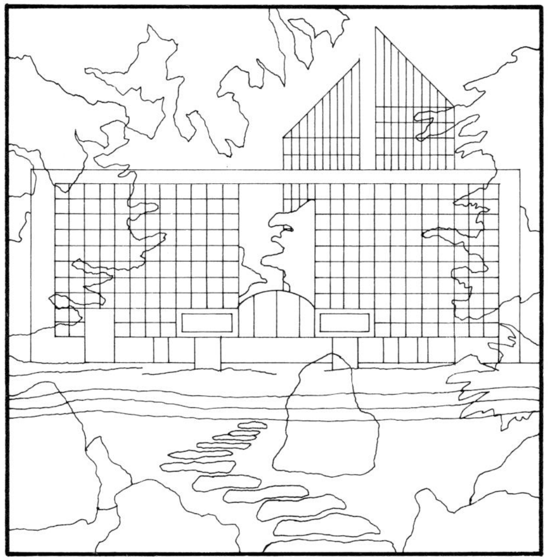

The introduction of foreground information is the key to the visual credibility of this hybrid graphic. Again, based on selected source material, add elements to the foreground which, in being controlled by a single vanishing point, animate this important sector of the image as a perspective.

N.B.: Apart from overlapping forms, extending the perspective of the foreground permits the designer to exploit the depth illusion via size and height variation in frontal objects.

3

The rendering stage offers the opportunity of exploiting other visual depth cues such as light and shade, texture, and aerial perspective.

N.B.: Two basic systems of value gradation should operate during both the drafting and rendering stages: darker values climbing to lighter in the vertical plane, and darker values receding to lighter in the horizontal plane. These progressions represent the visual cue of aerial perspective (atmospheric haze) and can be underlined by using diminishing line weights.

Photographs as Design Aids

1

Photographs can function as an invaluable aid throughout the design process. For example, a montage of sequential prints carefully taken for assembly into panoramic views can inform one about the broader aspects of a site and its surroundings.

These make excellent formats for either checking or conveying the implications of the intended mass.

2

Photographs of a site are also useful for an in-context examination on tracing-paper overlays of different ideas for the trial massing and detailing of façades.

3

Site photographs can be used as underlays in producing directly traced same-size analytical drawings or design graphics that focus upon particular aspects of an image.

More simply, they act as helpful source material when setting up the basic coordinates in perspectives and also serve as references for color and details when creating realistic freehand graphics.

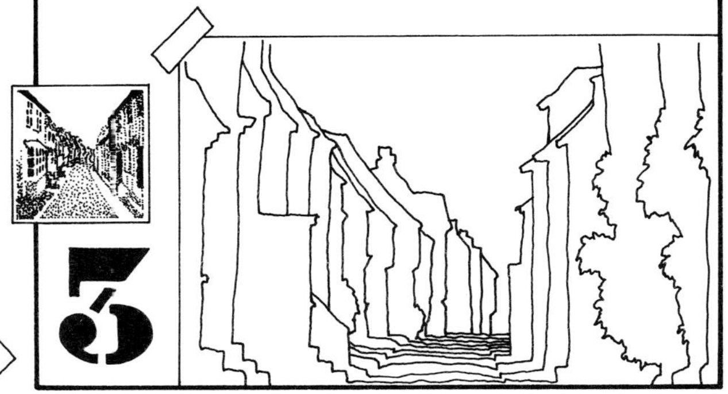

4

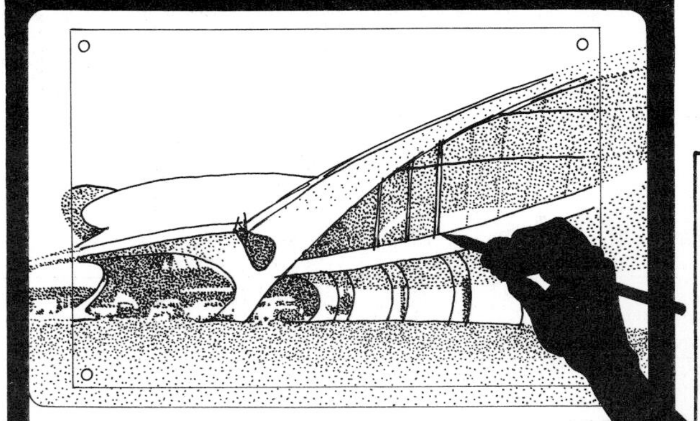

By using a sheet of drawing paper as a projection screen--and working in the light of slides enlarged in a projector, or prints rescaled in an indirect projector (episcope)--large and convincing pen or pencil drawing can be rapidly produced.

5

Analytical information, spatial zoning, or basic design goals can be quickly diagrammed using markers either directly on more complex photographs or onto transparent overlays.

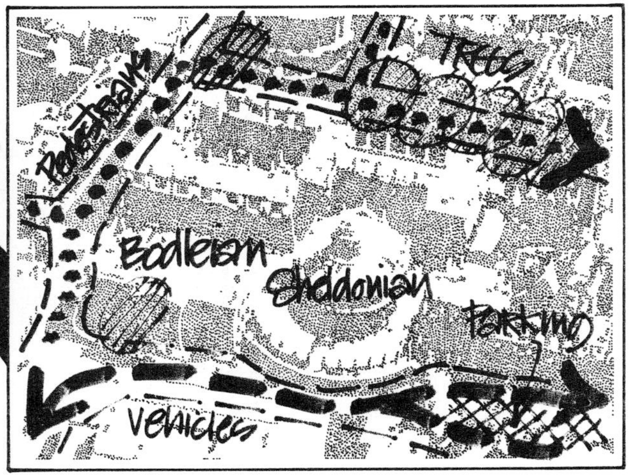

6

Photomontage, an underexploited design medium, is another fast method of transmitting potent imagery, using photographic components culled from a variety of sources.

N.B.: A method of experimenting with this medium is to assemble cut-out photographic elements directly on the platen of a photocopier.

Photocopying Sketch Models

A great way of quickly transforming the three dimensions of small-scale paper design models into two is to place them upside down on the platen of a photocopier and print them.

1

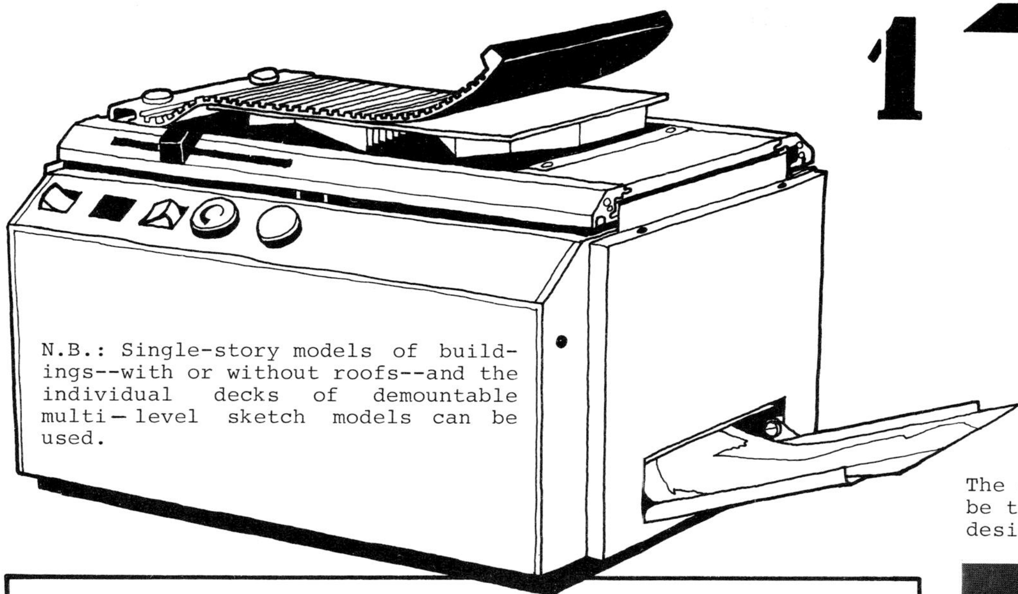

N.B.: Single-story models of buildings--with or without roofs--and the individual decks of demountable multi-level sketch models can be used.

2

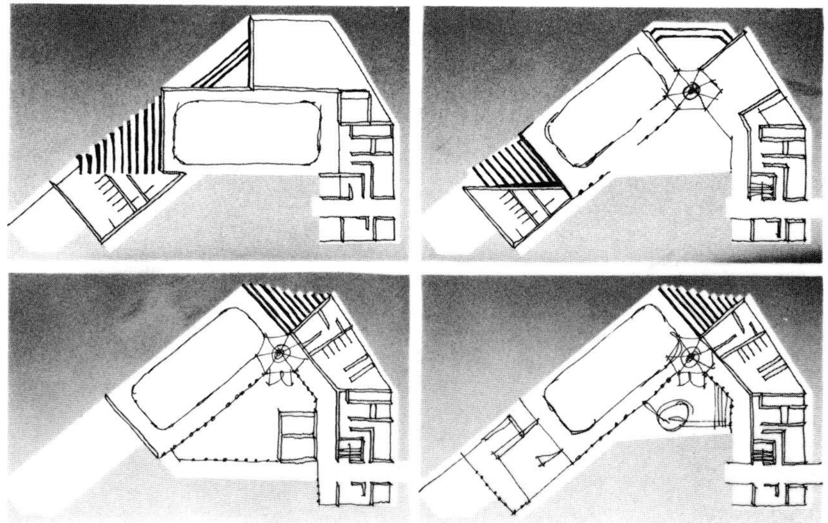

The development of a design idea in a sketch model form can similarly be tracked in a series of prints recording strategic points along the design route, for later use in wall presentations.

Another byproduct of this process is the resultant ability to develop further the design idea by working directly into the photocopied image, using pen or pencil.

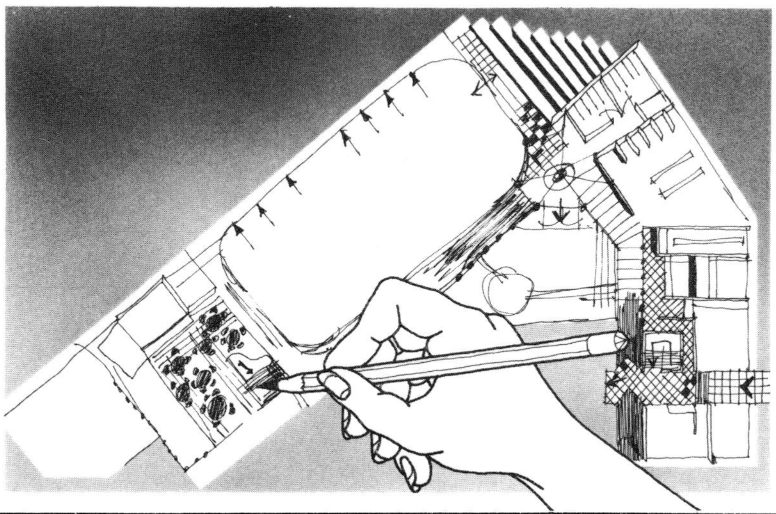

3

4

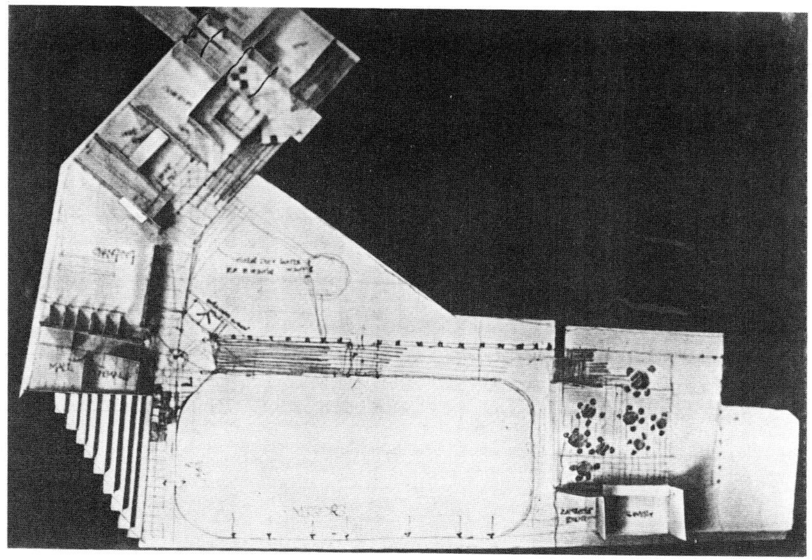

A third-year architecture student's initial sketch proposal for an ice rink was transferred from his paper model to a photocopied print for extension to the drawing form using a felt-tip pen.

How to Photocopy Convincing Perspectives

1

A convincing graphic of a building design concept can be quickly made by introducing a drawing into a photocopy made from a 10 x 8" print of a photograph of the intended site.

2

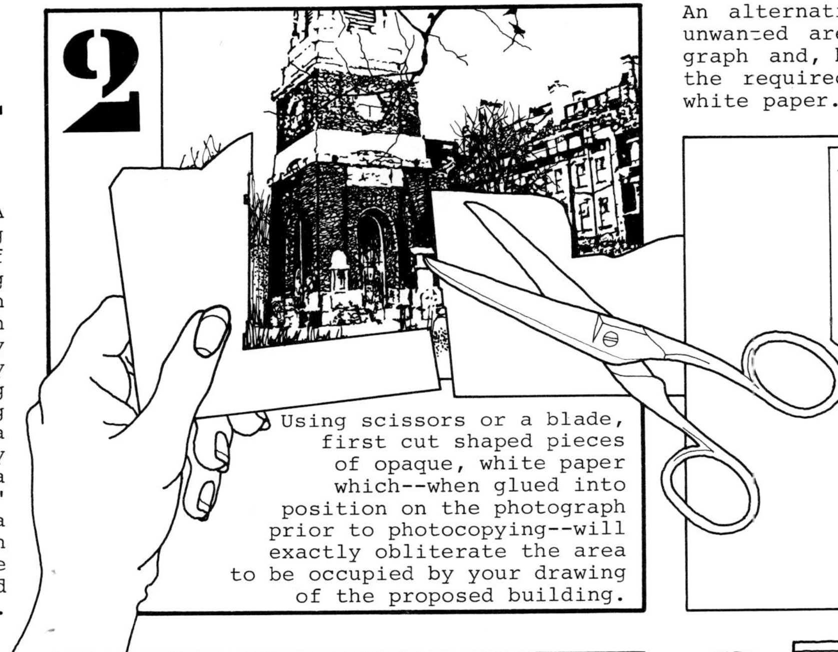

Using scissors or a blade, first cut shaped pieces of opaque, white paper which--when glued into position on the photograph prior to photocopying--will exactly obliterate the area to be occupied by your drawing of the proposed building.

3

An alternative is to cut away the unwanted areas of the actual photograph and, before photocopying, glue the required sections to a sheet of white paper.

4

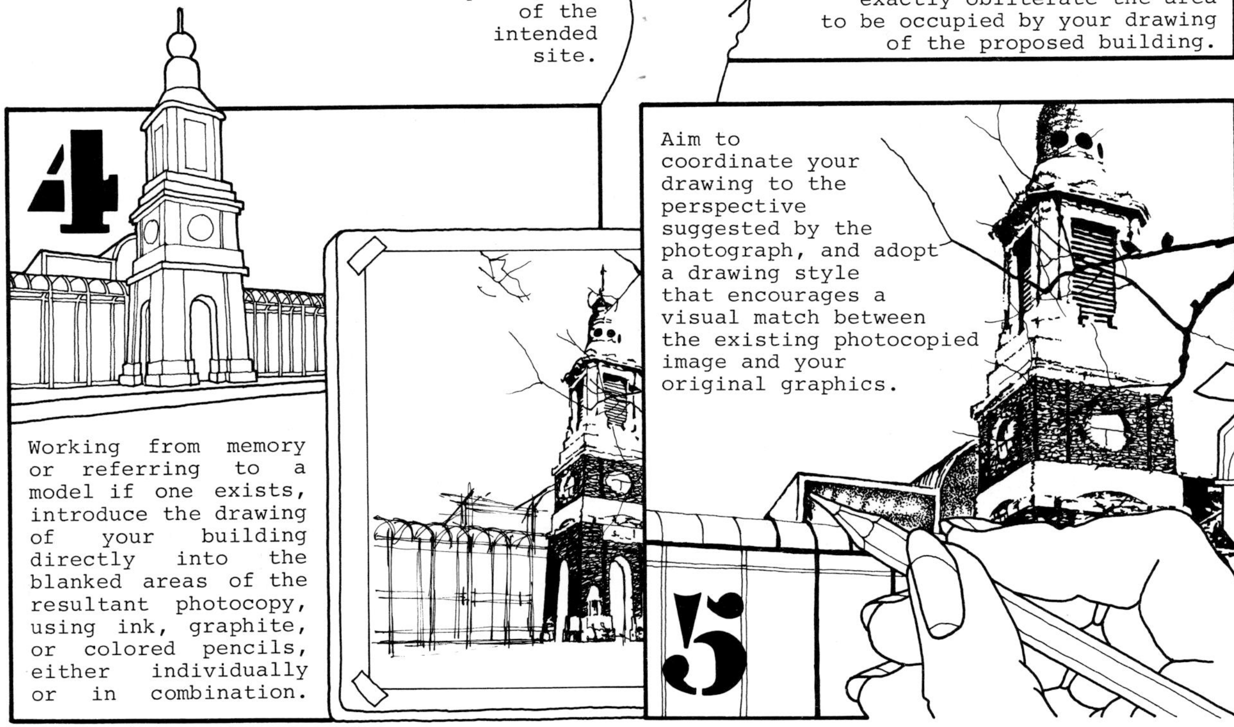

Working from memory or referring to a model if one exists, introduce the drawing of your building directly into the blanked areas of the resultant photocopy, using ink, graphite, or colored pencils, either individually or in combination.

5

Aim to coordinate your drawing to the perspective suggested by the photograph, and adopt a drawing style that encourages a visual match between the existing photocopied image and your original graphics.

6

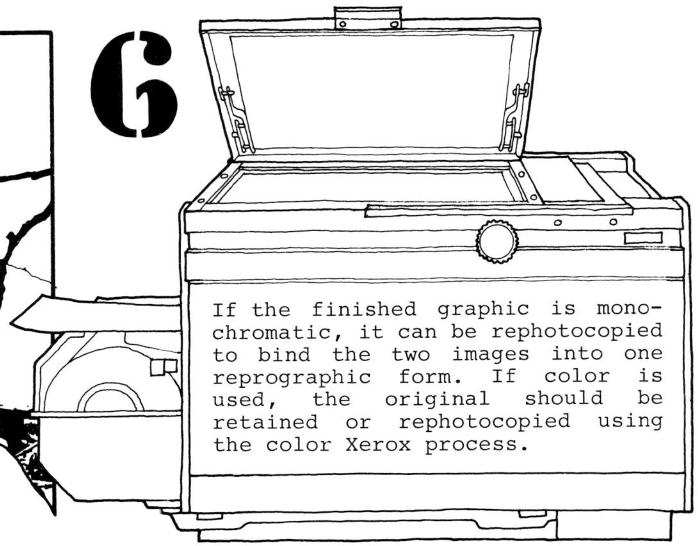

If the finished graphic is monochromatic, it can be rephotocopied to bind the two images into one reprographic form. If color is used, the original should be retained or rephotocopied using the color Xerox process.

The image can now be included as an illustration in a brochure, employed in wall presentations for critiques, or simply act as an aid to visualizing a developing design idea.

Second-Stage Photocopied Perspective

This is a sketch design for a music faculty building in Soho, London. This fifth-year student project was worked on a photocopy of a site photograph that had been selectively pruned to retain existing design elements and remove the pieces that created blank areas for the artwork. Mediums used include pencil, felt-tip pen, and markers.

How to Produce Super-Realist Artwork

Most Super-Realist artwork is derived from photographic source material. The source might be a single image or a montage combining a variety of different photographic images.

1 After selecting the source material, superimpose its image with a grid. A duplicate grid should then be drawn to the required scale in light graphite on the drawing board.

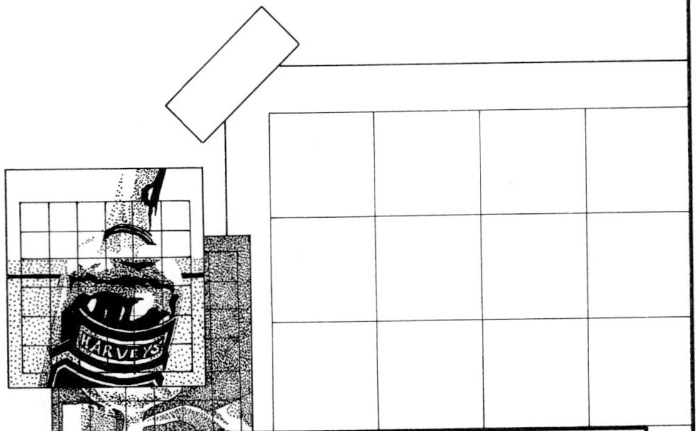

2 A close inspection of any photograph will reveal its formation as a pattern of subtle, obvious, and complicated abstract shapes. In monochromatic photographs, these shapes are defined by changing values, whereas in color photographs the shapes are determined by changes in hue. The secret of producing convincing Super-Realist artwork is to recognize these shapes and transfer them meticulously and accurately in line to the artwork, regardless of their apparent insignificance.

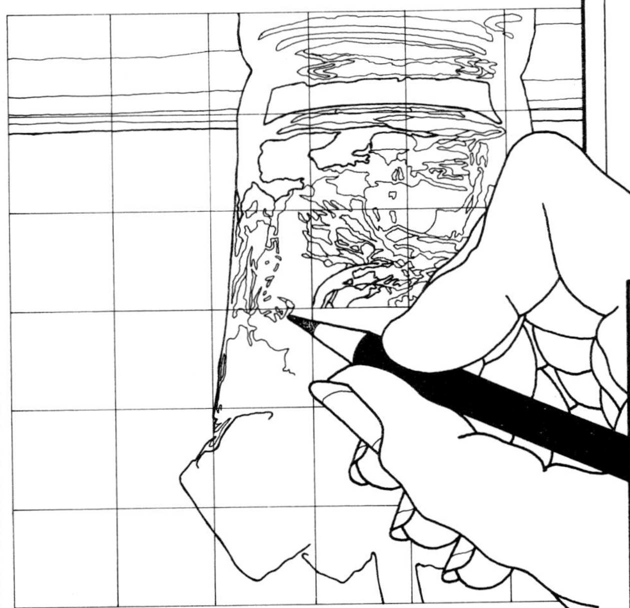

This stage, then, involves the transfer in pencil line of the precise outline of each value- or color-shape, into its appropriate rescaled linear "container" on the artwork grid.

N.B.: Avoid outlining obvious forms, as is done in conventional line drawings. A useful way to encourage concentration on the abstract pattern of shapes is to have both the source image and the artwork in an upside-down position as you work with them.

3 After completion, each shape can now be filled with its corresponding value or color. As the linear network of transferred shapes simultaneously embraces all visual cues in the original image, an even, flat application of medium should be attempted.

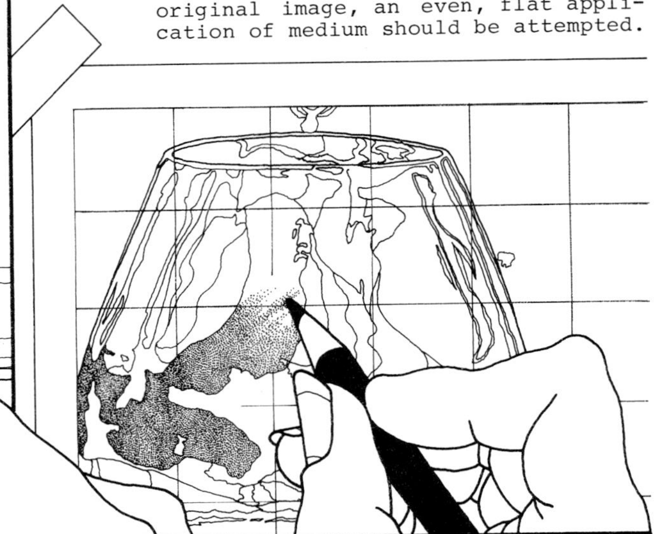

4 Different grades of graphite and drawing pressures will achieve the required range of values when rendering in pencil. Make sure, however, that a structured application of graphite carefully establishes the character (i.e., the hardness or softness) of the edge of each shape.

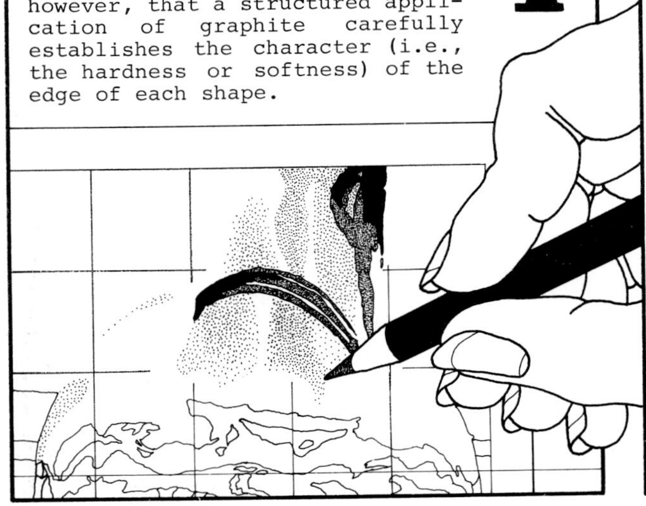

5 More diffuse edges of darker values can be achieved by a controlled rubbing of the graphite with the finger or a wad of cotton wool. An alternative method of structuring "out-of-focus" zones is to use a series of ascending tonal bands.

How to Produce Super-Realist Artwork

6

When working in color, use an opaque paint such as gouache as the medium. In this case, each color shape seen in the source image is in turn translated into carefully matched mixtures of pigment. Each color mix is then applied to the artwork in a layer thick enough to obliterate both the guideline pencil drawing and the paper support.

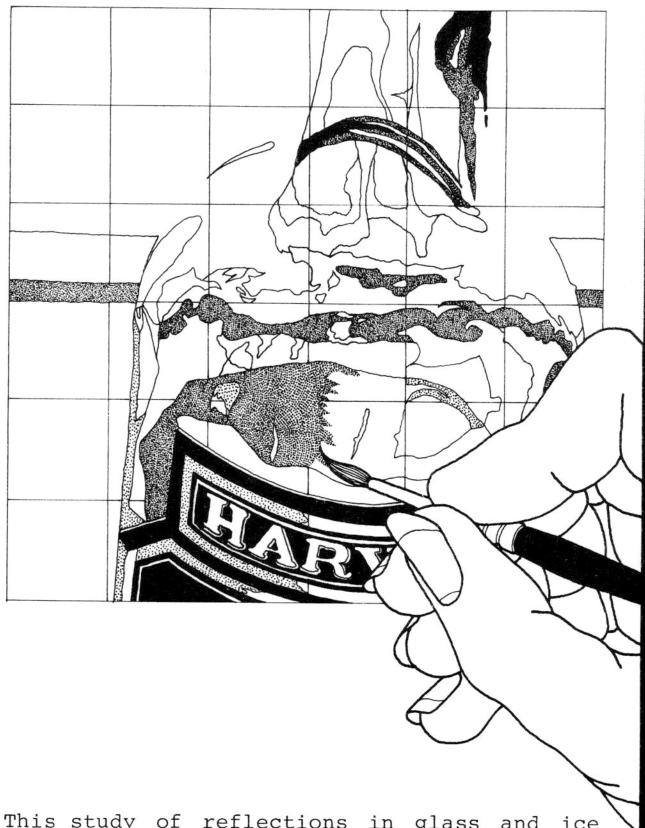

This study of reflections in glass and ice was entirely produced from magazine ads and painted in precise patches of gouache over a meticulous pencil line drawing. It is interesting to note that this first-year student's painting's reappearance as a photographic print transforms it back into its original mode of representation.

How to Make Composite Perspectives

1 The composite method of image building can achieve professional-looking perspectives and short-circuit the time spent in setting up vanishing points and lines of convergence.

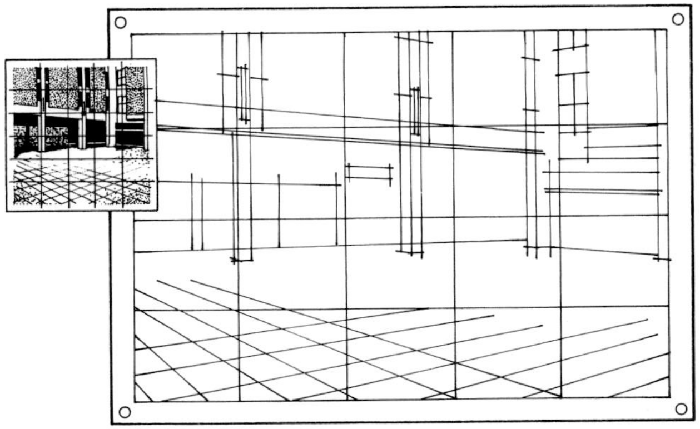

First, draw a grid over a photographic print of the site area taken with this graphic in mind and enlarge the same grid on the drawing board.

2 Working directly from the photograph, transfer the information, square by square, into the artwork using graphite, ink, paint, or a medium of your choice. Work the total image, as all further graphics will be superimposed.

3 Place a sheet of tracing paper over the artwork area to be occupied by the drawing of the designed form. Sketch its basic form until you are satisfied that its perspective appears compatible with that of the background.

4 Transfer the tracing-paper image to drawing paper and work up in a medium sympathetic to that of the site drawing. When finished, carefully cut out and spray-adhesive mount the image into its position on the artwork.

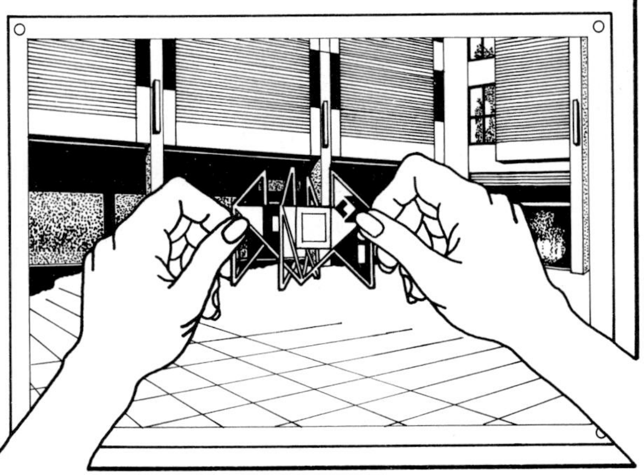

5 Figures and other ancillary forms can now be introduced into the image, first checking their scalar relationship to the main graphic, using the tracing-paper sketch method.

6

These can be worked on separate sheets of paper and copied directly from newspaper or magazine photographs to the scale required. When finished, cut out and spray mount them onto the format.

Composite Perspective Drawing

This design is for a portable information unit integrated into its shopping-mall setting, by a first-year architecture student. Its seven middle- and foreground components began separately from photographic sources then were spray mounted onto the background image, derived from a site photograph. The perspective was initially drawn in pencil and extended in India ink washes before being overworked in technical and fiber-tip pen.

N.B.: In order to speed up the image-building process, actual magazine photographs of figures--found to be in scale with their intended location in the perspective--can be cut out and glued directly onto the background graphic.

How to Produce a Photomontage

An excellent method of communicating a highly realistic impression of a building design in context with its proposed location is to introduce a photograph of a model to a photograph of the site.

1

Depending upon what the image is intended to convey, and after reviewing all possible vantage points, take a photograph of the site, allowing plenty of foreground detail.

N.B.: The print should not be smaller than 10 x 8" (250 x 200mm).

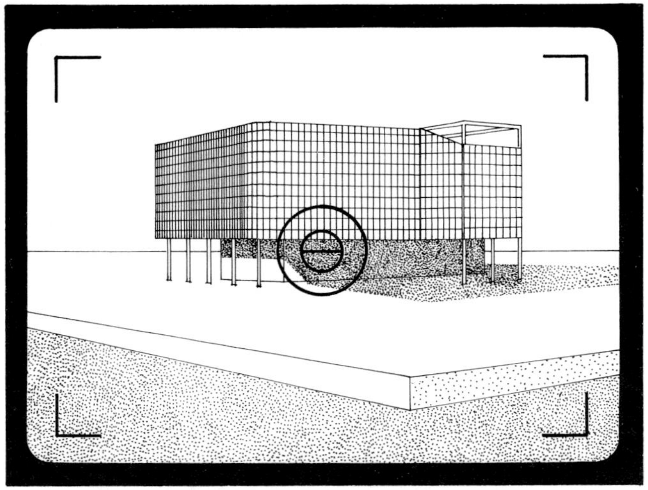

2

After aligning the model to the appropriate viewpoint and arranging lighting conditions coincident with that of the site print, photograph the model.

3

Next, place a sheet of tracing paper over the developed site print and make a sketch outlining the predicted shape of the building's proportions in relation to the proportions of its setting.

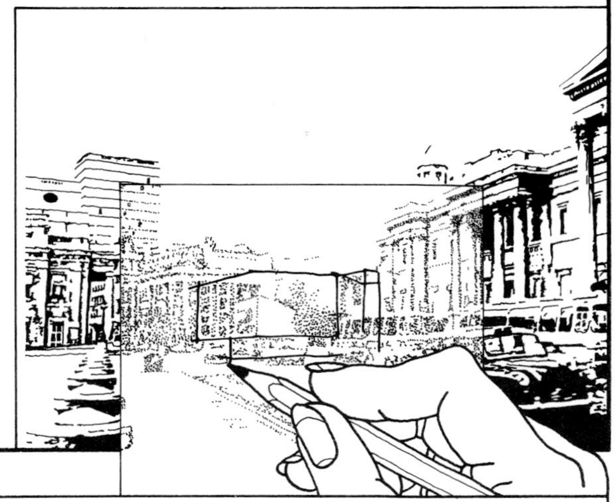

4

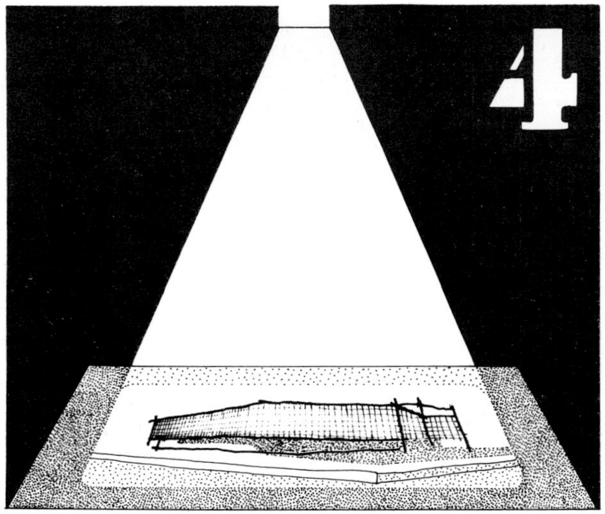

When placed on the enlarger easel, the sketch acts as a template against which the projected size of the model on the negative is determined before exposure.

5

Using a sharp scalpel, trace-cut the photograph of the model from its print. Leave an area below the building image, which will later act as a tab when gluing the photo into the site print.

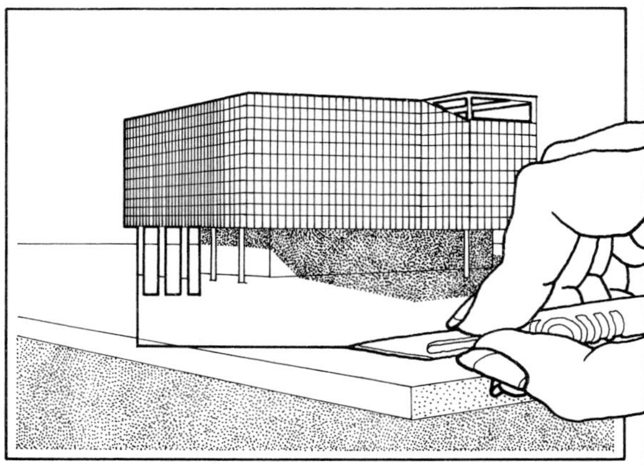

6

Finally, trace-cut the baseline and any vertical forms that will surround and overlap the image of the building on the site print. Insert the model image and carefully glue the tab to the back of the site print together with any other overlapping edges.

Second-Stage Photomontage

Here is an investigation via photomontage of the impact of a building design on a site adjoining Trafalgar Square. Produced from site and model prints by a fifth-year architecture student, each original montage was rephotographed to achieve the fusion of a second-stage print. These were then used as presentation graphics in a design competition.

N.B.: A useful tip to improve the impression of the photomontage illusion is to lightly sand the back edges of overlapping areas on both model and site prints with fine-grade glasspaper prior to gluing. The resultant reduction of the print paper's thickness helps to increase the visual integration of the two images.

Photoperspectives: Drawing-Photograph Combinations

1

When a model is not available, another method of producing composite images with a strong element of realism is to make a drawing of the designed form for incorporation into a site photograph.

This need not be a totally exposed view, but a convincing glimpse of the proposed building seen within a framed or partially screened context.

2

Photograph the site and develop as large a print as possible of the selected view.

N.B.: Several photographic agencies offer a cheap super-enlargement to poster size from prints. Although not of high quality, such prints are ideal for this form of graphic.

Next, place tracing paper over the print and, in response to its perspective, sketch the basic form of the building design. When satisfied as to its appropriateness, transfer it via tracing onto the drawing board.

N.B.: Perspective coordinates for proposed buildings are easily found by projecting lines back from rectilinear forms in the site photograph to their vanishing points.

3

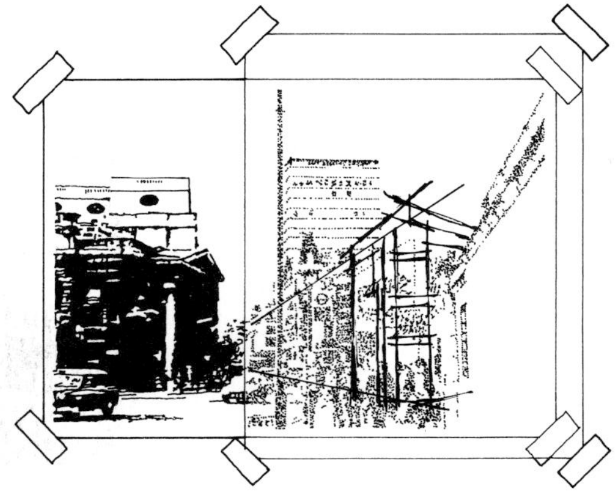

If it is planned not to produce a second-stage photograph from the artwork, the next phase is all-important. The quality and degree of rendering should be guided exclusively by a constant reference to the visual character of the site print. For example, a sharp and strongly contrasting image will dictate a similar graphic for the design, possibly employing a crisp pen technique. Conversely, a more diffuse or grainy print might suggest soft graphite or a wash rendering.

4

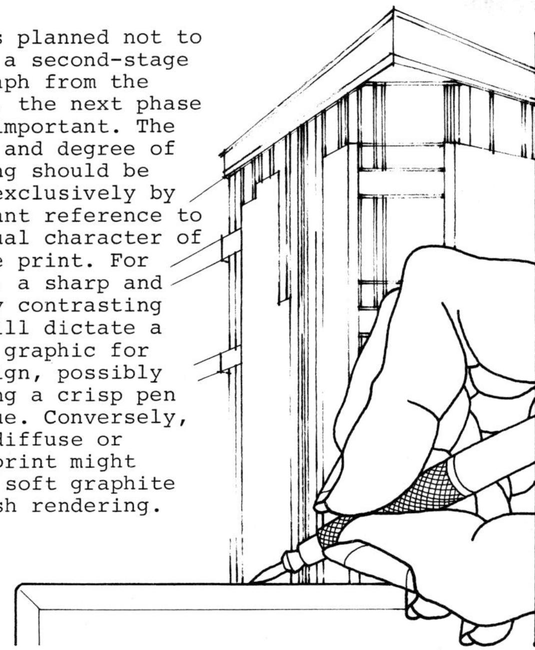

By taking advantage of the available possibilities for a greater fusion between the appearance of the drawing and the parent site print (correct angle of light, shadows cast by objects in the print onto planes in the drawing, nearer forms in the print overlapping the drawing's edge, etc.), a greater degree of realism will be achieved.

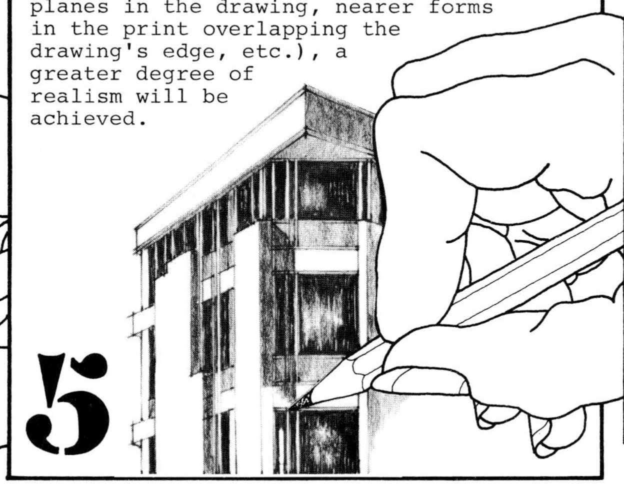

5

Finally, cut out the drawing and spray mount it onto its print support or insert it, using the photomontage method described on page 94.

6

Photoperspectives: Drawing-Photograph Combinations

If the montage of drawing and print is to be transformed into the overall fusion of a second-stage photograph, more license can be taken with the drawing. For example, even a basic line drawing will appear convincing in the final print.

7

8

When dealing with more complex buildings, a large drawing of their design can be photographed for reduction into a print and subsequent introduction to the site photograph via the photomontage technique described on page 94.

Two photoperspectives by Paul Chemetov

This direct combination of a pencil drawing and a photographic print was produced by a fifth-year architecture student to assess the impact of his design for a picture gallery and restaurant on a site adjacent to the National Gallery in Trafalgar Square, London.

How to Diazo Print Shadows from Models

By providing diazo prints that record accurately the effect of shadows cast from a model of a proposed building on its setting, this technique both replicates and extends the function of the Heliodon (an instrument for measuring shadows cast from scale models in relation to given points in the sun's azimuth).

The required equipment comprises a 500-watt tungsten spotlight to simulate the sun, and a sundial to fix its coordinates in relation to the model.

1

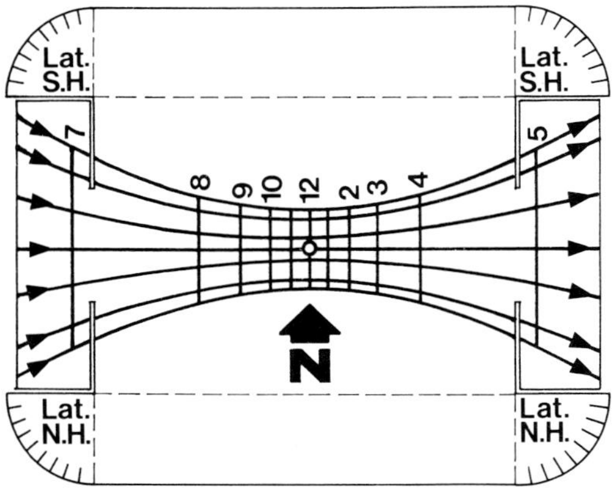

2

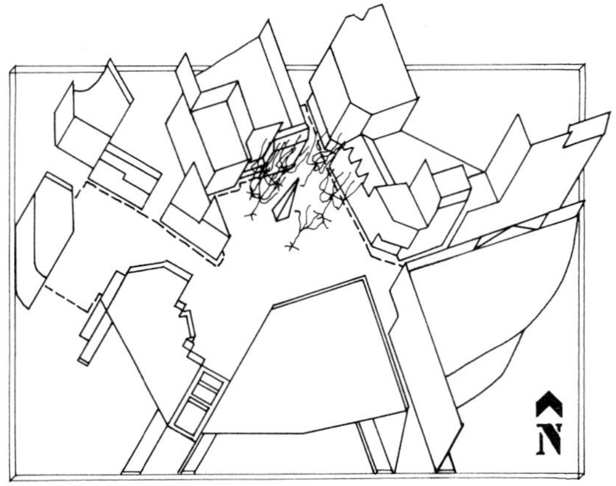

A scale block model of the building design should be glued to a base of clear acetate or glass. Other related vertical objects such as walls, existing buildings, or trees should also be added and glued to the transparent base, which, incidentally, might also include a delineation of the surrounding layout plan.

3

The next stage requires positioning the model and sundial on the drawing board. Locate the sundial as close as possible to the edge of the base of the model and coordinate both north points.

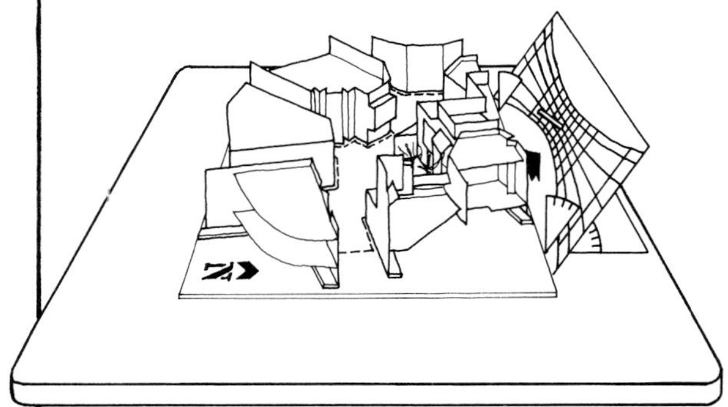

This setup is then positioned approximately 5'-0" (1.5m) below a freestanding or fixed directional spotlight.

4

Prior to exposure, it is wise to check the various shadow readings--each tracked by the sundial under the spotlight. For instance, a lateral tilting of the model will obtain various readings from the year cycle; rotating the model will find readings from the day cycle. A good starting point for a series of diazo prints would be a noon reading taken during the summer solstice, winter solstice, and equinox, as they determine extremes of shadow caused by significant points in the sun's azimuth, i.e., its highest, lowest, and midway points respectively.

N.B.: If available, the Heliodon's tilting turntable--being capable of being locked into any position--can be utilized to fix the position of the model in relation to the spotlight. Otherwise, this stage relies upon jacking the model into the required position for each reading prior to subsequent exposures.

5

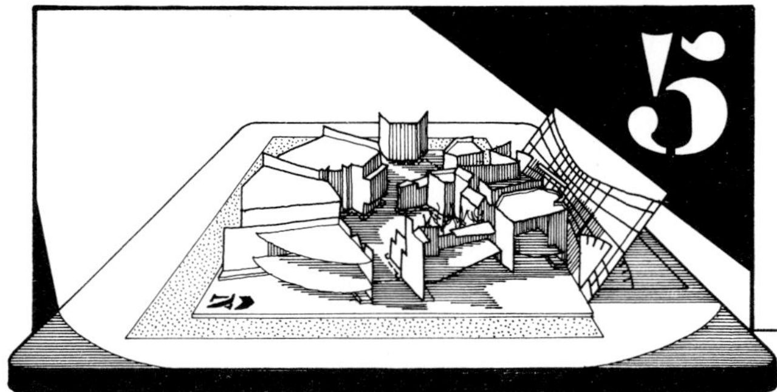

After the position of the model has been determined under the spotlight for the first print, switch off. Then, in a blacked-out room, carefully insert a sheet of unexposed diazo print paper between the model's transparent base and the drawing board. Then, switch on the spotlight and expose for approximately ten minutes.

N.B.: The use of an ultraviolet light would, of course, shorten considerably the length of exposure.

6

When the exposure process is completed, protect the light-sensitive print surface until developing it by diazo in the normal way.

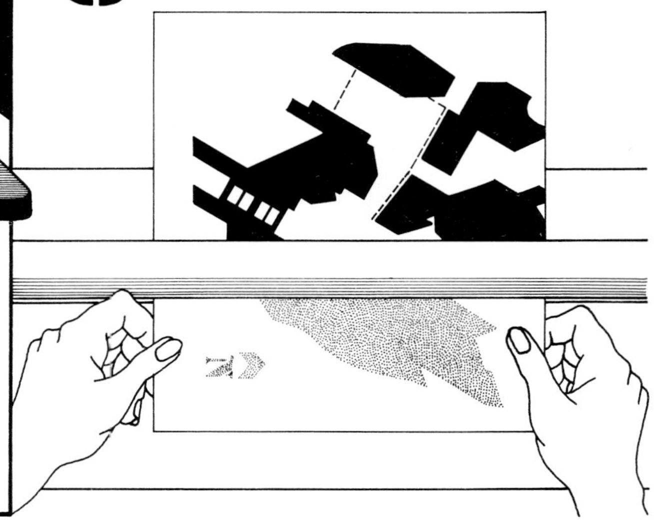

Diazo Printed Shadows from a Model

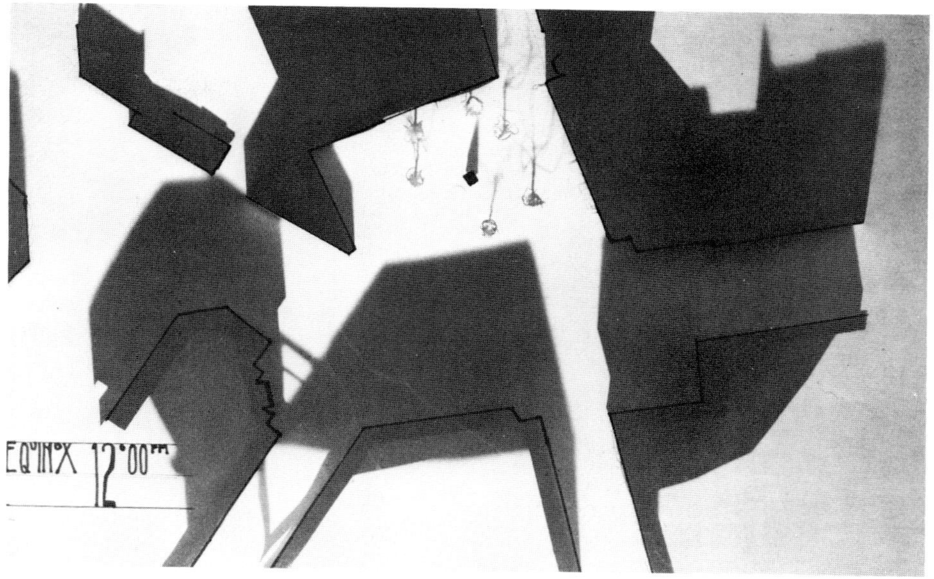

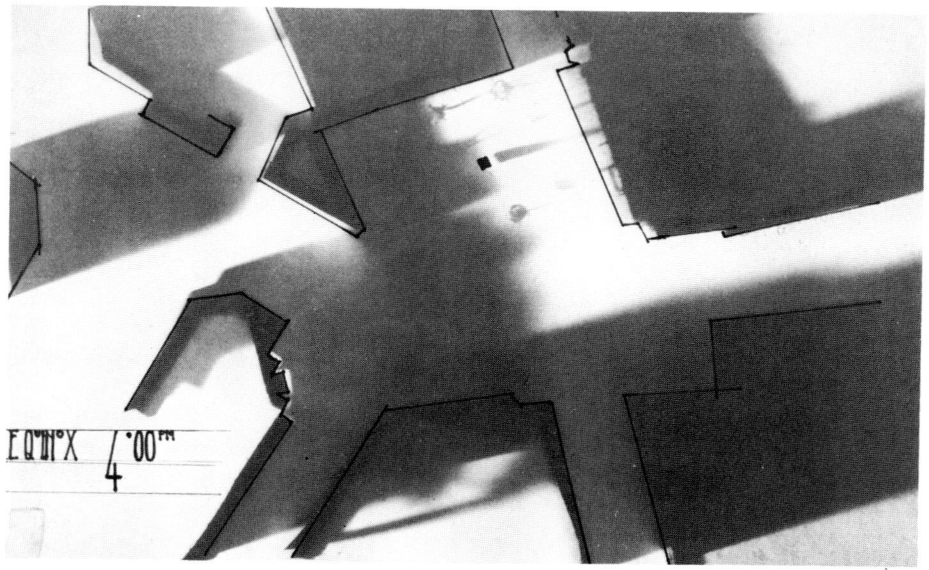

Four diazo recordings of shadows taken at different points in the day and year cycles. The model from which these readings were taken was a 1:500 block model built from cardboard on an acetate base to simulate an existing Oxford city square. The study was made to test the impact of shade and shadow on the space prior to the development of design proposals for the area. This method was devised by Peter Ireland as part of a second-year-architecture project.

Increasing Realism in Photographs of Models

After photographing a presentation model of his proposed building, an architect once was bemused to find that his clients--on seeing the projected color transparencies--believed that what they saw was a real building. He realized that the powerful illusion of scale was caused by his inclusion of cut-out photographs of figures--a simple method that induces a strong impression of realism in color or monochrome slides and prints taken of models built to 1/4" = 1'-0", 1/2" = 1'-0", and 1" = 1'-0" scale (metric equivalents 1:50, 1:20, and 1:10).

1

First, select a series of appropriately scaled figures from color magazines and cut them out, allowing a margin.

N.B.: The selection should avoid the more "posed" postures and concentrate instead on frontal, side, and rear views of people describing unself-conscious body positions.

2

3

Spray-mount the cutouts to a sheet of thick paper. Then cut them out again, this time to their exact shape, using a sharp scalpel.

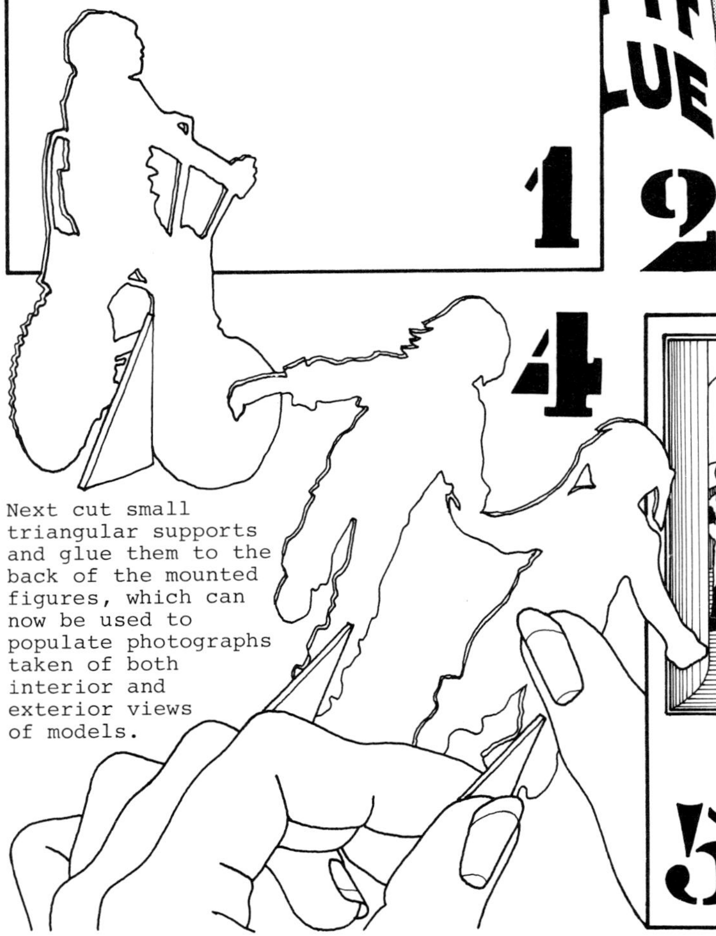

4

Next cut small triangular supports and glue them to the back of the mounted figures, which can now be used to populate photographs taken of both interior and exterior views of models.

5

When deploying figures in models, aim to avoid the rigidness of a stage-set. Locate figures in natural situations, such as overlapping in groups, turning corners, partly seen from behind objects--as they would be seen in reality.

6

Prior to photographing, check the figures' compositional arrangement in relation to the intended format of the subsequent photograph. Also, make sure that each figure faces square-on to the camera lens, or else distortion will occur and the illusion be lost.

5 THE PRESENTATION PACKAGE

Tips for Combining Lettering with Drawings

1

AVANT GARDE
MICROGRAMMA
MEDIUM EXTENDED
HELVETICA MEDIUM
STENCIL
COMPACTA OUTLINE

When combined with drawings, lettering should be integrated carefully as a design component into display layouts. The selection of simple and efficient letterforms used in a consistent fashion will aid clarity in communication, with degrees of importance in their message being achieved by variations in size, boldness, color, and location in the layout.

As a general rule, avoid oversized lettering, overelaborate letter types, and, especially in main titles, the mixing of capitals with lower case, and the underlining of important words.

2

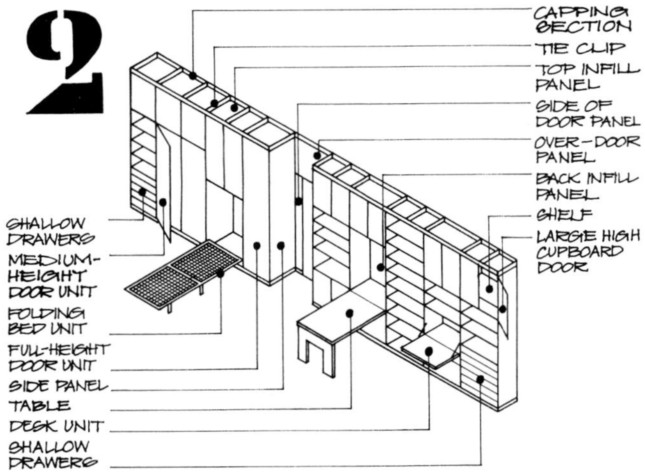

An efficient method of annotating drawings is to stack written information into two blocks, either above and below or to either side of the drawn image. Labels can then be clearly keyed in to their graphic counterparts without making the drawing confusing.

When annotating directly an element of a drawing, aim to create compact blocks of information. Also, when labeling areas, as in plans, choose a lettering size that sits comfortably inside the space. For instance, when lettering irregular shapes, position labels at their visual centers.

3

① BOILER ② SHELVES ③ MICROWAVE ④ FRIDGE ⑤ PORCH ⑥ FOOD CBD ⑦ SINK ⑧ WASHING ⑨ DRYING ⑩ WARDROBE ⑪ BED ⑫ STORAGE

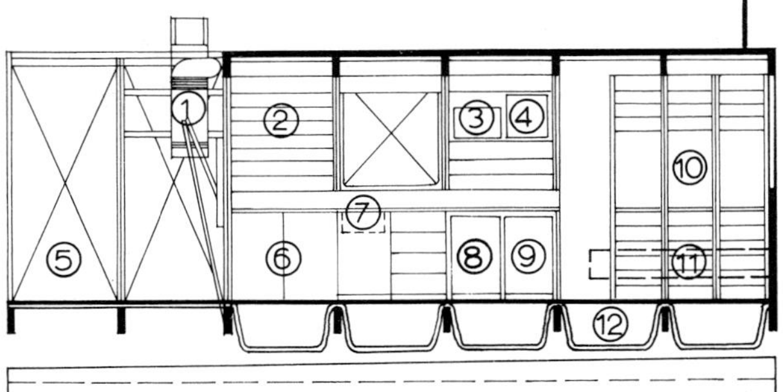

Another method is the annotation of drawings with numbers. These refer the viewer to a legend which, within the overall sheet layout, is located clearly in relation to the drawing.

4

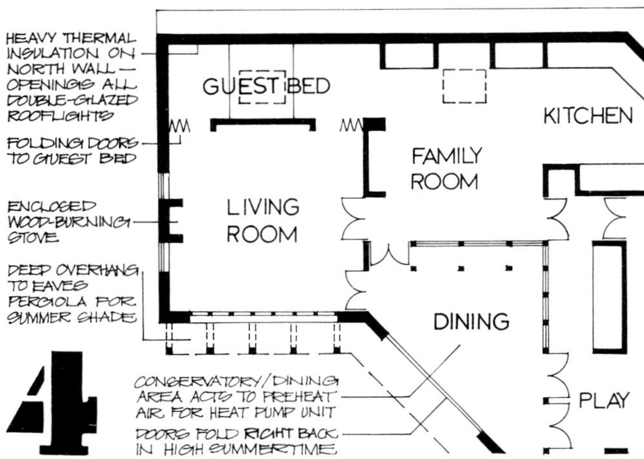

5

Complicated drawings will require that lettering be organized both inside and outside the drawn image. They also benefit from a hierarchy of letter sizes, each layer of written information functioning in different ways and being read at different distances from the drawing. In such drawings, main titles should be read in conjunction with the whole sheet. Subtitles (type of drawing, name, scale, etc.) should be legible without interference with the drawing; labels (functions of various spatial zones, etc.) should be clearly perceived as part of their drawn zones; and captions (references, details, construction information, etc.) should be clearly related or keyed in with their drawn counterparts.

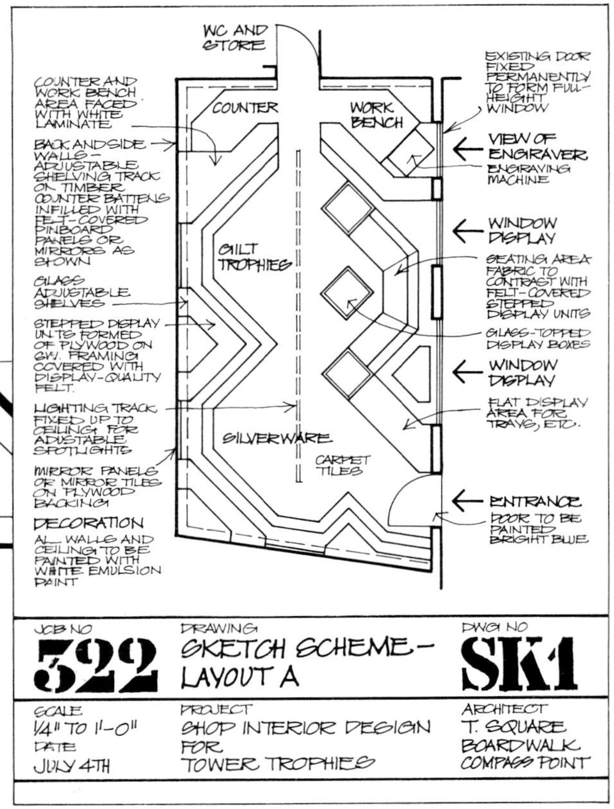

Tips for Combining Lettering with Drawings

The idea that lettering should be the first element on a design presentation sheet to hit the eye often leads to an oversized annotation that either disrupts or overpowers the drawn image.

6

This site cross-section, for instance, attempts to communicate formal massing in a slice of space. The use of excessively large letterforms placed in close proximity to its base causes the two elements to attach; the lettering dominates and thereby contaminates the central graphic image.

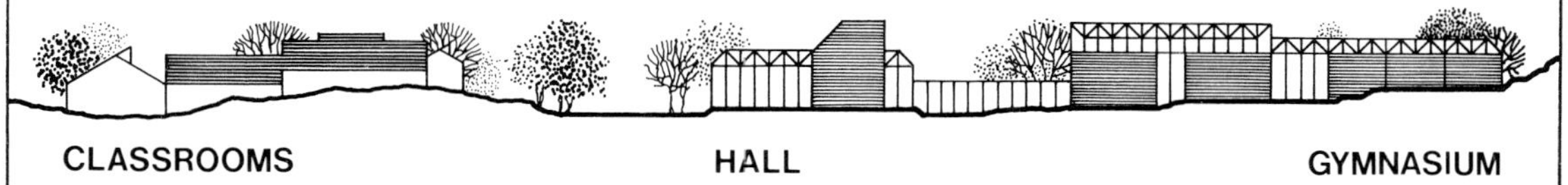

A more sympathetic method of titling in this situation is to enlist a smaller, clear typeface that, in keeping a respectful distance from the drawing, informs without having its graphic message distorted.

7

A good method of juxtaposing titles with drawings is to design the titles so that their blocks either begin or end in direct relationship to the main edge of the drawing. This system is simple to operate and can be used on presentation sheets carrying either individual or groups of drawings.

8

Two forms of letter spacing are in common use: mechanical and optical ("eyeballed"). Optical spacing involves the arrangement of letters by eye, a positive-negative exercise creating visually unified elements. Mechanical spacing refers to sheets of instant lettering and some stencils that incorporate registration marks that regulate the distance between letters.

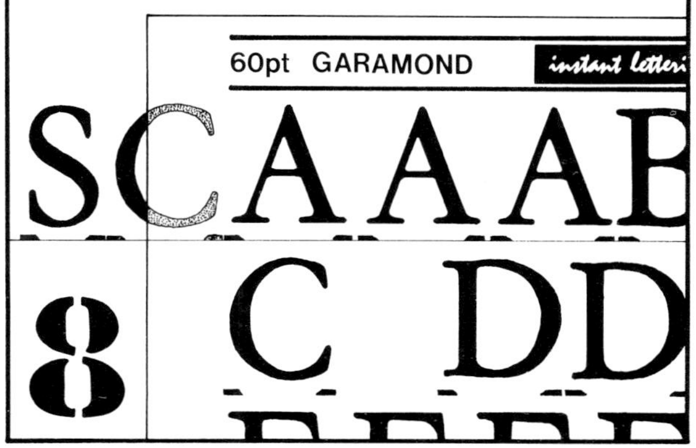

9

As mechanical forms of spacing generally pay no need to the different spacing demands made by the various characters, and as there is no set distance for spacing, a good tip for beginners is to practice optical spacing by positioning letters as closely as possible without their actually touching.

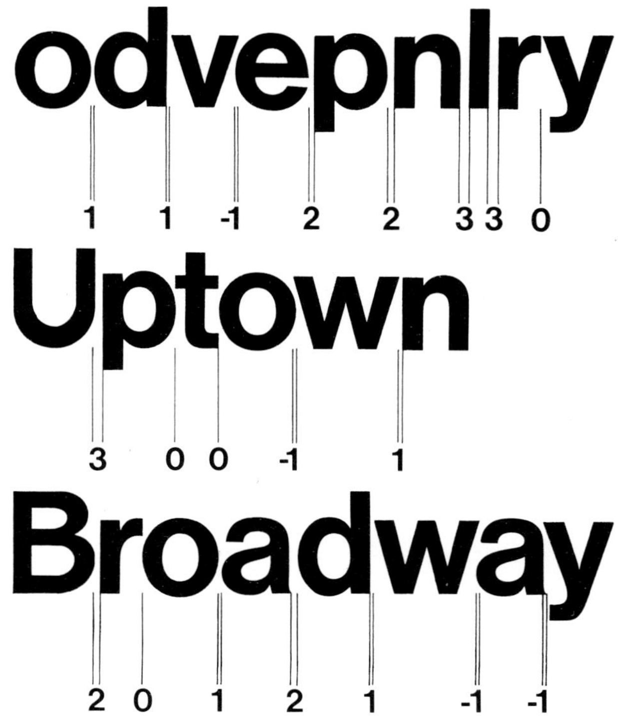

These are examples of a spacing system devised for New York's Metropolitan Transit Authority. They illustrate a "mechanical" spacing method that takes into account the various spacing requirements of different types of letterform when juxtaposed in words. The top line illustrates units of spacing required by letters when those of similar and dissimilar character become neighbors. The second and third line exemplifies this spacing system applied to typical words used in subway signs.

How to Use Overlays in Presentations

Complex design solutions can be communicated using the overlay method in wall displays and brochures. The progressive build-up of superimposed layers of information is mainly used to explain in-depth site appraisals and intricate planning proposals, but it can be utilized for many forms of design communication.

Overlays can be worked on tracing paper or on acetate sheets. However, the latter are more successful when more than two layers of information are involved.

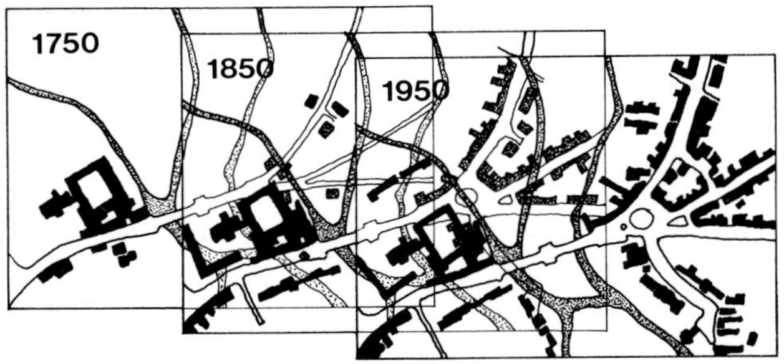

1

2

Labeling and titling can occur at the various stages in overlay presentation. However, as with all the other information contained on the sheets, make sure that labels or titles do not conflict on completion of the overlay sequence. One method is to employ a color-coded system, i.e., different colors of lettering at different levels--with the strongest colors being on the lower sheets.

3

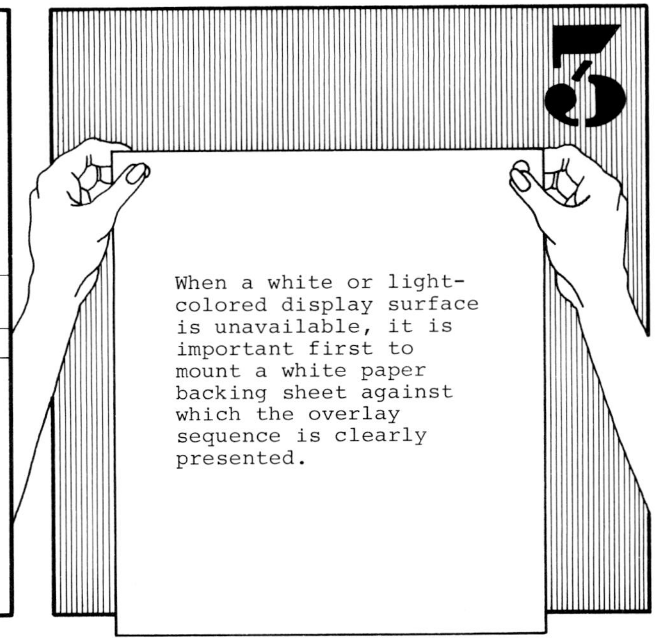

When a white or light-colored display surface is unavailable, it is important first to mount a white paper backing sheet against which the overlay sequence is clearly presented.

The set of overlay material can be pinned directly to the display surface. The pinning operation--as with the binding of brochures--acts as registration and should be carried out carefully.

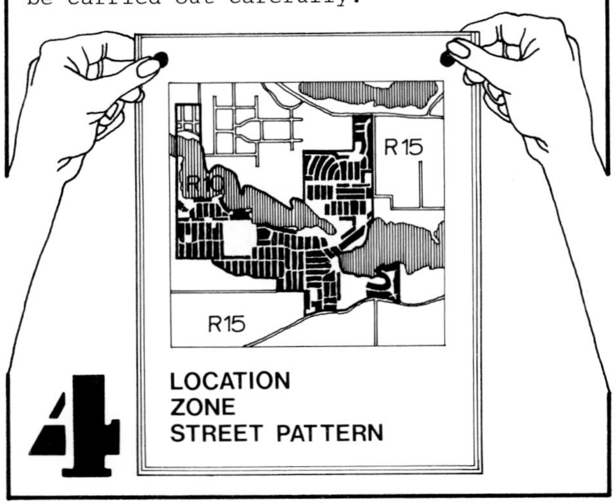

4

5

Hanging is better than pinning because it avoids the chore of having to hold or temporarily pin back from the format the sheets awaiting their turn for overlay.

The hanging method simply necessitates punching two holes through the set of overlays, which are then reinforced with eyelets. The sheets are then hung in sequence on hooked pushpins or substantial chart tacks, leaving the designer free during presentation.

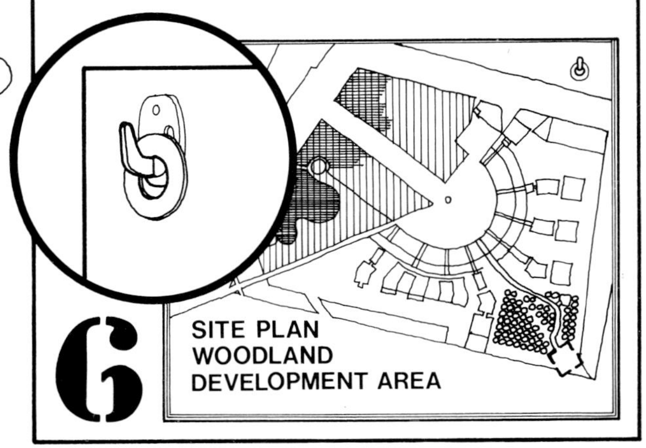

6

Experimenting with Overlays

One of the many ways of employing overlays in design presentations is to use progressive cross-sections--composed of opaque dry-transfer color and ink on acetate--to unfold large interior spaces.

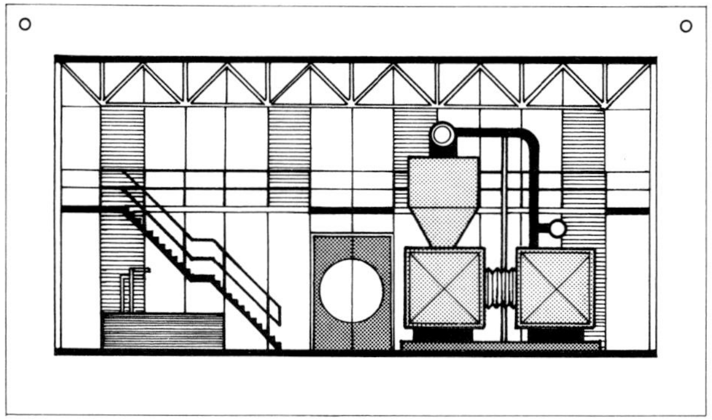

1 Being presented first, the farthest section might incorporate an interior view of the back wall elevation together with objects placed immediately in front of its plane.

2 A second overlay might then introduce a section taken at a convenient point near the middle of the interior.

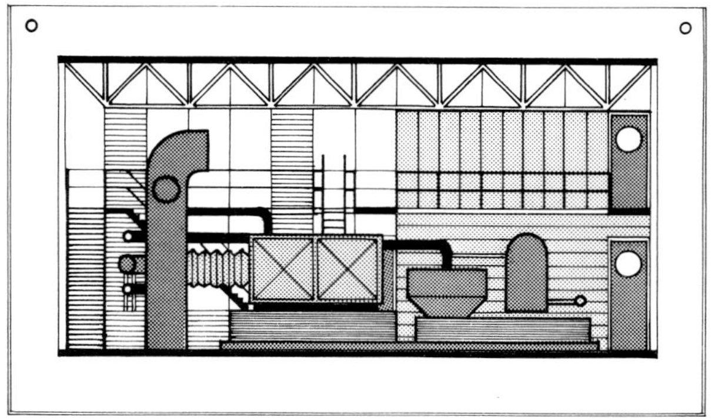

N.B.: Selection of the point at which this, and the subsequent section, occur is made in response to the availability of views through unworked areas of clear acetate.

3 An overlay reconstruction of an interior design concludes with a third section taken at a point just inside the near elevation.

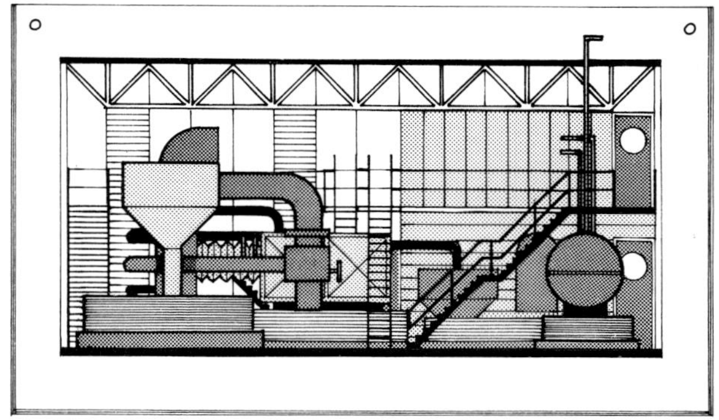

N.B.: The sequence can be extended by adding a fourth overlay which, in carrying the exterior front elevation, places the observer outside the building.

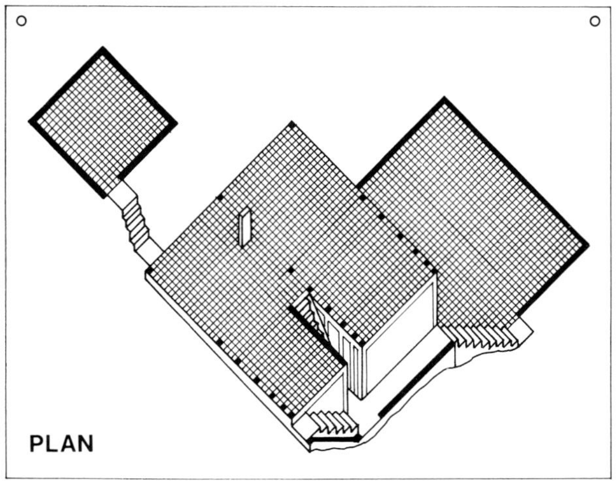

4 Another overlay sequence, again using opaque dry-transfer color and ink on acetate, reconstructs a building design in the horizontal plane. In this sequence, the plan represents the first layer of presented information.

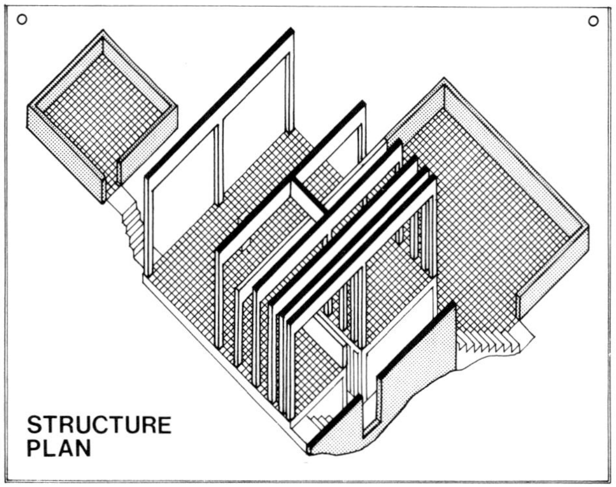

5 The second overlay superimposes structural elements, partition walls, and, if scale or viewability allows, furniture and figures.

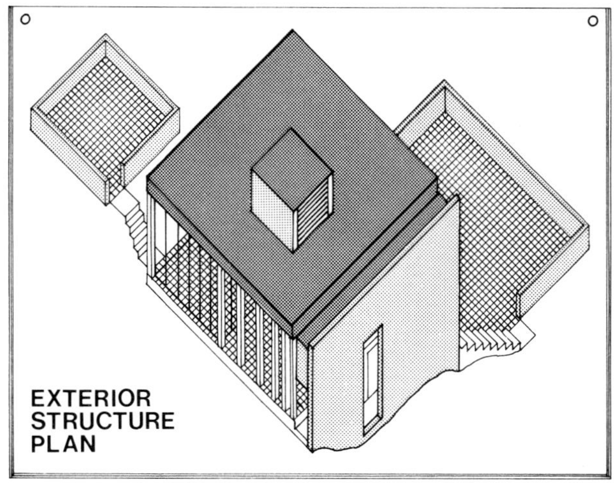

6 This sequence is completed by a third layer of acetate that overlays the external envelope--the result representing a regular axonometric.

Presenting with Projectors

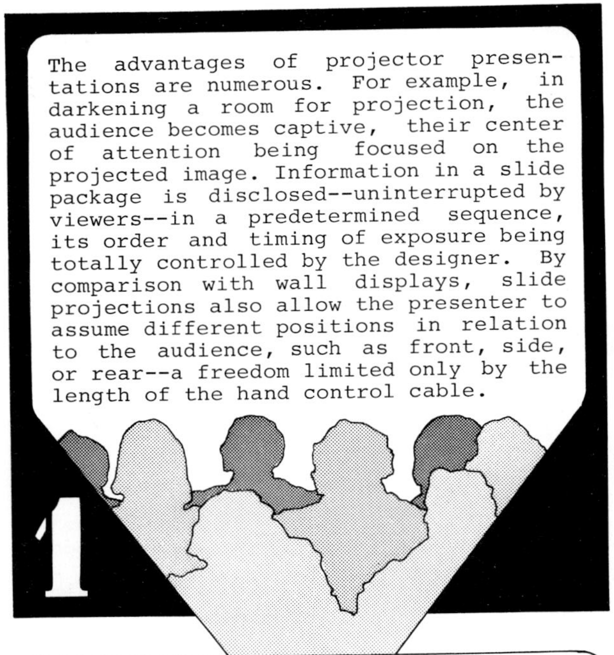

1

The advantages of projector presentations are numerous. For example, in darkening a room for projection, the audience becomes captive, their center of attention being focused on the projected image. Information in a slide package is disclosed--uninterrupted by viewers--in a predetermined sequence, its order and timing of exposure being totally controlled by the designer. By comparison with wall displays, slide projections also allow the presenter to assume different positions in relation to the audience, such as front, side, or rear--a freedom limited only by the length of the hand control cable.

2

All forms of image can be combined as a means of disclosing various design concepts, such as images photographed from magazines or all kinds of artwork photographed in color or in monochrome, together with lettering, composite images, and even diagrams.

3

Statistical diagrams such as graphs, tables, bar charts, and so on can be made more visually exciting for projection as slides by adding color and support imagery. A fast method is to photograph a diagram integrated with relevant magazine photographs. This technique can convert a potentially dull visual into a professional-looking and digestible screened image.

4

When producing orthographic drawings for conversion via photography into slides, the designer should be aware of the contrast needed for clarity in projection. Simple drawings using strong ink lines together with dry-transfer tone or color work well for such images.

5

Live commentaries can take advantage of a pointer, an indicator projecting an illuminated arrow to draw attention to screened detail. Pointers are sometimes built into the projector, into the hand control, or supplied as separate devices.

N.B.: Most projectors allow slide shows to be projected by remote control. Spoken commentaries can also be tape recorded to synchronize with an automated or manual display. Specific moods can also be induced by adding tape-recorded music or appropriate sound effects. For the former, tracks from popular albums can be used.

6

There is also the visual diversity of multiscreen projection. Two, three, four, and up to eight banks of projectors are sometimes enlisted to project visual fragments of information.

N.B.: It is important that multiscreen displays not contain overly complex information--particularly in written form. If text or detailed graphics are used, these should be screened for longer periods within a preplanned sequence of presentation.

Tips for Rostrum-shooting Artwork

1

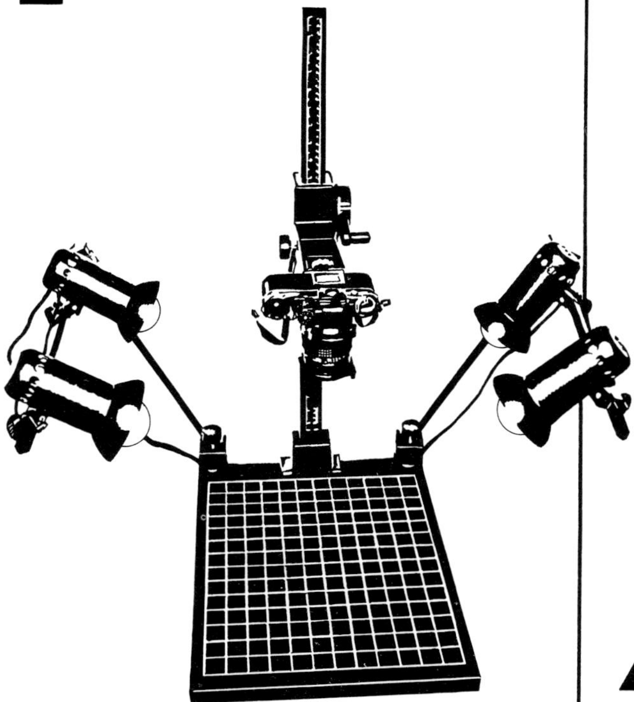

Rostrum photography using a copying stand is the alternative to the use of tripod with flash or floods. Even illumination is provided by four lamps positioned above the copying board and, for this reason, direct sunlight should be avoided when in use. If color-balanced lamps are not provided, attachable blue filters are recommended when photographing most colored artwork. A macro lens should be fitted to an SLR camera loaded with a film of the slowest possible speed. Focusing is a meticulous operation involving moving the entire camera back and forth. For exposure, set a delayed action to eliminate camera shake. During focusing and exposure, care should be taken to avoid shadows cast by the user onto the artwork.

2

Make sure that the artwork format is compatible with the proportions of the ultimate transparency. Also, especially when producing perspectives for conversion into slides, make sure that artwork responds to a clear frame of reference. Otherwise, the appearance on the projected slide of unworked areas of paper around the frame will tend to countermand the illusion of perspective depth.

3

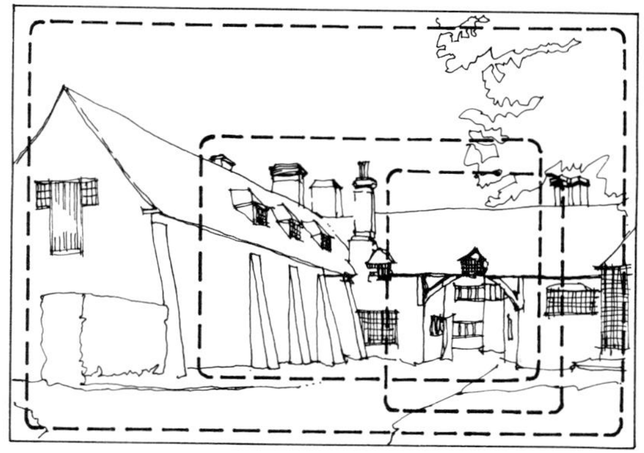

The macro lens allows several different slide images to be made from one perspective drawing. For example, a two- or three-stage sequence of slides can be derived using selected frames of reference, and working from "inside" the perspective to its outer frame. In such sequences, the close-ups (those taken inside the perspective) will obviously magnify the nature of the technique and paper texture.

4

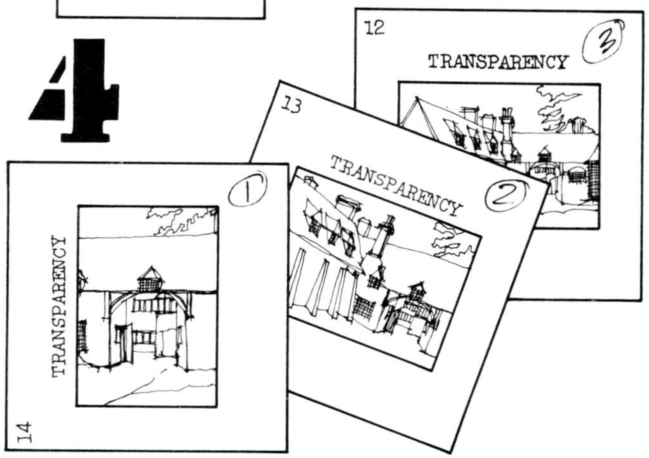

When presenting short slide sequences made from a single drawing, project those taken "inside" the format first so that the audience's realization of the singular nature of their source is delayed.

5

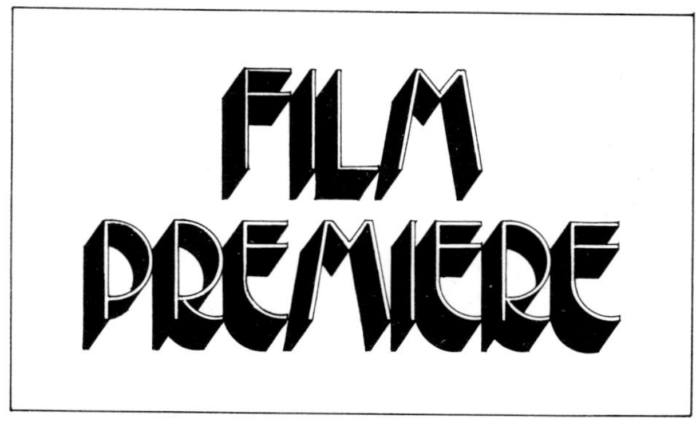

The copying stand is also useful for photographing three-dimensional material. For instance, a simple but effective method for titles is to glue strips of paper end-on to pre-drawn lettering on a backing sheet. When illuminated obliquely--achieved by switching off two side lamps--the resultant light and shadow effect offers a dramatic source for slide-presented credits etc.

Slide Presentation Techniques

1

A

A 35mm color slide presentation of a site analysis is a fast, professional method of orientating critique or client panels prior to their confrontation with design proposals.

For example, a presentation package might include series of slides processed from shots photographed progressively along a pre-planned route around and about the site environment. In functioning as serial vision "stills," these could take the viewer on a "walk" through the space of the design setting and, if required, focus on factors having particular impact on the ultimate design proposal.

B

Also, in order to avoid time spent explaining shot locations, a series of corresponding slides could be made from rostrum photographs of the site plan. Before each shot, a **V** symbol--cut from colored paper--can be positioned on the plan to denote location and direction of each of the on-site photographs. After processing, each site plan location slide is then paired off with its on-site counterpart for a twin projection. During the presentation sequence, the **V** on each successively projected site plan "animates" to the position from which the view on the adjoining image was photographed.

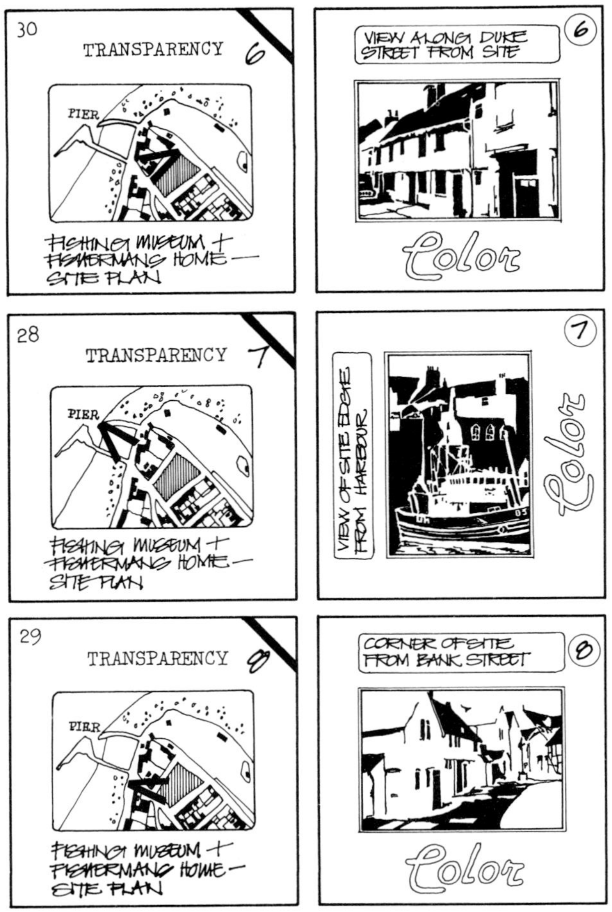

2

An alternative use for slides made from on-site photography is as a source for analytical drawings. For this purpose, slides are projected onto a sheet of drawing paper for their traced transformation into a more diagrammatic monochrome or colored artwork.

After rostrum shooting and processing, slides of analytical drawings can then be paired . . .

3

. . . with their on-site source images in a twin projector sequence which, apart from taking the viewer on a site tour, also displays two perceptions--one via the mechanical eye of the camera, another using the analytical eye of the designer.

Slide Presentation Techniques

4

Slide presentations are also useful for introducing a building design within its setting. Site drawings, traced from on-site slides projected onto drawing paper, could then receive composite drawings of the proposed architecture viewed from different vantage points.

5

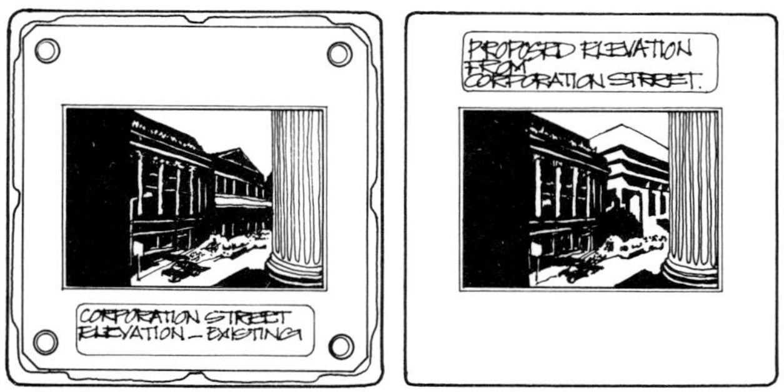

These could then be photographed on the rostrum, processed as slides, and then twin-projected alongside their source slides for a "before" and "after" impression to communicate the impact of the form on its environment.

6

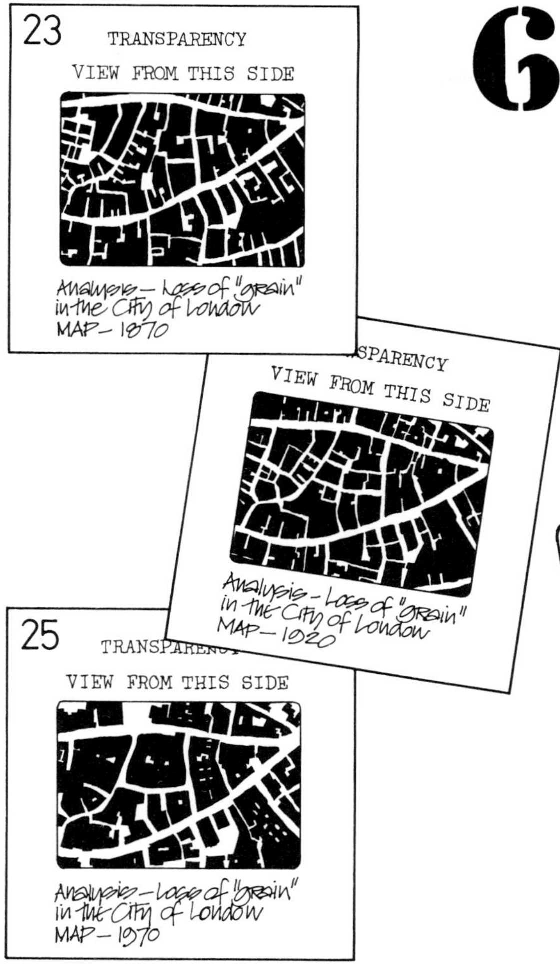

A progressive buildup of the elements in a complex design analysis, urban growth patterns, and phases in the construction of buildings and the like can be presented in an "animated" form. Stages in the assembly of monochrome or colored artwork destined for transformation into 35mm slides are simply rostrum photographed for a projected sequence in which each screened image brings a component of information not present in the last.

7

Apart from including some of the sequences already described, a more ambitious slide presentation could package the entire design process, from initial key ideograms to final presentation drawings. Also, modelscope photographs processed as slides could take viewers on a trip around the inside of models.

Making Slides for Projector Presentations

As slide presentations are often remote-control projections, some form of written narration is required. In "silent" presentations, the insertion of credits, captions, etc., into the slide package greatly enhances one's communication prowess.

A basic method of making do-it-yourself credits is to produce rostrum photographs that exploit the colors of dry-transfer lettering affixed to contrasting self-colored backgrounds, monochrome or colored site prints, or appropriate photographs culled from color magazines.

1

A further possibility is the production of composite slides, i.e., a double exposure combining either lettering or line drawings or both with a colored image. This process requires a slide copier and two 35mm color slides. The first slide should be a slide-mounted "litho" film negative taken of lettering, a drawing, or a combination of the two, the second a color transparency taken of a suitable background.

4

2

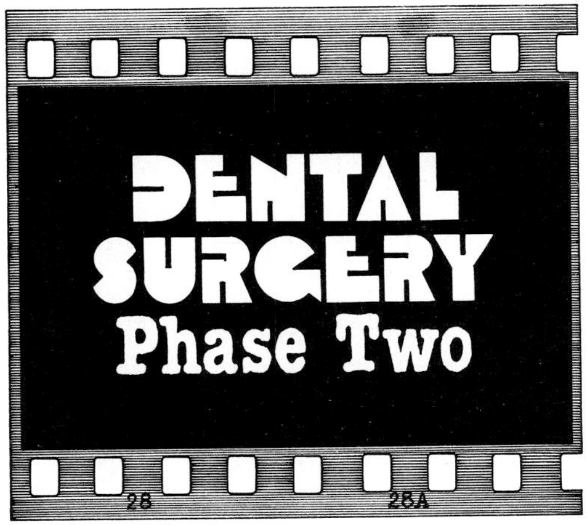

Another method is to rostrum photograph typewritten or black dry-transfer lettering on a white background using 35mm "litho" or line film. The resultant negative is then slide-mounted to project its reverse image, i.e., white on black.

Next, place the background color slide into the slide carrier on the slide copier, focus, and shoot, using color film. Then remove the original slide and, if not using a multiple-exposure camera, rewind the film back to its original position. Finally, insert the slide-mounted "litho" negative into the slide carrier, focus, and reshoot as a double exposure.

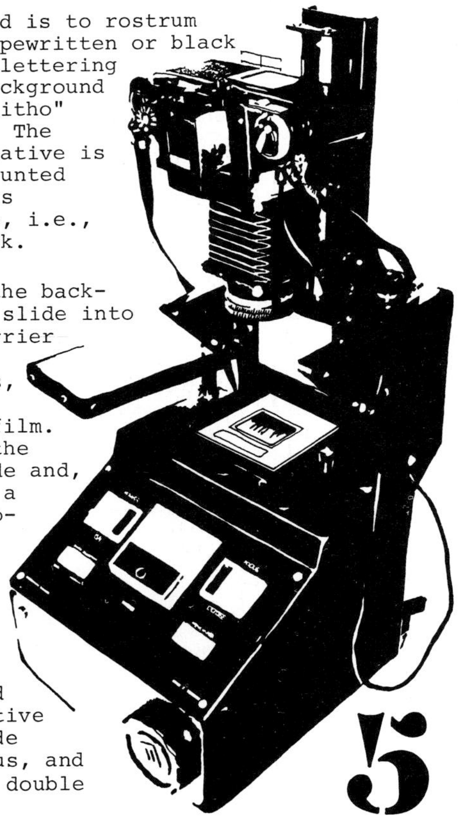

5

Using the same process, line or line and hatched drawings made in black-on-white paper can be rostrum photographed to project them as a reverse image. All kinds of linear artwork can be used as source material, even thumbnail sketches achieving the same potential conversion into images with billboard proportions.

3

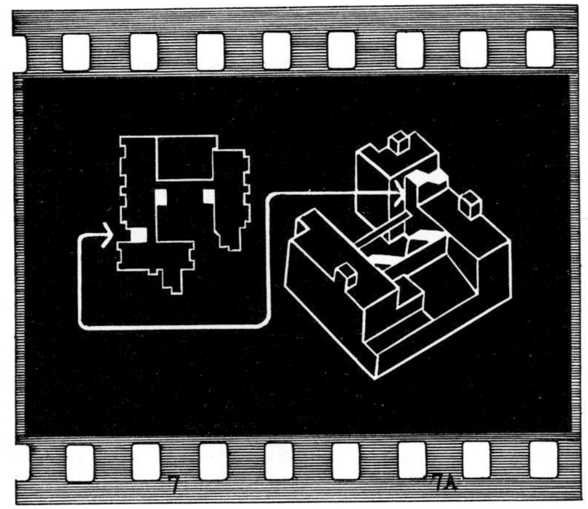

6

The processed result is a composite image of a color slide superimposed on a white image, the latter resulting from the opaque areas on the "litho" negative acting as a stencil, allowing only the light of the image to fall on the reexposed film.

Making Slides for Projector Presentations

When making slides it is important to predetermine the position of the drawing or lettering on the negative so that its subsequent superimposition coincides with the more opaque areas on the reexposed frame of the recipient color film. For instance, if parts of a title or drawing on the negative are double exposed so that they coincide with transparent areas on the color image, they will be lost.

7

8

This problem can be overcome, however, during the second exposure by inserting a colored gel between camera and negative. The subsequent shot then causes the lettering or drawing on the negative--together with the color of the gel--to be exposed on the color film as an opaque image.

Another exciting dimension of composite slide making is the fusion of a model or a drawing of a building design with a color slide of its proposed setting. This process requires a setup in a blacked-out room comprising a projector, a back-projection screen (which could be made from a suspended, battened sheet of heavy-duty tracing paper, or a thin, white bedsheet), and camera with tripod.

9

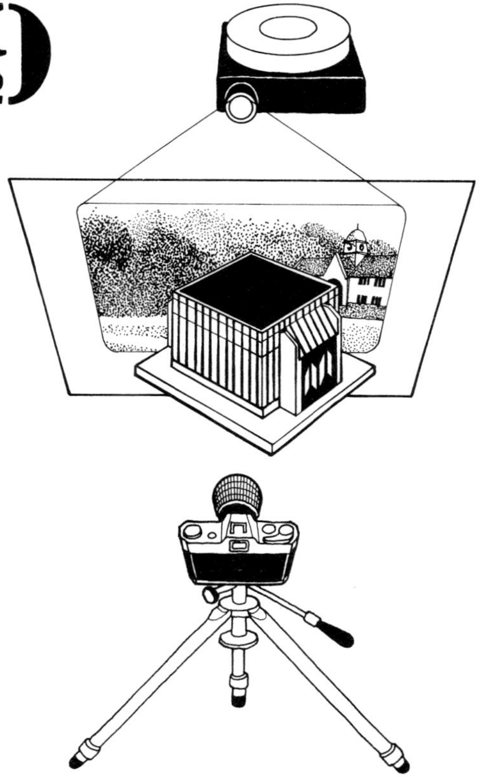

The site slide is then back projected onto the screen, with the model supported or suspended in front of the screened image. N.B.: In order to allow a drawing to take part in the composite slide, it should be heat mounted to a card and then cut to shape prior to insertion from the side or suspension from above, between camera and screen.

10

The next stage is critical. The model or drawing must be side illuminated so that stray light does not fall on the screen. This is done by a careful positioning of the model or drawing in front of the screen, together with the manipulation of the black-out curtain so that a chink of daylight falls across the faces.

11

Finally, check the composition through the viewfinder, shoot the composite image, and process.

N.B.: The use of a telescopic lens will compensate for any focal discrepancy caused by excessive distance between the face of the model or drawing and the screened background image.

Tips for Designing Brochure Layouts

1

Within a highly competitive job market, the brochure has become a widely used vehicle in design communication--either to clients, or to advertize one's ability to potential employers, astute students compiling and mailing brochures of their work when making long-distance job applications. Brochures act as miniature exhibitions that, like slide presentations, reveal their contents sequentially but with greater emphasis on written information. Being portable and conducive to reproduction, they can function to store or proliferate ideas. They can also complement or duplicate wall displays for circulation to a wider audience. When duplication is the intention, originals should be produced to a size acceptable for reduction by the reprographic process in mind.

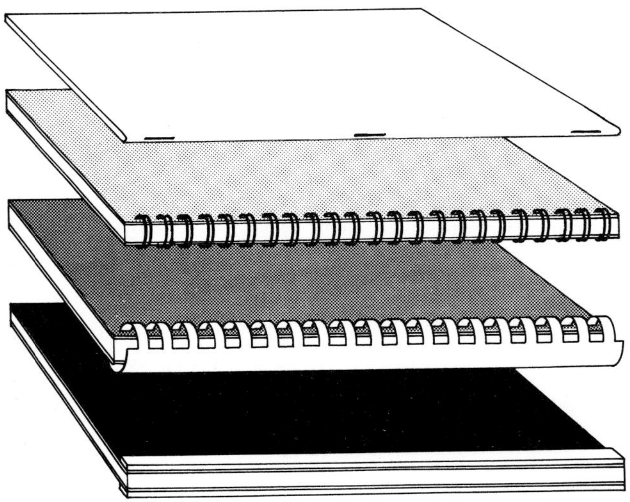

4

For more permanent binding, brochures can be stapled, spiral bound in plastic or wire spines or, for a really professional appearance, assembled via the vinyl rivet method.

2

Table of Contents

	Introduction	1
1	Survey of situation	6
2	Appraisal of potential	21
3	Design proposals	62
	Conclusion	82
	Index	86

Many styles exist for brochure presentation, but each is likely to consider a uniform method of ordering its contents. A basic framework might include title page, preface, introduction, an organized system for paragraphs and sections, and, if applicable, a conclusion, bibliography, and index.

N.B.: Spelling mistakes and factual or typing errors do not instill confidence in readers. Therefore, it is wise to have the draft text checked by an independent reader.

5

Text for do-it-yourself brochures can be handwritten or typed with titles and headings in instant lettering, several manufacturers producing a "typewriter" typeface that works well when combined with typing. The more confident can introduce drawings directly onto page formats; otherwise, photographs, color Xerox reductions or enlargements, or regular photocopy reductions can occupy whole pages, or be aerosol-spray mounted into the text.

N.B.: It is important that all illustrations be keyed into the text and, whenever possible, located on the same format as their reference.

3

When brochures are intended to double as a wall display, their binding method should allow for rapid disassembly. Binding methods that allow this transformation without page disfigurement are proprietary springback folders and slide-on plastic spines.

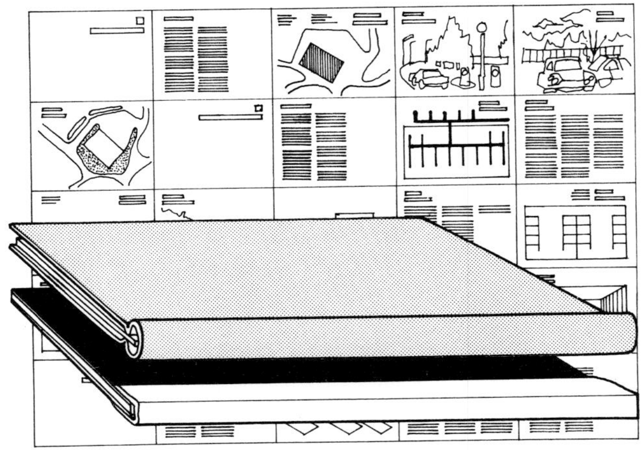

Before embarking on ink drawings destined for a dual role in reduction, check that nib sizes are compatible with the degree of intended reduction. For example, the thickness of lines in a drawing reduced to a quarter of its original size will reduce by half. Also, avoid overelaborate lettering styles, as they do not reduce well. This table shows a minimum size of line thickness, instant lettering point size, and height of stencil letterform in relation to a reduction ratio. The key to the reduction ratio is obtained by dividing the width of the original by the width to which it is likely to be reduced.

6

REDUCTION RATIO	MINIMUM TECHNICAL PEN NIB SIZE	MINIMUM INSTANT LETTERING POINT SIZE	MINIMUM STENCIL HEIGHT
3:2	0·15	12 pt	3 mm
2:1	0·2	16 pt	4 mm
3:1	0·3	24 pt	6 mm
4:1	0·4	36 pt	8 mm

Tips for Designing Brochure Layouts

The use of a grid should accommodate all the essential ingredients of a brochure's design. It should establish column widths, picture and caption areas, and margins.

A basic, easy-to-read layout for portrait format brochures using photographic illustrations is the single column of typewritten text with a width dictated by that of a regular and compatible print size.

This format allows the insertion of prints into text, a direct location with their reference prescribing page layouts.

7

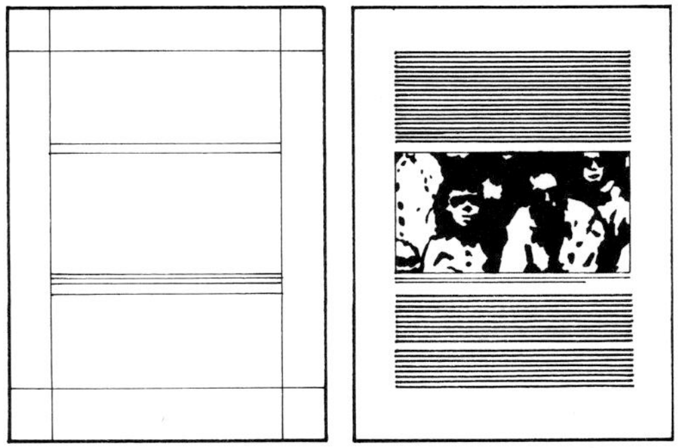

As a general rule, always allow a generous center-spread margin so that the inside edges of columns of text and illustrations do not disappear down the central gutter when the brochure is opened. However, stapled and spiral-bound brochures are easier to handle when their contents are filled with illustrations. The latter allow foldout material to be inserted . . .

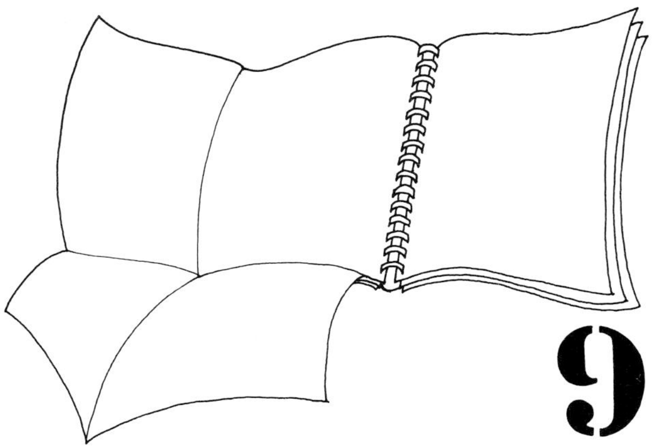

9

Another flexible arrangement for portrait formats is a double-column layout: a wider column incorporating text and key illustrations, a narrow one containing key illustration captions together with support illustrations located whenever possible adjacent to their text reference.

8

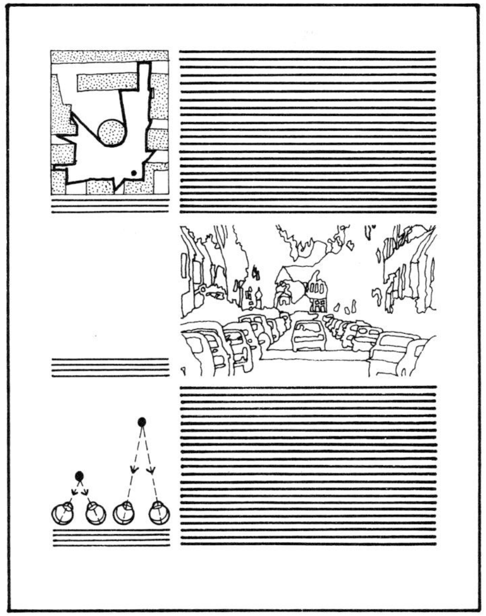

10

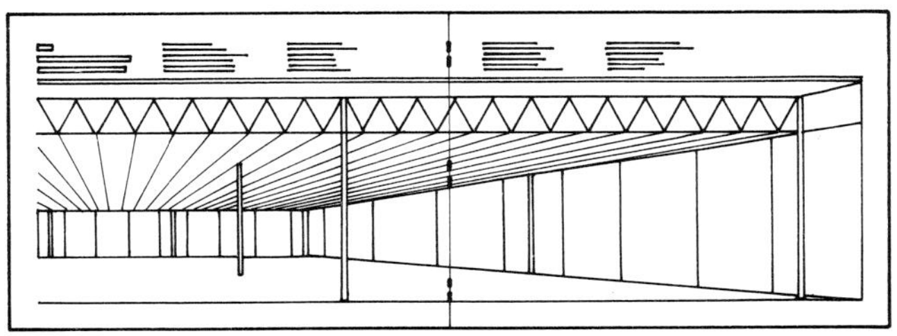

. . . while the former offer the potential of double-page spread exploitation.

11

The wider landscape formats are easier to design and more digestible to peruse when organized into a series of columns. These can be designed against a grid to carry either:

A

Solid text

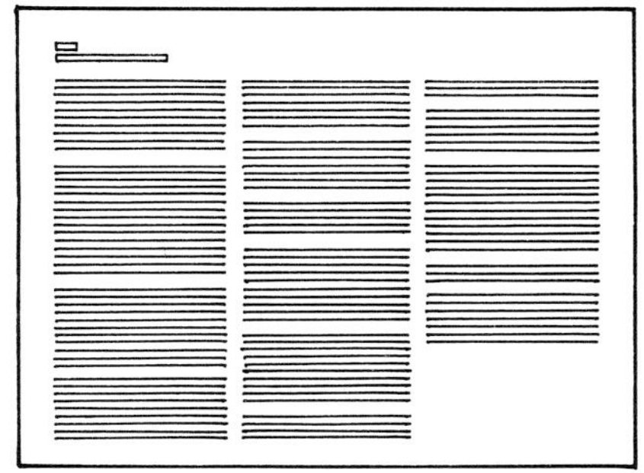

B

Related combinations of text and illustrations.

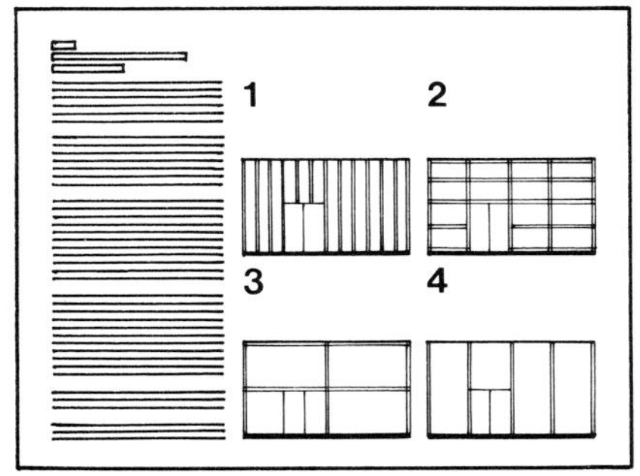

C

Full-page illustrations with annotation responding to the three columns.

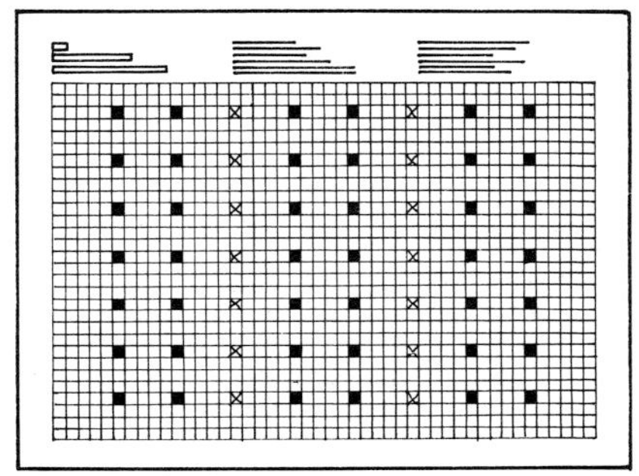

N.B.: It is important not to overcomplicate drawings for brochures; simple, confident linework creates a clean impression and is better equipped to survive reduction.

How to Make Professional-looking Brochure Covers

1

Using a straightedge and a sharp cutting knife, cut a series of windows into a sheet of white, thick paper, thin card, or the custom opaque vinyl sheet supplied with the plastic rivet binding method.

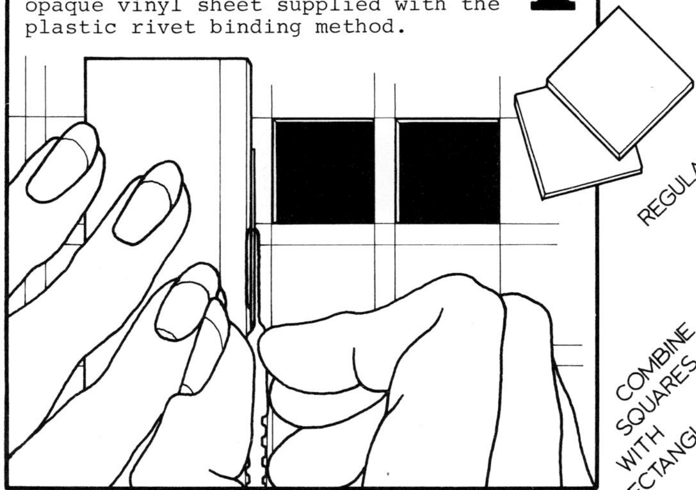

2

The arrangement of the window design might be thus . . .

3

If working with paper or card, laminate the "window frame" to the face of a second blank sheet of the same size and material. Use the aerosol adhesive method, spraying the back of the "window frame."

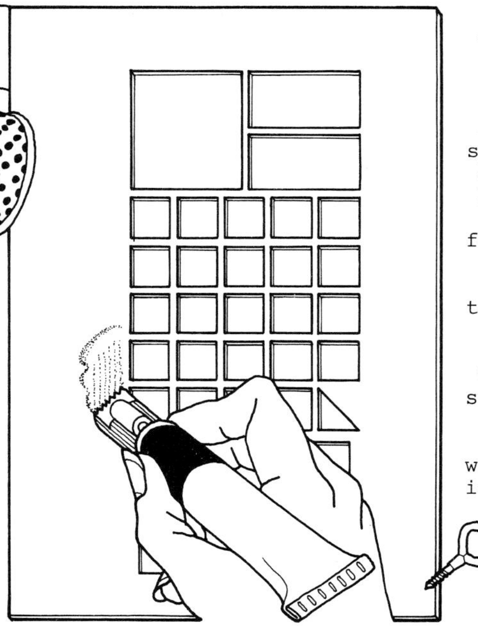

If working with vinyl, carefully and sparingly apply clear spirit-based glue to the back of the "window frame" prior to laminating it to the vinyl support sheet. This avoids surplus glue squeezing into the windows during bonding.

4

5

The result is a cover design in white on white relying exclusively on light and shadow to achieve its subtle visual effect. When bound into the brochure, its low relief also offers a pleasing tactile quality.

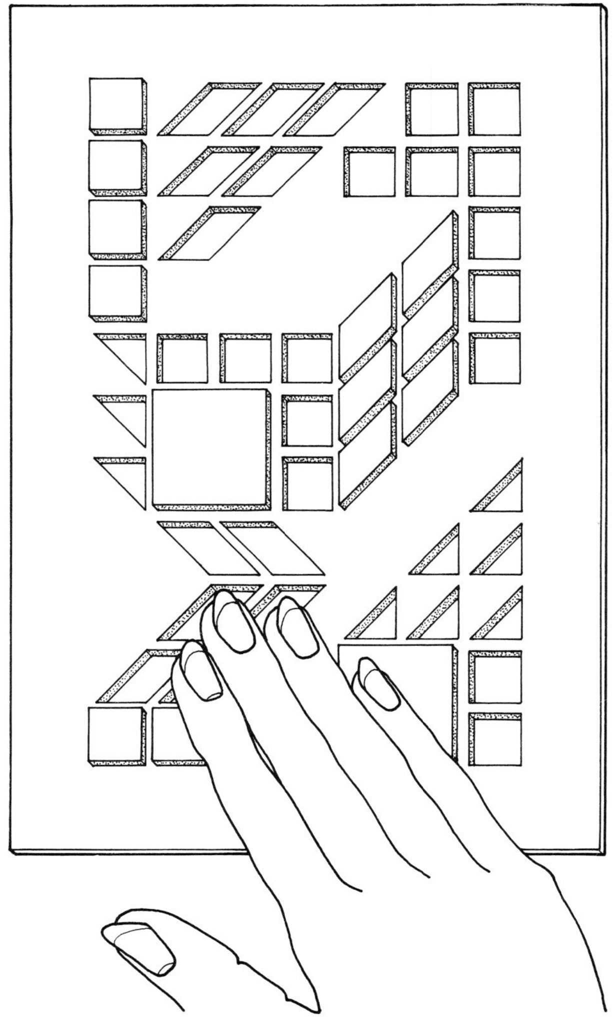

Adding Color and Titles to Brochure Covers

1

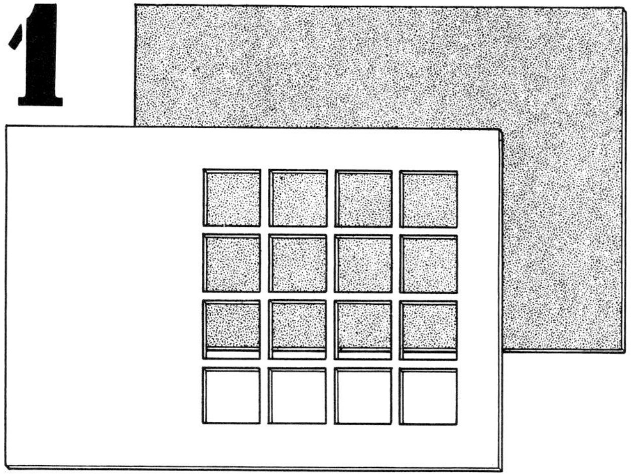

The binding method of vinyl supplied with plastic rivet is available in a range of basic colors. By selecting two contrasting hues and following the double-skinned lamination process a basic color combination can be achieved.

2

For covers designed to incorporate titles and the like, stenciled or dry-transfer lettering can be applied--either before or after lamination--to a predesigned title window.

N.B.: Dry-transfer lettering is available in colors: red, blue, green, yellow, black, and white.

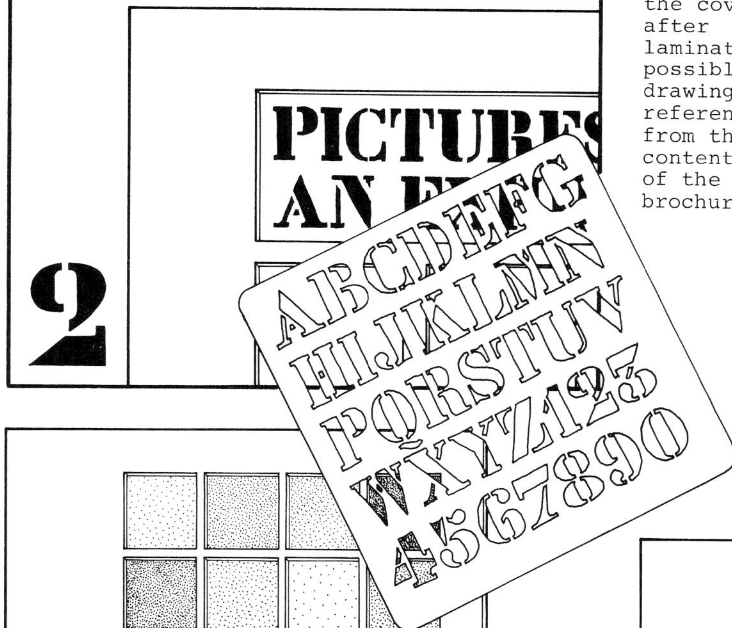

3

Alternatively, dry-transfer lettering can be applied to an additional clear acetate "dust cover"--its location aligning with a contrasting window panel color when bound into position.

4

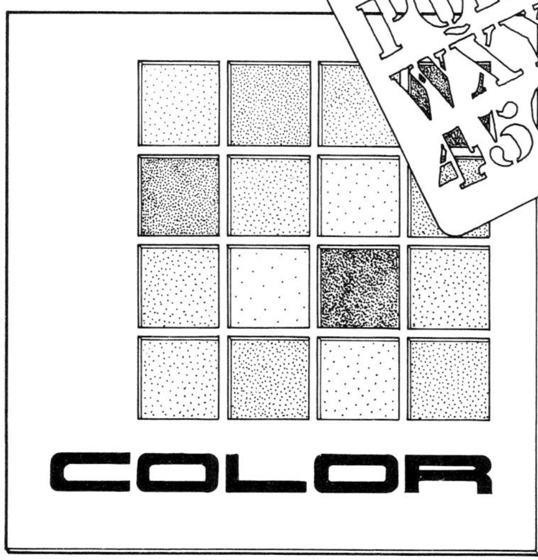

A multicolored cover is easily produced by spray mounting different colored papers to the support sheet. These are then individually contained by the laminated "window frame."

5

Further developments--with or without titles--of this simple method are:

Additional shapes added to the cover after lamination--possibly drawing reference from the contents of the brochure.

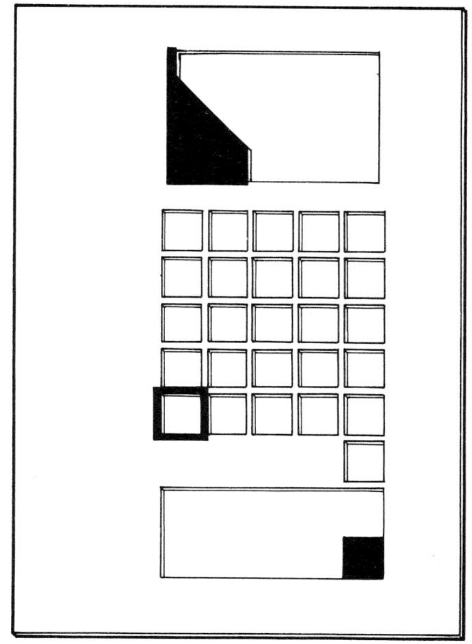

The spray mounting of photographic images culled from color magazines to reinforce the subject area of the brochure.

How to Make a Linocut

1

The materials required for linocutting are a set of interchangeable cutting heads and a handle, a small rubber-sleeved roller and a sheet of glass, water- or oil-based printing ink, and a sheet of lino.

N.B.: Lino grades thinner than 1/4" (6mm) should be strengthened by gluing them to a Masonite backing support.

2

The design can be transferred to the lino either by direct pencil drawing or by tracing it using carbon paper placed under a same-size master.

Begin gouging outlines and fine details using the finer cutting head. Then introduce thicker lines and remove larger areas of the "negative" with the medium and large cutting heads.

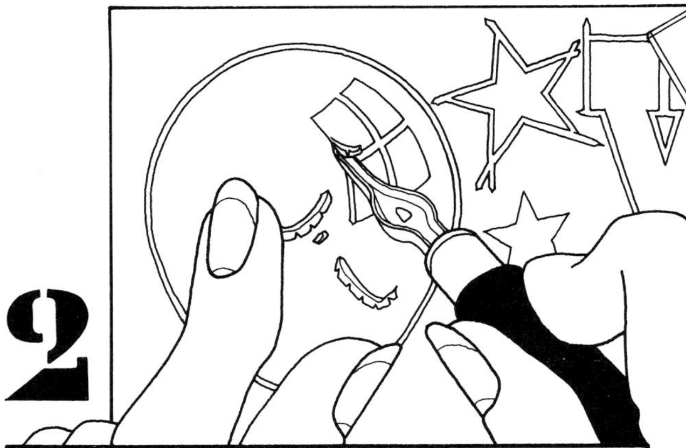

3

When the lino block design is completed, load the roller with the selected ink color. Rolling up is done on the sheet of glass, the distinctive "hiss" signaling its readiness for application to the lino.

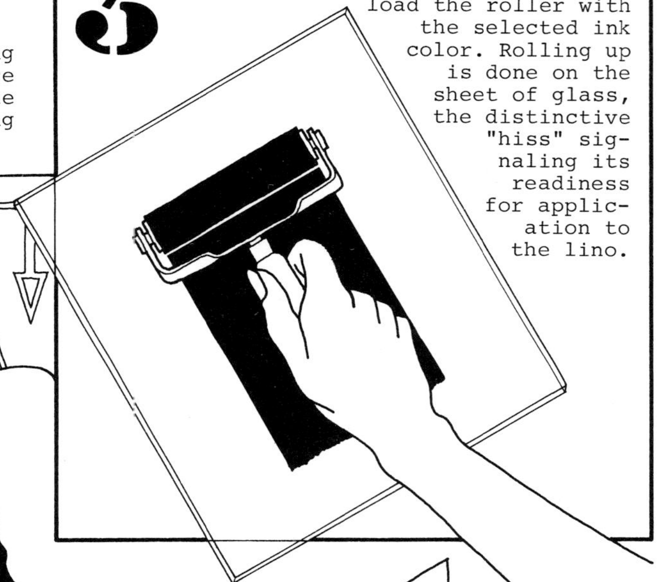

4

Roll up the lino block. In order to apply an even, thin film of ink, work the roller along the length and breadth of the block.

5

Finally, place a sheet of paper over the inked-up block and burnish. This can be done by hand burnishing using a clean roller, or rubbing with the back of a wooden spoon.

N.B.: All kinds of thinner papers, especially tissue paper, are excellent for printing. However, avoid the nonporous or heavily coated papers.

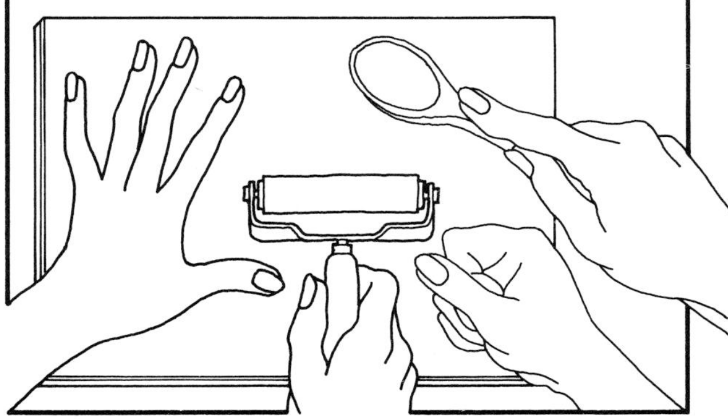

6

Carefully peel away the paper from the block.

Linocut Brochure Cover

On the right is one of a set of three linocut brochure covers designed and printed by John Craig. A pencil guideline drawing was sketched directly onto the surface of soft-composition lino laminated to plywood. This was made during his visit to the location of the design study area. Later he cut away the silhouette image from the lino block, removing the sky area and foreground details. The main title was also cut away at this stage, but from pencil-drawn guide-lines transferred to the block after tracing from an instant lettering catalogue. The result was then printed onto a range of colored papers using black printing ink.

1

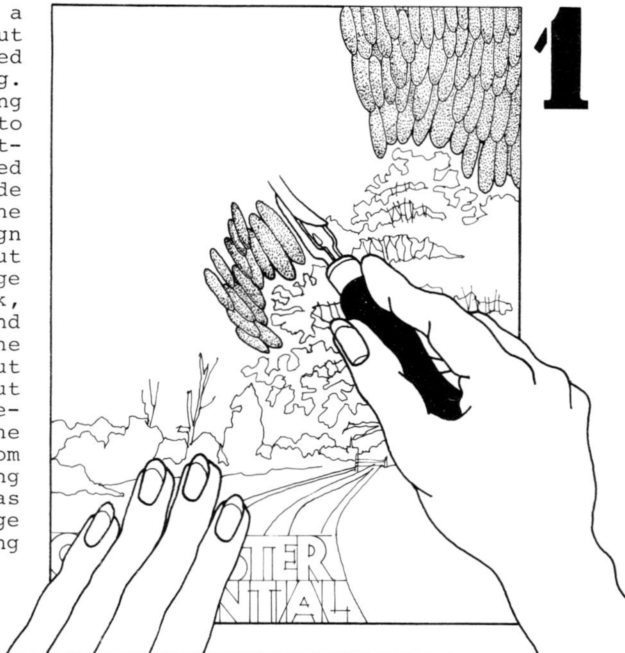

Next John fashioned a series of small lino blocks for subtitles, each strip of linocut lettering corresponding to the contents of each report, and again he transferred to the lino after tracing from a catalogue. These were then rolled up in red printing ink and "rubber stamped" into the area of colored paper representing the sky mass. Slight deviation in the position of each imprinted subtitle gave individual covers within the set a distinctive character, each achieving three colors for the price of two.

2

Linocut by John Craig (Aldington, Craig, & Collinge).

How to Make "Animated" Graphics

1

An exciting method of creating eye-catching exhibition graphics, posters, etc., is to introduce two images--one to the left-hand face and one to the right--on a corrugated surface. This method was first used on Victorian trams and later adopted by Op artists such as Yaacov Agam and Carlos Cruz-Diez. The process affords the opportunity of combining two types of graphic information in one format, which "animate" in response to spectator movement.

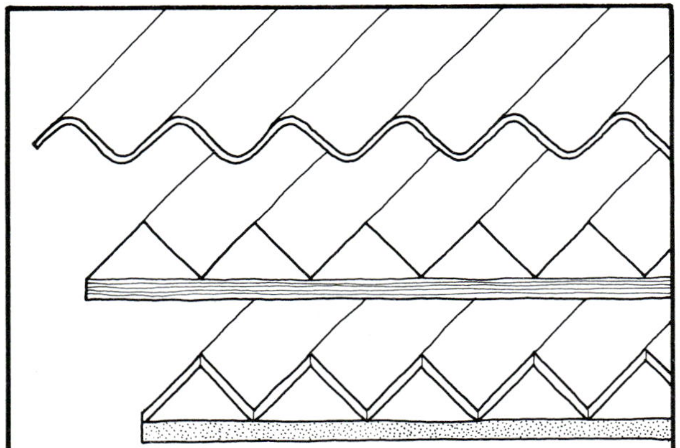

2

Corrugated metal or plastic is ideal but expensive. However, alternative surfaces can be constructed by gluing triangular-section timber strips to a base-board, or from cardboard strips glue assembled on a plywood or chipboard support.

3

Next two images should be chcsen, one perhaps composed of lettering, the other pictorial--duplicate images of either, or mirrored combinations of words and pictures.

4

Paint the two images in monochrome or color onto sheets of card or paper cut to the size of the format. Obviously, the width of the left or right image will be the sum total of all the left or right-hand face widths.

5

Then, using a cutting knife and straightedge or a guillotine, cut the two images into strips corresponding to the number and size of the corrugated faces.

6

Finally, progressively glue the left-hand and right-hand image strips onto their respective corrugated support faces.

How to Make "Animated" Graphics

The completed image makes a visually attractive graphic, especially in corridor-type spaces. Approaching from one direction, spectators can perceive a totally different image . . .

7

8

. . . from that seen in another . . .

9

. . . the two images melting into an abstract fusion when viewed from the front.

10

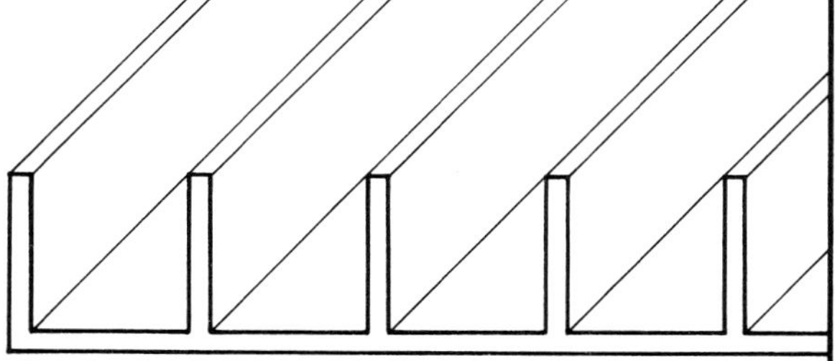

Another method of creating "animated" graphics is a surface constructed of vertical fins on a baseboard. Again, these can be glue assembled in cardboard or, for more permanence, built in timber. This format offers a "readable" central image, with separate images seen from the left and the right.

The process of image lamination is the same as the latter except that three images are involved instead of two. A short-cut is to stick the laminated strips of two of the graphics back to back and to glue them end-on in sequence to a support laminated with the third image.

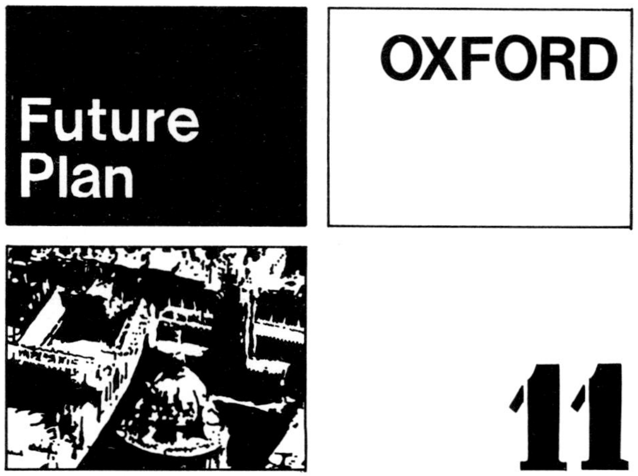

11 12

The viewing principle of both formats works at any size. They function equally well at small poster size, the size of an interior wall, or as an external elevation of a large building. N.B.: Bold, hard-edge graphics work best on both formats.

How to Design Exhibition Panel Layouts

1

Exhibitions are concerned with "showing off" developing ideas or themes whose messages can either make forceful statements or remain neutral in character, allowing the observer to form opinions. An exhibition's message therefore should be established at the outset. Other basic decisions concern the range of visual material to be included (this helps determine the number and size of panels) and whether the material is to be transformed into camera-ready mechanicals for professional photographic enlargement. The following hints, however, are directed mainly at the creation of a small do-it-yourself exhibition using individually mounted photographs, drawings, and other artwork.

First, assemble the range of existing material, and make notes and drawings describing the potential material planned for inclusion.

2

Next, organize the material into a proposed sequence of panel content. At this stage it is useful to consider each panel as the page of a book, deciding whether the content is to be exhibited chronologically or in a series of themes.

3

Once the material is arranged in a logical pattern, make a series of sketch layouts for each panel. When doing so, consider the overall texture of the format by controlling the composition of value, density, and scale. Also, resist the temptation to over-saturate the panels with too much information.

4

A practical aid to layout design is a simple grid against which images, titles, and captions can be organized as related elements. In acting as a harness, the grid will help bring a sense of continuity to the visual texture of each format, such as a positive-negative relationship between black and white areas.

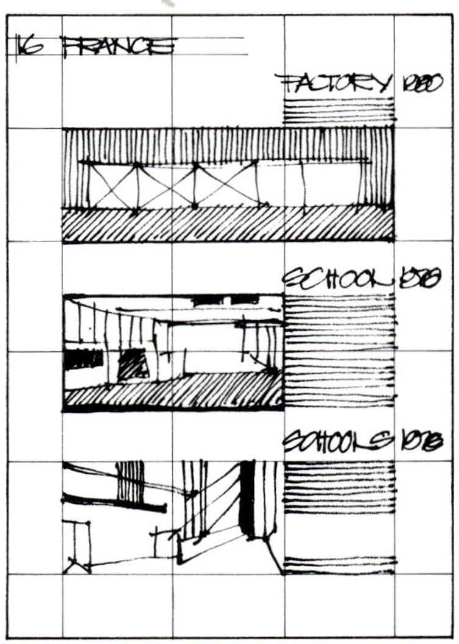

5

Variety in format will be achieved by changes in panel layouts. For example, large, punchy images should be used to introduce and climax the panel sequence. Similarly, large images dispersed at regular intervals throughout the chain of panels will act as "breather" points, as visual pauses to aid the digestion of information.

6

The introductory panel, particularly, should encapsulate something of the essence of the show. This should also create some visual drama and, if necessary, serve the double function of a design for the exhibition poster.

How to Design Exhibition Panel Layouts

7

Once the overall and individual panel layout is established, and as a final check before producing finished panels, it is wise to make trial mockups of each panel to half or full size. Panel formats can be rescaled quickly using a larger version of the original layout grid drawn on paper. This can then receive directly drawn graphics to simulate each panel or be produced as would a mechanical, comprised of pasteups. For this stage, black and gray felt-tip pens on white paper will simulate line and half-tone images.

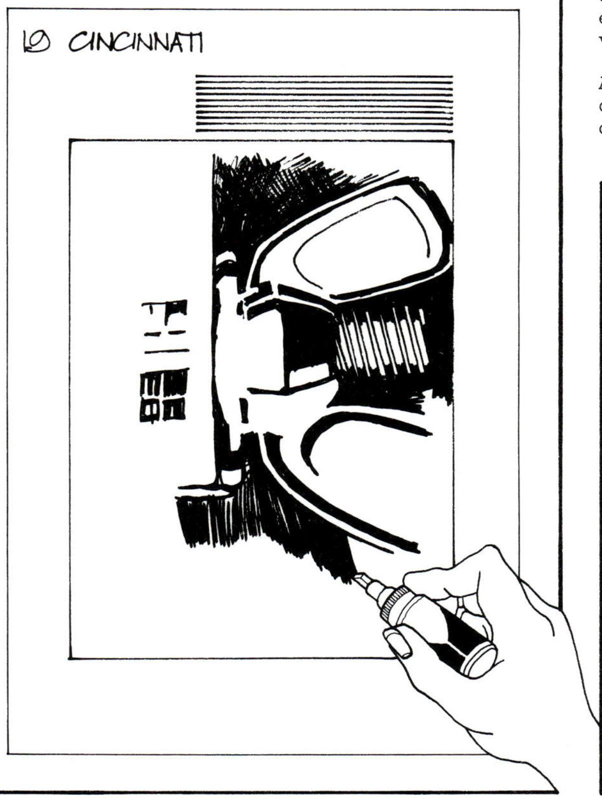

8

Completion of the felt-tip-pen mockup of each panel allows the exhibition to be previewed in a simulation of its final form.

After making any adjustments or alterations on the mockup, begin the final production of correctly sized photographic and artwork.

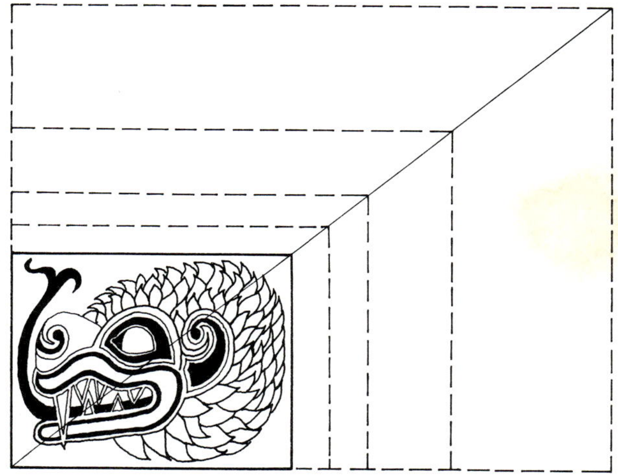

9

A fast method of rescaling rectangular formats during both mockup and final production stages is via a diagonal line which, when drawn through diametrical corners, projects correct proportion to any given scale.

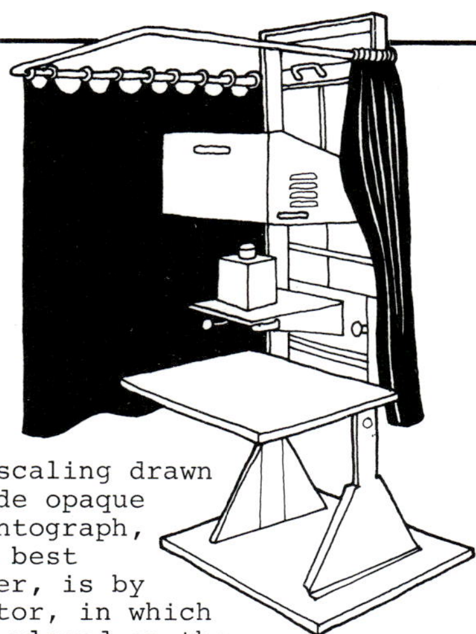

10

Methods of rescaling drawn artwork include opaque projector, pantograph, and grid. The best method, however, is by direct projector, in which the master is placed on the copyboard and its rescaled image projected through a lens-and-mirror system for direct copying onto the drawing surface.

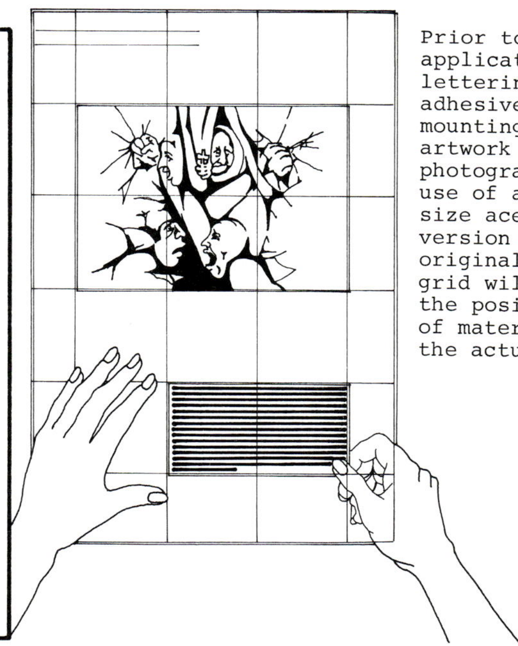

11

Prior to the application of lettering and the adhesive spray mounting of artwork and photographs, the use of a full-size acetate version of the original layout grid will control the positioning of material on the actual panels.

Lettering and Legibility in Exhibition Panels

There are a variety of methods for applying lettering directly to exhibition panels. These include dry-transfer and vinyl letters (available in black, white, and color), stenciled lettering, and photographically blown-up typewritten characters applied as cut-out plates.

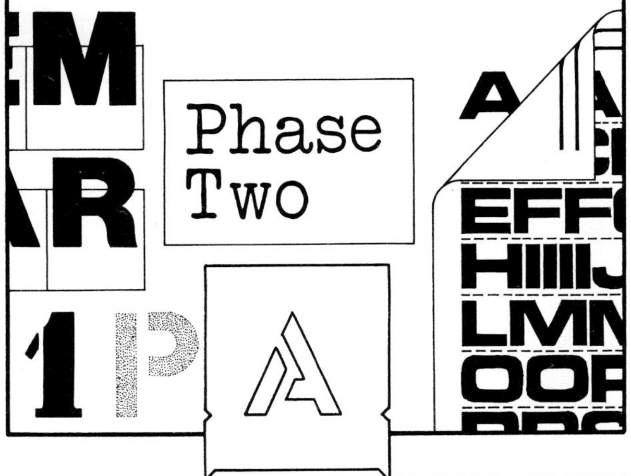

2

However, overall legibility of lettering should be an early design consideration when communicating to a standing or walking audience because, unless the recipient is already deeply interested in the subject matter on exhibition, the brain has a low threshold of mental tolerance. For instance, observational research conducted in London art galleries found that the average time spent in viewing individual paintings was around five seconds. Three levels of spectator tolerance should therefore be considered:

a) The "tourist" spectator who, in moving quickly from panel to panel, absorbs the main theme of the exhibition.

b) The half-committed spectator whose less casual stance allows him to absorb primary and secondary information.

c) The fully committed spectator who, being interested in the material, is prepared to drain the exhibition of its information.

These various spectator stances can be translated into a basic design layout which, via the relative positions and sizes of lettering and images, can cater to different levels of perception.

3

For example, a continuity of bold panel titles, the panel numbering system, and a key image or group of images will accommodate the first level of perception.

4

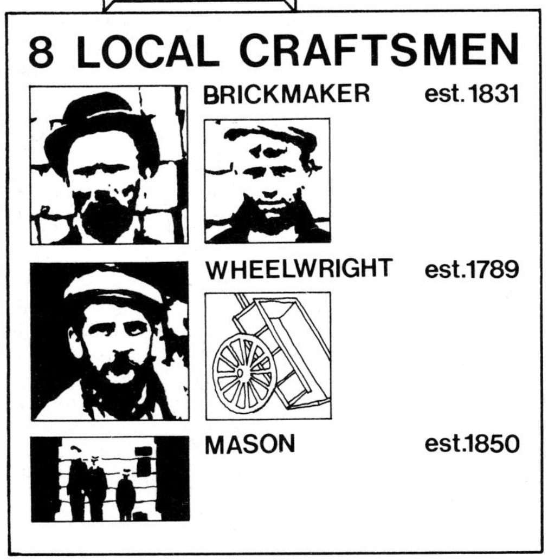

Medium-sized lettering for caption headings annotating the primary and secondary images draws the spectator into the second level of perception.

5

A smaller typeface, in elaborating caption headings, uses not more than a hundred words to avoid overkill.

The translation of the three levels of engagement into three different styles of letterform should occur only on larger panels. This is not recommended for smaller formats as this could appear fussy and disturb the visual grain of exhibited material. Finally, justify lines of text, and captions. Care in spacing to achieve this neater effect appears far more professional than the ragged edges of unjustified caption blocks.

BRICKMAKER est. 1831

Josiah "Bullnose" Stock (far left) was the grandson of the founder of the brickworks, Noah I. Squint. His eldestson, Joseph (left) carried on the family business & formed it into a major industrial company in this region.

6

How to Make an Exhibition Panel

1

Plywood 24" x 24" x 3/8" (610 x 610 x 9mm) makes an excellent small-panel format for exhibition of small-scale artwork and photographic prints; two lumberyard sheets of 8' x 4' (2440 x 1220mm) or 10' x 4' (3050 x 1220mm) offer sixteen or twenty panels respectively without wastage.

The plywood sheets can be cut down to panel size with a circular saw, using glasspaper to smooth any rough edges.

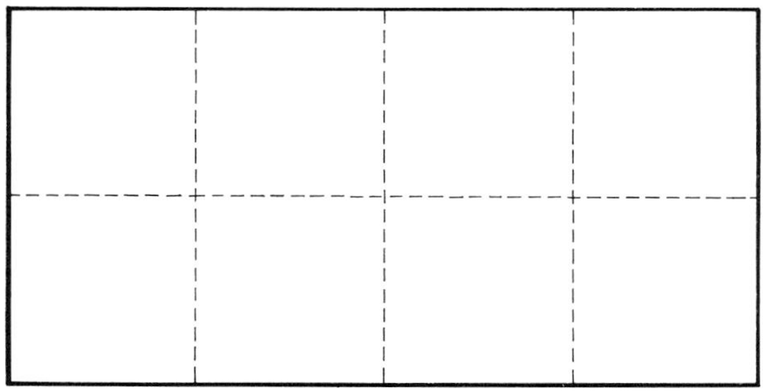

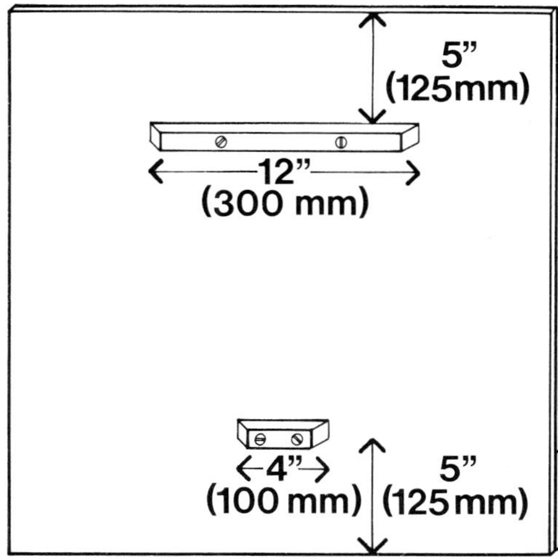

2

The panels can now be painted, aerosol sprayed, or stained in a pigment with a matte or satin finish. The choice of color should relate to the nature of the display material, e.g., black for color prints or more agressive monochrome artwork, white or neutral for sensitive graphics, or, indeed, any hue that aids the projection of the display.

Each panel requires two 3/4" (19mm) square-section timber strips as housing for the hanging system. These should be cut to length with mitered ends and glued and screwed into position on the back of each panel.

3

4

Heavy-duty nylon fishing line is adequate for the hanging cord. This can be fixed to the upper housing with eyelet screws, or simply double stapled using a heavy-duty staple gun.

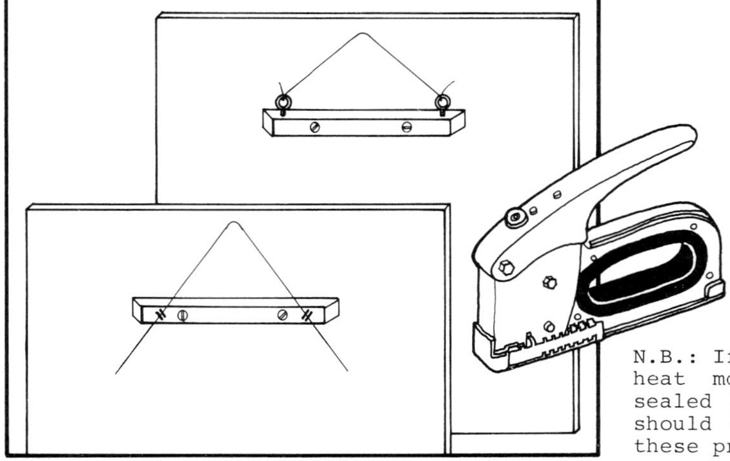

5

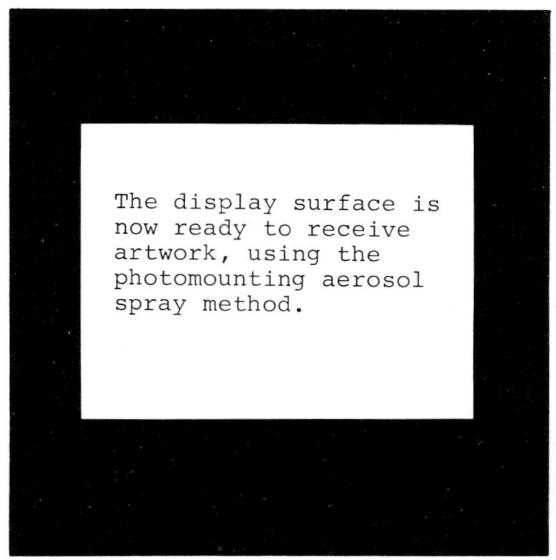

The display surface is now ready to receive artwork, using the photomounting aerosol spray method.

N.B.: If the exhibition material is to be heat mounted, or the final display heat sealed (see page 126), the housing system should not be affixed until after either of these processes.

When the panel is hung, the lower housing strip acts as a spacing device, retaining the board in a vertical viewing position.

6

Touring Exhibition: Wells Coates

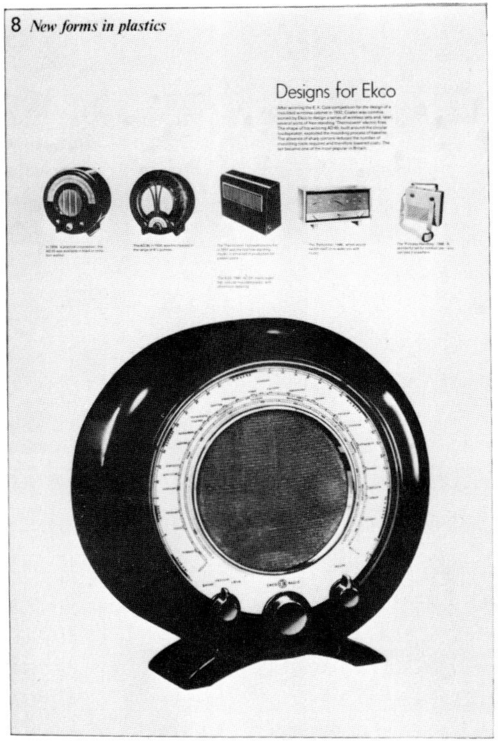

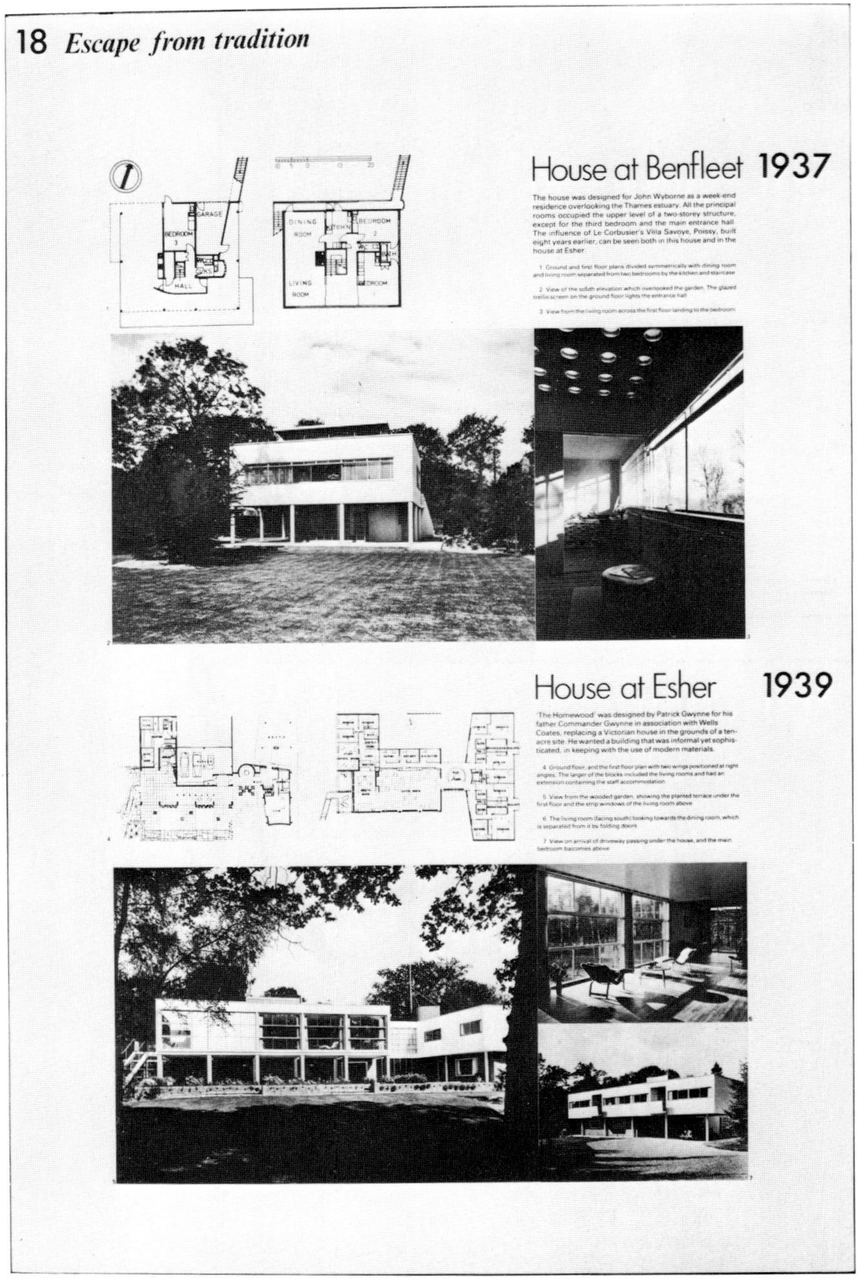

Three panels from a set of twenty-one comprising an exhibition celebrating the multifarious design achievements of architect Wells Coates. This touring exhibition was designed and produced by a group of fifth-year students together with faculty at the Department of Architecture, Oxford Polytechnic.

How to Protect Exhibition Panels in Transit

1

If an exhibition is to tour, a simple method of protecting the edges of its panels is to frame them with L-section aluminum having mitered corners. Use a section of aluminum with an inside face dimension slightly greater than the thickness of the panel. This affords a raised edge on the face of the panel so that if it is accidentally dropped face down it ensures that the display surface is protected.

Touring exhibition panels will also require a crating method that allows ease of handling, access, and adequate protection during the rigors of transit.

This type of crate is found to be ideal. It is constructed from 1/4" (6mm) plywood panels stiffened with a 2" x 1" (50 x 25mm) softwood exterior frame, the latter providing hand-holds, thus removing the necessity for additional handles.

N.B.: If exhibition panels are not framed, it is recommended that the interior of the crate be lined with baize.

The runners are 1" (25mm) square battens screwed into position before final assembly. These should be located so as to allow a groove just wide enough to receive each panel snugly and to allow a minimum of 1" (25mm) between the loaded panels.

N.B.: Panels should be loaded in a back-to-back and face-to-face sequence.

A 1" (25mm) thick sheet of foam rubber should be inserted at each end of the crate so that any lateral movement in transit is cushioned.

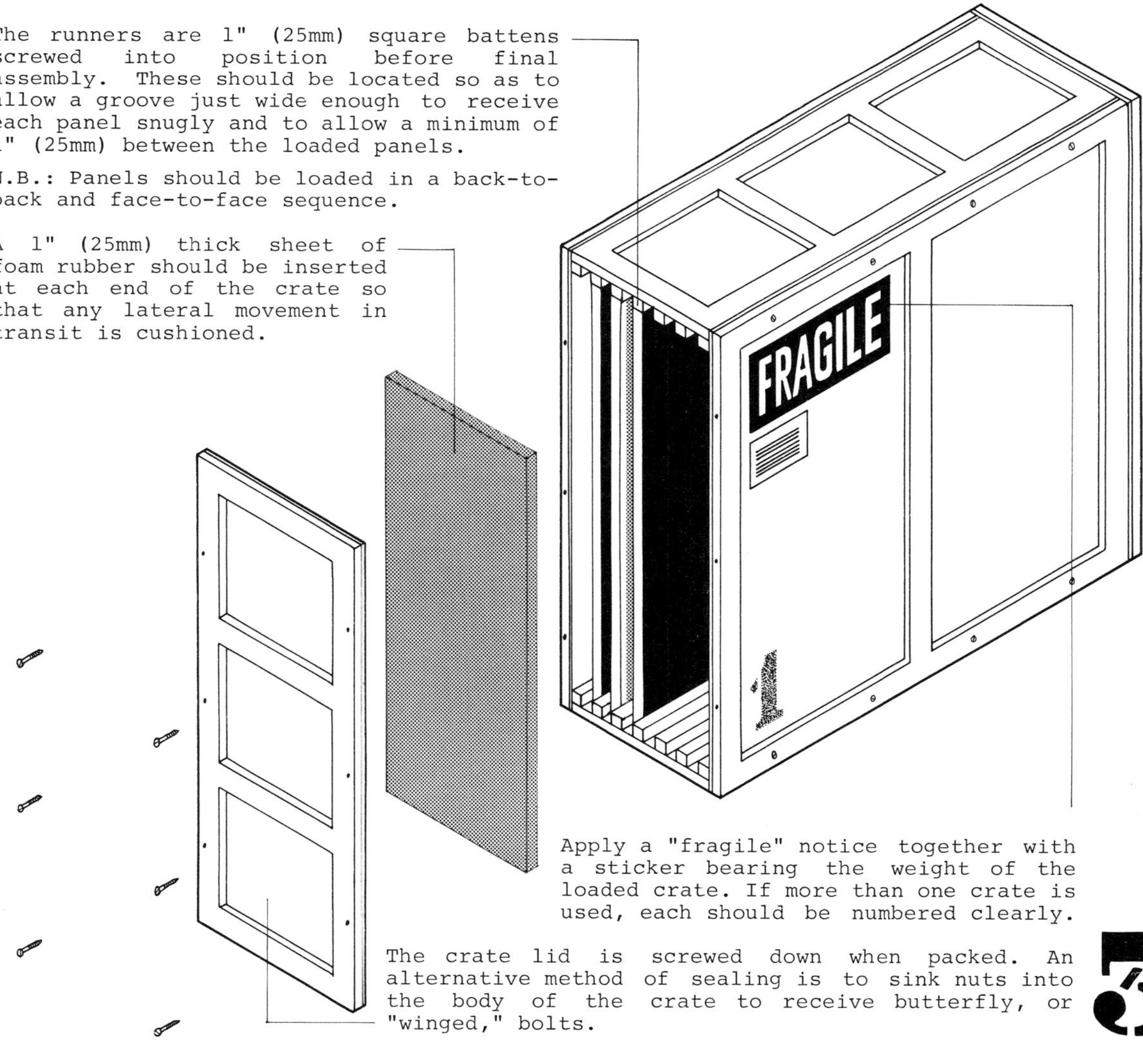

Apply a "fragile" notice together with a sticker bearing the weight of the loaded crate. If more than one crate is used, each should be numbered clearly.

The crate lid is screwed down when packed. An alternative method of sealing is to sink nuts into the body of the crate to receive butterfly, or "winged," bolts.

3

2

When cut to size, mitered, and drilled, the frame should then be glued and screwed into position.
Apply epoxy resin adhesive to the inside faces of the aluminum sections before screwing them into the back of the panel through countersunk holes.

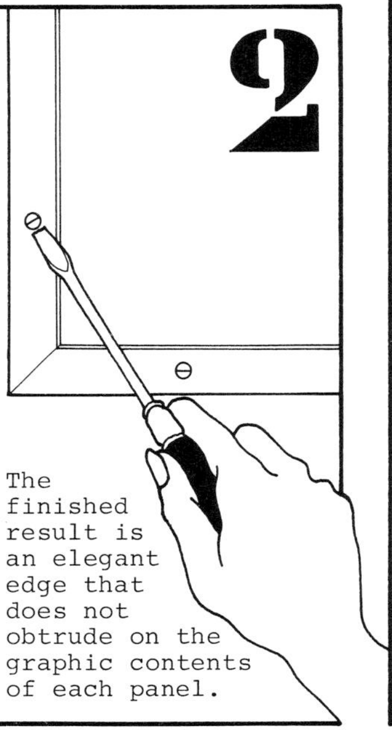

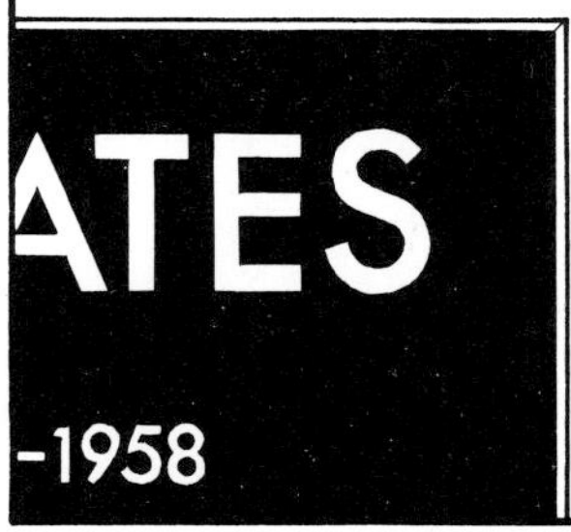

The finished result is an elegant edge that does not obtrude on the graphic contents of each panel.

Heatsealing Artwork and Exhibition Panels

Heatsealing is a lamination process in which a layer of transparent plastic film is bonded to artwork surfaces as protection against dirt and scuffing. Apart from extending the life of architectural drawings, another use is in presentations when, for instance, the surface of a heat-sealed graph can be drawn over using felt-tip pens, marks being wiped off for immediate reuse.

1

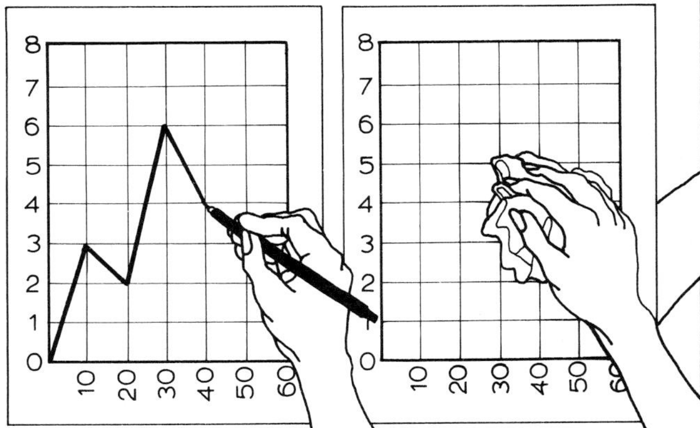

Before bonding, first cut a piece of heatsealing film to the required size, then separate it from its backing sheet.

N.B.: Film is available in matte luster and glossy finishes. However, matte is recommended for display work, especially that which includes photographs--and also for felt-tip overwork.

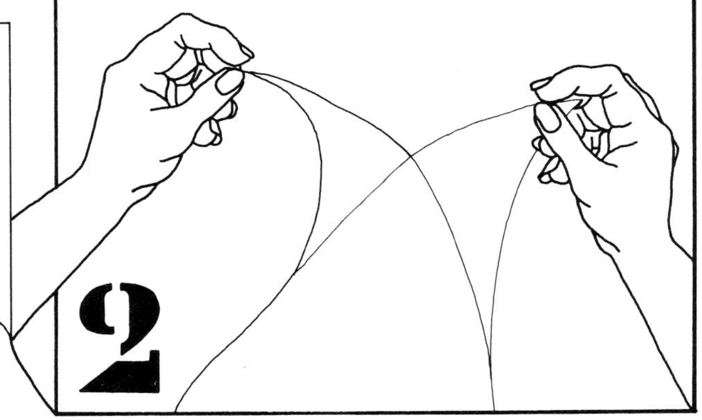

2

3

Lay the film over the artwork-display surface and carefully smooth it over with the flat of the hand, avoiding air pockets and wrinkles.

Next, cover the face of the artwork with a clean sheet of paper before insertion for 20 seconds in a heat mounter that has reached its operational heat.

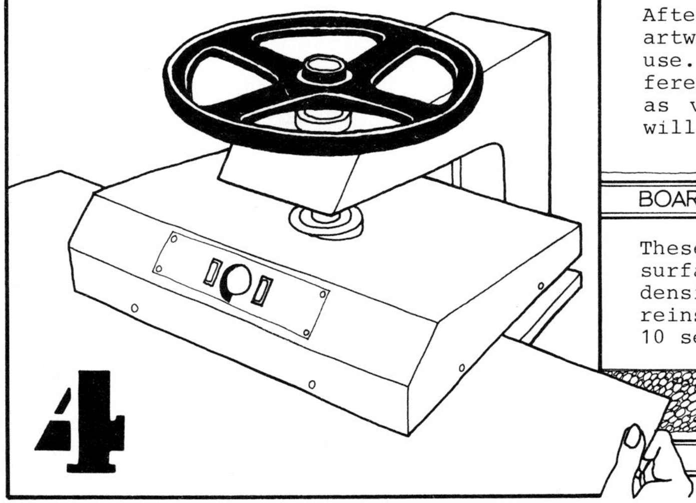

4

5

After removal from the heat mounter, flat artwork surfaces will be bonded and ready for use. However, if the surface comprises different thicknesses of artwork elements, such as vinyl letter forms, their raised edges will cause air pockets around their perimeter.

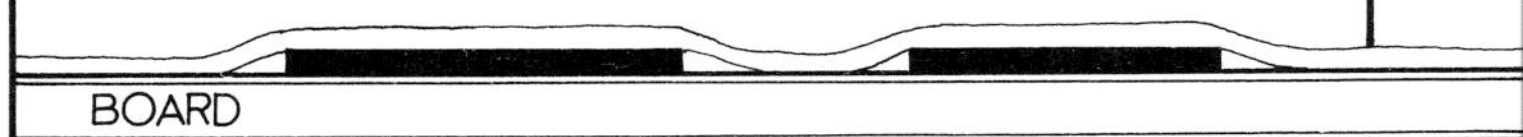

These can be removed by overlaying the surface with a proprietary sheet of high density, heat resistant foam plastic, and reinserting in the heat mounter for a further 10 seconds.

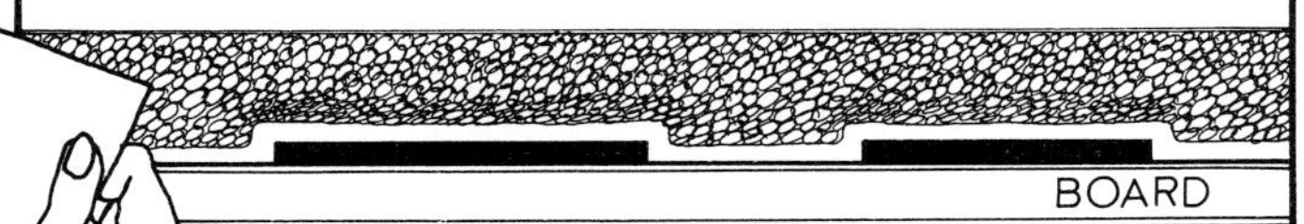

6

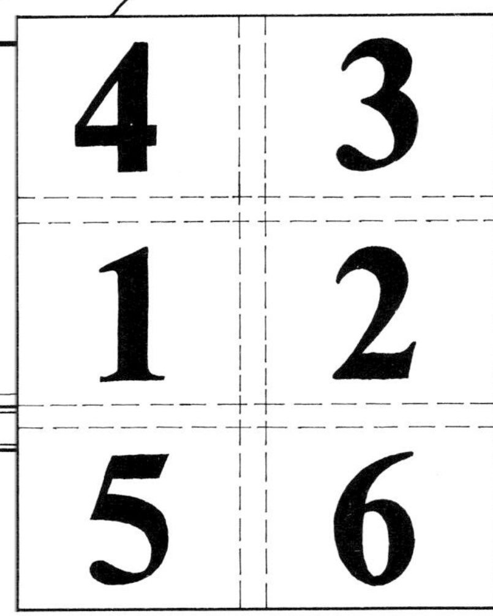

When heatsealing, or heat-mounting artwork larger than the platen size, it is advisable to follow a progressive pattern of insertions. This avoids any buildup of air in the middle of the laminated surface.

Artwork Lamination: Roll-on Plastic

1 When laminating finished artwork with the rolled version of high-tack clear plastic film, place the artwork onto the roll and cut off a sheet allowing a minimum of 1/2" (12mm) all-around overlap for folding over the edges.

2 Release about 4" (100mm) of film from its backing paper and crease the latter across its full width.

3 Carefully position the exposed film on the edge of the artwork format and lightly press down, making sure that it is evenly attached without stretching.

Gradually work across the surface of the artwork, releasing the backing paper parallel with the surface.

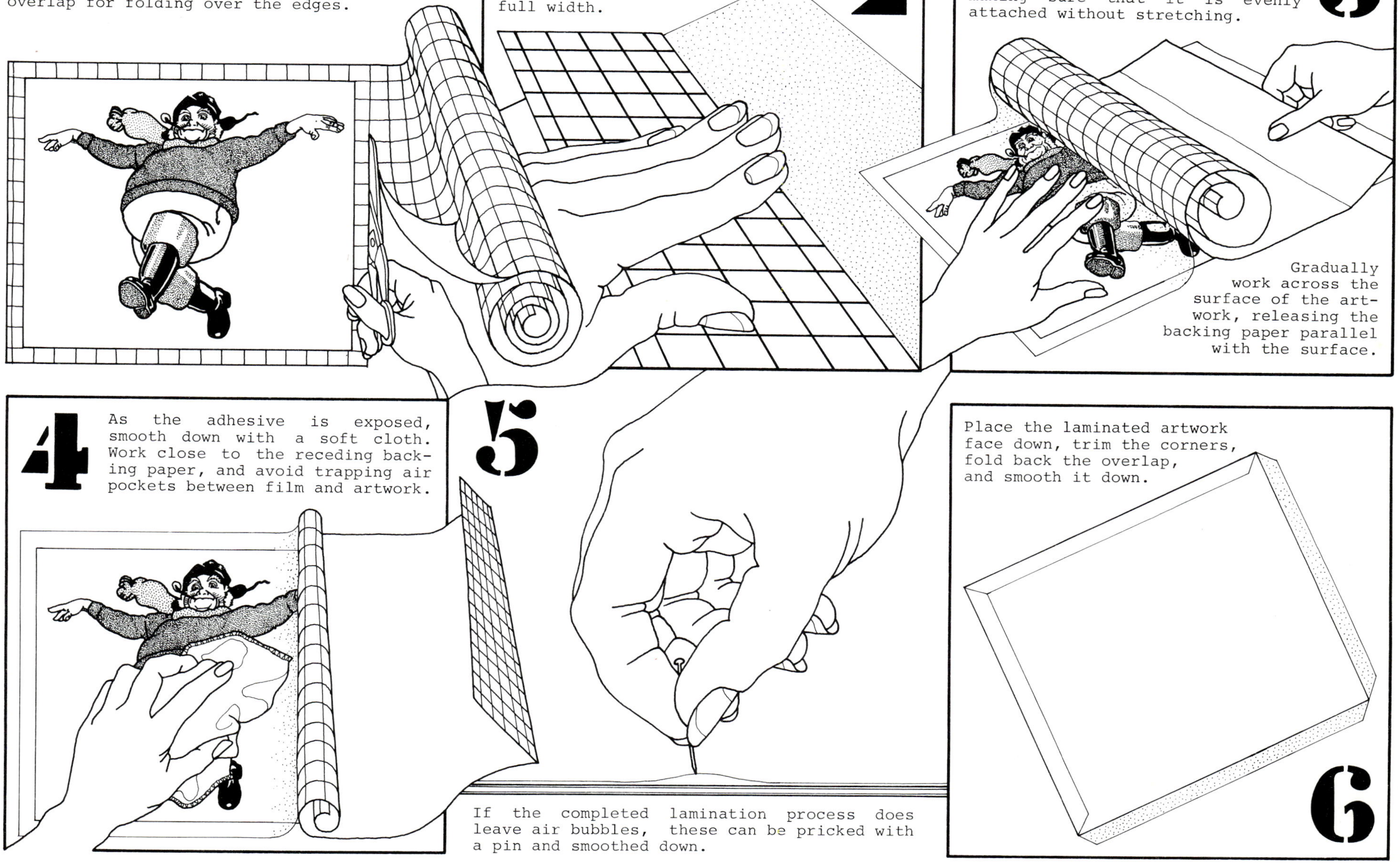

4 As the adhesive is exposed, smooth down with a soft cloth. Work close to the receding backing paper, and avoid trapping air pockets between film and artwork.

5 If the completed lamination process does leave air bubbles, these can be pricked with a pin and smoothed down.

6 Place the laminated artwork face down, trim the corners, fold back the overlap, and smooth it down.

INDEX